Pragmatics Online

Pragmatics Online examines the use and interpretation of language and communication in digitally mediated contexts. It provides insight into how meaning is communicated online, with a focus on how users negotiate and navigate the constraints and resources of social media sites and other online contexts.

The book introduces key concepts in the study of digital contexts and online communication, and discusses how these can be understood from the perspective of pragmatics. Each chapter examines a different topic and includes an overview of key research alongside original pragmatic analyses of data. Topics include sharing and liking, emoji and emoticons, memes, and clickbait. Kate Scott focuses on how ideas and topics from pragmatics can be applied to mediated contexts, irrespective of the particular media.

The book is an essential guide to the pragmatics of online discourse and behaviour for students and researchers working in the areas of digital pragmatics, language and media, and English language, linguistics, and communication studies.

Kate Scott is a senior lecturer at Kingston University, London (UK). Her research focuses on cognitive pragmatics, and she has published on the pragmatics of digitally mediated communication, exploring topics including hashtags, clickbait, and memes.

Language and Digital Media
Series editors: Carmen Lee and Camilla Vásquez
Series co-creator: David Barton

Language and the study of it are changing rapidly in the age of digital media; our use of language is gradually shaped by and is in turn shaping new media. Exploring the interplay between digital media and language in society and covering a broad selection of research contexts, books in *Language and Digital Media* investigate both language online and people's practices around it, including how they create and how they use online texts. Each title includes both an overview discussion of the topic as well as analysis of data. Presenting rigorous research, yet written in an engaging and accessible manner, the series is key reading for students and researchers across language, linguistics, communication and media studies.

Language, Creativity and Humour Online
Camilla Vásquez

Pragmatics Online
Kate Scott

Mobile Messaging and Resourcefulness
A Post-Digital Ethnography
Caroline Tagg and Agnieszka Lyons

For more information on any of these and other titles, or to order, please go to https://www.routledge.com/Language-and-Digital-Media/book-series/LADM

Pragmatics Online

Kate Scott

Routledge
Taylor & Francis Group

LONDON AND NEW YORK

Cover image: © Getty Images

First published 2022
by Routledge
2 Park Square, Milton Park, Abingdon, Oxon OX14 4RN

and by Routledge
605 Third Avenue, New York, NY 10158

Routledge is an imprint of the Taylor & Francis Group, an informa business

© 2022 Kate Scott

British Library Cataloguing-in-Publication Data
A catalogue record for this book is available from the British Library

Library of Congress Cataloging-in-Publication Data
Names: Scott, Kate, 1976- author.
Title: Pragmatics online / Kate Scott.
Description: Abingdon, Oxon ; New York, NY : Routledge, 2022. | Series: Language and digital media | Includes bibliographical references and index.
Identifiers: LCCN 2021035539 | ISBN 9781138368415 (hardback) | ISBN 9781138368590 (paperback) | ISBN 9781003254201 (ebook)
Subjects: LCSH: Pragmatics. | Social media--Semiotics. | Communication and technology. | Interpersonal communication.
Classification: LCC P99.4.P72 S36 2022 | DDC 401/.45--dc23/eng/20211118
LC record available at https://lccn.loc.gov/2021035539

ISBN: 978-1-138-36841-5 (hbk)
ISBN: 978-1-138-36859-0 (pbk)
ISBN: 978-1-003-25420-1 (ebk)

DOI: 10.4324/9781003254201

Typeset in Times New Roman
by SPi Technologies India Pvt Ltd (Straive)

Contents

PREFACE

Technology develops quickly and relentlessly. I wrote the majority of this book during the Covid-19 pandemic. During this time, I went from using video-conferencing technology once in a while to using it daily as my main channel of communication. As I went from being a hesitant novice to a confident expert user, it was impossible not to be aware of the shifting digital landscape around me and the communicative practices that were shifting in response to this. Users of digitally mediated communication adapt quickly. Their practices develop in line with the technology. However, this pace of change poses a challenge to researchers working on online communication. It is almost impossible to keep up to date with all the possibilities for interacting and communicating online, and it is easy to feel as though your work will be out of date before it is even finished.

At its heart, this book is about communication in context. The phenomena and case studies function to illustrate how we adapt to changing communicative contexts and how we use the resources available to us to communicate. The approach taken is to think about how technology affects the context in which communication takes place, and to examine the strategies that users develop to navigate (and in some cases exploit) this. Even if, by the time you read this book, the sites discussed have fallen out of favour, you should still be able to appreciate the connection between the contextual and technological constraints under which users were operating and the strategies that they adopted. Even if the online landscape looks very different in ten years' time, the brains and cognitive systems that we use when operating the technology will not have changed very much.

Many of the examples in this book draw on data from social media sites. Examples that are not publicly available have been reproduced with permission. Publicly available examples have been anonymised, except when they have been posted by public figures, such as politicians and journalists, or when they were posted on behalf of companies or organisations.

I have followed the convention of referring to the speaker/writer/communicator as *she* and the hearer/reader/addressee as *he* in cases where this clarifies meaning and helps the reader to assign reference. No further meaning should be inferred from this use of pronouns.

ACKNOWLEDGEMENTS

I would like to thank Elsevier for granting me permission to reuse work from previously published journal articles in this book. Sections from Chapter 3 are reprinted from *Journal of Pragmatics*, 184, Scott K., The pragmatics of rebroadcasting content on Twitter: How is retweeting relevant?, pp. 52-60. Copyright (2021). Sections from Chapter 4 are reprinted from *Journal of Pragmatics*, 81, Scott, K., The pragmatics of hashtags: Inference and conversational style on Twitter, pp. 8-20, Copyright (2015), and from *Discourse, Context and Media* 22, Scott, K., 'Hashtags work everywhere": The pragmatic functions of spoken hashtags, pp. 57-64, Copyright (2018). Sections from Chapter 7 are reprinted from *Journal of Pragmatics*, 175, Scott, K., You won't believe what's in this paper! Clickbait, relevance and the curiosity gap, pp. 53-66, Copyright (2021).

Thank you to Carmen Lee and David Barton for approaching me to write this book, and to anonymous reviewers for their feedback on early proposals. Thanks to Carmen Lee and Camilla Vásquez for their comments on the first draft. All mistakes are, of course, my own. I am grateful to Hannah Rowe and Eleni Steck at Taylor & Francis for their support, encouragement, and patience.

I have been lucky enough to work with an amazing group of mentors and colleagues who have guided and inspired me in my work in pragmatics. There are too many to mention, but particular thanks go to Robyn Carston, Billy Clark, Tim Wharton, Dan Sperber, and, of course, Deirdre Wilson. A special mention must also go to Ryoko Sasamoto for her support, encouragement, and friendship.

I would not have got through the last two years without the fantastic support of my wonderful Kingston colleagues Fan Carter, Sara Upstone, and Aybige Yilmaz. Thank you for the happiness! Finally, thank you to Esam Bakhsh for keeping me sane over the last year. You mean the world to me.

1

INTRODUCING PRAGMATICS ONLINE

This book is about digitally mediated communication. However, at its heart, it is a book about people, and it is about how people use the resources available to them to communicate with each other. Pragmatics is the field of linguistics that is concerned with how we use language in context. Exploring language and communication online from a pragmatic perspective, reveals just how strong our urge to communicate with each other is, and how resourceful we are when it comes to achieving this. As we shall see over the course of the book, online contexts differ from offline contexts in important ways, and, indeed, online contexts differ from one another in various ways too. However, communicative acts are performed by human beings, and the underlying mechanisms that drive the production and interpretation of those communicative acts are the same online, as they are offline. As Locher (2010) puts it, 'online communication is as real as offline interaction'. While new technologies may offer new opportunities and new resources, they are only as effective as the people who use them. There is no reason to believe that our basic human abilities and behaviours change when we go online. Many of the analyses and discussions in this book have arisen from the assumption that we expect to find the same general processes at work whether we are communicating online or offline.

The focus of this book is digital online technologies. However, humans have used technology to mediate communication throughout history. Whether

DOI: 10.4324/9781003254201-1

it be the telegraph, the printing press, or simple writing instruments, communicative technologies have always affected the context in which communication takes place. As humans, we have been adapting our communicative strategies to the available technologies for as long as those technologies have existed. The differences in the way we interact online and offline must be understood in relation to the context in which the communication is taking place.

Pragmatic theories, frameworks, and analyses which take contextual factors into account are crucial in understanding this aspect of communication, and they are at the core of the discussions in this book. In this first chapter, we introduce the general field of pragmatics, including some key terms, ideas, and theories that will be used in the rest of the book. Then we look more closely at digitally mediated communication, and we will start to think about the ways in which it is different to face-to-face communication. A range of characteristics will be introduced to help us to grasp the differences between different platforms, and between online and offline communication. These discussions introduce key themes and they will provide us with the building blocks and the vocabulary for the more detailed analyses in later chapters.

PRAGMATICS AND PRAGMATIC THEORIES

Communication is context-sensitive. When we communicate with others, the interpretation of our messages almost always depends on the context in which those messages are produced and understood. This is the case whether we are communicating face-to-face or at a distance, and whether we are using spoken, signed, or written forms of language. It is also the case when we communicate non-verbally via gestures, facial expressions, or body language. To understand what someone means by what they say, we must consider the context in which the utterance has been produced and the intentions of the person who has produced it. To do this we draw on a range of information. We might draw on information from the physical environment to work out who or what someone is talking about. We might use information from the prior discourse to help us to disambiguate a word or phrase. We might use information that we gather from the speaker's facial expressions or tone of voice to decide whether someone is asking us something or telling us something. In each of these cases, we use information from the context to help us work out what the speaker was intending to communicate. These processes are the focus of pragmatics, and the goal of pragmatics is to understand and explain how we communicate in context.

Those working in pragmatics are traditionally interested in those parts of language which are context-sensitive. They might, for example, study deictic expressions which cannot be fully interpreted without reference to the context. Another major branch of pragmatics is concerned with the study of what speakers implicate by their utterances, and many scholars study how non-literal uses of language, such as metaphor and irony, can be used to convey meaning. When we communicate we do not only transfer factual information. We also interact with others in a social context. We use the words that we say to perform speech acts. We promise, persuade, beg, assert, question, and warn, and we also tailor our utterances to the social context in terms of how direct, indirect, or polite we choose to be. All of these tasks fall under the umbrella of pragmatics.

Pragmatics is a broad discipline, and it encompasses a range of approaches to the study of language and communication in context (Mey 2001; Verschueren 2009; Locher and Graham 2010; Chapman 2011; Kecskes 2014). Much of the existing work on the pragmatics of online communication has focused on socio-cultural factors and on the participatory practices that take place online. This research has revealed a wealth of insights into how users' manage interactions, relationships, and audiences online, how they construct and perform identities in mediated contexts, and how they navigate multi-lingual and multi-cultural discourse contexts. Work in these areas often overlaps with sociolinguistics, conversational analysis, and discourse analysis. I will make reference to some of this work in the discussions that follow throughout this book, and we will see how users employ digital resources for relational and (im)politeness purposes (for example Darics 2010; Langlotz and Locher 2012; Arendholz 2013; Rudolf von Rohr and Locher 2020), how they construct identities online (for example Zhao et al. 2008; Skovholt et al. 2014), and how they signal affiliation and group membership (for example Zappavigna 2012, 2018; Miltner and Highfield 2017). This remains a fruitful area for research, and as technologies develop and online practices evolve, the possibilities for future work in interpersonal and intercultural pragmatics continue to grow.

The discussions in this book, however, will take a broadly theoretical approach to pragmatics, and the main focus will be on how we can understand the communicative behaviour that we find online in terms of a general theory of communication and pragmatics. As Chapman (2011: 8) explains, theoretical pragmatics is concerned with 'the question of how meaning can in general be communicated … given the finite resources of a language and the vagaries of context'. As we shall see in the second half of this chapter and in Chapter 2, we often have different resources available to us when we communicate online, and digitally mediated contexts can be vague and unpredictable in new and interesting ways. This makes digitally mediated communication an exciting area for analyses and discussions from the perspective of theoretical pragmatics. In the rest of this chapter, I set the scene for these discussions and analyses. I begin with a brief overview of two key theoretical frameworks in pragmatics: speech act theory and relevance theory. The concepts, definitions, and principles assumed by these theories will form the basis of many of the analyses and discussions that follow in later chapters.

Speech act theory

Speech act theory (Austin 1962; Searle 1965, 1969) emerged as a way to understand and analyse the things we do when we speak. As we saw above, we can do a range of different things when we use language. We can make statements and assert facts, but we can also ask questions, make requests, give warnings, and issue commands, amongst various other things. Understanding the type of act that a speaker is performing is a key part of a hearer's task when interpreting an utterance. If, for example, a hearer interprets an utterance as a suggestion when it was intended as a command, we have a case of misunderstanding.

Work in speech act theory has aimed to classify different speech acts and to describe the conditions under which they may be successfully performed. According to Arielli (2018), we can understand the things we do online in the same way that we can understand the things that we do with words. A status update, he claims, is an assertion, an act of liking is an expressive, and a friend request is a directive. That is, these different online acts are, according to Arielli, also different types of speech act.

A key contribution of speech act theory is the observation that, not only can we do different things with words, but we perform different kinds of acts every time we speak. Austin (1962) proposed a distinction between locutionary acts, illocutionary acts, and perlocutionary acts. A locutionary act is the act of producing the utterance itself. It is the act of making the sounds or producing the written marks. An illocutionary act is the type of act that the utterance performs. A request is a different illocutionary act to a command, for example, and a promise is a different illocutionary act to a dare. Most of the work in speech act theory has been focused on the study of illocutionary acts and the illocutionary force that utterances carry. Finally, an utterance may perform a perlocutionary act. Perlocutionary acts are the effects that the utterance has on the hearer. So, for example, a command might have the effect of scaring the hearer, or a joke might make the hearer laugh. Illocutionary acts are part of the speaker's intended meaning, but perlocutionary acts may be intended or unintended.

Relevance theory

Relevance theory is a cognitive framework for understanding human cognition and communication (Sperber and Wilson 1986/95; Carston 2002; Wilson and Sperber 2012; Clark 2013). It is based on two key principles: the cognitive principle of relevance and the communicative principle of relevance. The cognitive principle of relevance states that human cognition is geared towards the maximisation of relevance. That is, we naturally pay attention to inputs and stimuli which we judge as likely to be relevant to us. Something is relevant to us if it leads to what are known as *cognitive effects*. Cognitive effects can be thought of as updates to the way we think about the world, or as changes to the assumptions that we hold. New information can change these assumptions, and if it does, then we say that the new information is relevant.

As we move around the world we hold assumptions about the way things are. For example, as I write this, I hold various assumptions, including those in (1) to (3).

(1)   It is Monday today.

(2)   I have four eggs in my fridge.

(3)   If it rains tomorrow, I will not have to water the garden.

New information is relevant if it interacts with the assumptions that we hold in one of three ways. First it might strengthen an assumption that we already hold. If I open my fridge and see four eggs in the carton, this visual information will strengthen my assumption that I have four eggs left in my fridge. If, on the other hand, I look in my fridge and see an empty egg carton, this new information will contradict and eliminate my previous assumption. Contradicting and eliminating an assumption is the second type of cognitive effect. The final type of cognitive effect is a contextual implication. This results when a new piece of information combines with an existing assumption to yield a new implication. For example, if I get up tomorrow and see that it has been raining, this information will combine with the assumption in (3) to yield the implication in (4).

(4)   I will not have to water the garden.

The more cognitive effects that follow from an input, the more relevant that input is. However, processing new information requires effort. The relevance of an input is also affected by the amount of effort that is required to process it. The more effort required to process an input, the less relevant that input will be. The relevance of an input is determined by (a) cognitive effects, and (b) processing effort.

The relevance of a stimulus must be assessed relative to the context in which it is interpreted. We can think about context from various perspectives. We can think of it in physical terms as the place in which an utterance takes place. We can think of it in textual terms as the things that have been mentioned in the discourse up until that point. However, in the relevance-theoretic pragmatic framework, context is a psychological construct. It is the set of assumptions that the hearer holds and which he will use in his interpretation of the stimulus.[1] The information that it has been raining is relevant to me in the example above because it has been processed in a context that includes the assumption in (3). The same information might be completely irrelevant on a different occasion if it does not interact with assumptions in any way to yield cognitive effects. That is, if nothing follows from the fact that it is raining, the fact that it is raining is not relevant to me in that context.

Now that we can define relevance and context in this more precise manner, we can turn to the role that they play in communication. As we move around the world, we look for relevance, and we hope for relevance. However, it is only when someone openly and intentionally communicates with us that we can expect relevance. Intentional and overt acts of communication are what is known as ostensive acts of communication. Relevance theory can be particularly useful for the analysis of online communication because it is a theory of pragmatics that deals not just with utterances, but with all ostensive acts of communication. According to relevance theory, ostensive acts are special. This is captured in the communicative principle of relevance which states that 'every act of ostensive communication communicates a presumption of its own optimal relevance' (Sperber and Wilson 1986/95: 266–267). An ostensive stimulus will be optimally relevant if it satisfies both of the requirements of the definition of optimal relevance, as given in (5).

(5)   (a) The ostensive stimulus is relevant enough for it to be worth the addressee's effort to process it.

(b) The ostensive stimulus is the most relevant one compatible with the communicator's abilities and preferences.

What this means is that the addressee of an utterance, or any other ostensive stimulus, can presume that the communicator was aiming to make her utterance optimally relevant. The addressee can use this presumption in his interpretation. Based on clause (a), the addressee can assume that the utterance will be worth his while to process, and this leads him to the assumption that the speaker will not have put him to any gratuitous effort. In practical terms, this means that if a speaker produces a long-winded, detailed, or indirect utterance, the hearer will assume that she has done so for a reason, and will look for extra effects to justify the extra processing effort that has been demanded of him. Clause (b) sets the upper limit on what a hearer can expect. A hearer can only expect a speaker to produce an utterance that is compatible with her abilities and with her preferences. That is, a hearer cannot expect a speaker to say something that she does not want to say or that she is not able to say, even if it would be more relevant to the hearer if she were to do so. The addressee of an utterance will use these assumptions in his interpretation, and they lead us to the relevance-theoretic comprehension procedure, as given in (6).

(6)   Follow a path of least effort in deriving cognitive effects: test interpretive hypotheses (reference assignments, disambiguations, implicatures, etc.) in order of accessibility.
Stop when your expectations of relevance are satisfied (or abandoned) (Wilson and Sperber 2004: 613).

This comprehension procedure falls out naturally from the communicative principle of relevance and the definition of optimal relevance.

To assess the relevance of an utterance, a hearer must form a hypothesis about the speaker's overall intended meaning. This is everything that the speaker intended to communicate to her addressee when she produced the utterance. Part of her overall intended meaning will come from what she states or asserts. This is known as her explicitly communicated meaning. However, her overall intended meaning also includes anything that she intentionally implies or implicates. This is referred to as implicitly communicated meaning. According to relevance theory, inference is involved in constructing hypotheses about both aspects of a speaker's meaning, and both are therefore of interest from a pragmatic perspective. We consider these in more detail in the next section.

UNDERSTANDING SPEAKER'S MEANING

To work out what a speaker intends to communicate, a hearer must form a hypothesis about her overall intended meaning. This will include her explicitly communicated meaning and her implicitly communicated meaning. In this section, we look at the inferential processes that play a part in the utterance interpretation process, and we assume three levels of meaning: a basic-level explicature (or proposition expressed), higher-level explicatures, and implicatures. We consider each in turn, and focus on the role that inference plays in deriving each.

The proposition expressed

What a speaker means when she produces an utterance in context is, in almost all cases, much more specific and precise than the meaning that is encoded by the words and structures that make up the sentence itself. Consider the example in (7).

(7)   He sleeps with his bat by his bed.

Without access to the context in which it is spoken, it is impossible to know precisely what the speaker of (7) intended to communicate, even at a fairly basic level. Most approaches to pragmatics acknowledge a level of meaning that corresponds to the basic statement that the speaker has asserted. This is variously referred to as 'what is said', 'the basic explicature', or 'the proposition expressed'. This is the aspect of the speaker's meaning that we would generally consider to be truth evaluable. That is, we can determine whether what the speaker has said is true or false by comparing the proposition that has been expressed with the state of affairs in the world.

Part of the hearer's job when interpreting an utterance is to form a hypothesis about the proposition that the speaker has intended to express. The addressee of (7) will need to perform at least two pragmatic processes before he will be able to form such a hypothesis. He will have to decide who the pronoun *he* refers to. If it refers to one particular person, let us call him John, then it expresses one proposition. However, if it refers to a different person, let us call that person Ramy, then it expresses a different proposition. In the first case, it is a statement about John, and in the second, it is a statement about Ramy. Whether these statements are true or false will depend on different things. We say they have different truth conditions. How we assign reference to pronouns such as *he* and to other referring expressions directly affects the truth conditions, and hence the proposition that is expressed by the utterance.

The sentence in (7) also contains the lexically ambiguous word *bat*. To interpret the utterance the hearer must decide which of (at least) two meanings the speaker intended. Does the person referred to in the utterance sleep with an animal by his bed, or does he sleep with a piece of sporting equipment designed for hitting balls by his bed? Once again, the two meanings have different truth conditions, and we do not know what the explicit meaning of the utterance is until we choose between them. Reference assignment and disambiguation are two key issues in pragmatics. However, often we have to do even more pragmatic work to reach the meaning that was intended by the speaker. Consider the exchange in (8).

(8)   Jasmine: I've stubbed my toe!
      Pippa: Stop fussing! You're not going to die.

Think about the proposition that Pippa is expressing in the second half of her utterance in (8). It seems fairly clear that she is not telling Jasmine that she should stop fussing because she is immortal. Rather she is telling her that she is not going to die right now from this particular incident. To understand Pippa's utterance we must go beyond the (even disambiguated) words and enrich the proposition expressed to something like (9).

(9)   You're not going to die right now from stubbing your toe.

The enrichment in (9) is highly context-dependent. If we put the same uttered words in a different context, they are likely to lead to a different explicit meaning.

Disambiguation, reference assignment, and enrichment are all inferential processes, and so our pragmatic processing systems are involved in the derivation of the proposition expressed.

Higher-level explicatures

As we saw above, speakers can perform a range of different speech acts when they produce utterances. Speech act information can be captured via what are known as higher-level explicatures. The proposition expressed is the basic-level explicature of an utterance, and indeed, is often referred to as just *the explicature*. However, this basic explicature can then be embedded within a higher-level explicature which may include information about the speech act that the speaker is performing. For example, imagine that Sylvia produces the utterance in (10), intended as a promise. We can represent the speech act that she is performing as the higher-level explicature in (11).

(10) There will be cake at the party.

(11) Sylvia promises that [there will be cake at the party].

Higher-level explicatures also capture information about the attitudes and emotions of the speaker towards the explicature that she has communicated. Imagine that the example in (12) is uttered by Antonia.

(12) Sadly, there won't be any cake.

The truth-evaluable proposition that Antonia has expressed is given in (13). However, the higher-level explicature in (14) is also part of her intended meaning.

(13) There won't be any cake.

(14) Antonia is sad that [there won't be any cake].

We cannot say that we have fully understood a speaker's message if we have not correctly understood the attitudes and emotions that the speaker intends to convey. In example (12), the propositional attitude information has been communicated via the use of the word *sadly*. However, the speaker could have conveyed the same information via facial expressions and/or tone of voice. Both speech act information and propositional attitude information are understood as part of what is explicitly communicated (hence higher-level explicatures), rather than what is implicitly communicated. This is because they are a development of the basic-level explicature. They have truth conditions in their own right which are independent from the truth conditions of the basic-level explicature communicated by the utterance. Both the basic-level explicature and higher-level explicatures can combine with existing assumptions to yield implicatures. We turn our attention to implicitly communicated meaning next.

Implicitly communicated meaning

Even after we have disambiguated, assigned reference, and performed any other context-specific processes of enrichment to derive the explicit meaning, we may not have fully understood the speaker's overall intended meaning. Speakers often use their utterances to imply or implicate meaning that goes beyond the words. Consider the utterance in (7) again, but this time as the answer to a question, as in (15).

(15)   Lydia: Is Ramy really keen on cricket?
       Matt: He sleeps with his bat by his bed.

Not only does the context help us to assign reference and to disambiguate, but it also leads us to infer additional meaning beyond that conveyed by the explicit meaning alone. Now Matt's utterance is not just a statement about Ramy's sleeping habits. It is also an answer to Lydia's question, and most people would agree that it communicates that, yes, Ramy is really keen on cricket. To infer this extra meaning we have to draw on a range of different assumptions about how and why people behave in certain ways, and then use these to relate Matt's utterance to Lydia's question. Working out what a speaker is implicitly communicating is another pragmatic task, and the study of how hearers do this is a key concern of pragmatics generally.

Any propositions that a speaker intends to implicitly communicate are implicatures. Consider the exchange in (16).

(16)   Ben: Have you read *The Lord of the Rings*?
       Alice: I don't like long books.

Alice explicitly communicates that she does not like long books. She implicitly communicates that she has not read *The Lord of the Rings*. This is an implicature, and, more specifically, it is an implicated conclusion of her utterance. However, to reach this implicated conclusion, Ben has to access the assumption in (17) as a premise.

(17)   *The Lord of the Rings* is a long book.

This is necessary if he is to understand Alice's reply as an answer to his question. Alice has also intentionally communicated this assumption, and we say that it is an implicated premise. Both implicated conclusions and implicated premises are implicatures. That is, they are both intended implications.

Implicatures can vary in strength based on the evidence that the hearer has for deriving them as intentionally communicated. It would be fairly difficult to make sense of Alice's utterance in the context without accessing the implicated premise in (17), and so we can say that this is strongly implicated. We often find weak implicatures associated with poetic and figurative uses of language, such as metaphor. When Romeo utters the line in (18) in the famous balcony scene in *Romeo and Juliet* (Shakespeare 1597/1980), he is using a metaphor.

(18)   Juliet is the sun (II.ii.4).

It is hard to paraphrase exactly what is communicated by this metaphor, and different readers may derive slightly different implicatures. However, in terms of speaker's meaning, we can understand metaphors as achieving relevance by making a wide range of weak implicatures available to the hearer.

To understand what a speaker intends to communicate when she produces an utterance, the addressee must form a hypothesis about her overall intended meaning. This overall intended meaning is a combination of the proposition expressed, higher-level explicatures, and implicatures. Inferential processes are involved in the derivation of all three.

DIGITALLY MEDIATED COMMUNICATION

Online and digitally mediated communication comes in many forms. The main focus of discussions in this book will be sites and platforms that are part of what has become known as Web 2.0. As Barton and Lee (2013: 9) explain, Web 2.0 applications 'allow users to create and publish their own content online', and social networking, participation, and collaboration are core activities. In Web 2.0 environments, users not only consume online content, but they also produce it. Many of the strategies, techniques, and resources that we discuss in this book have emerged as user-generated solutions to the problems or limitations of digitally mediated communication. They have been developed or adapted by users, and then later incorporated into the functionality of the sites. Such innovation is only possible because users are participating and creating content, as well as consuming it.

We will touch on a number of different platforms and networking sites throughout this book, including Twitter, Facebook, WhatsApp, and YouTube. Each site offers its users slightly different options and means of communication. To consider the ways in which the technology and software influence and interact with utterance production and interpretation, we need a way to compare media both with each other and with face-to-face communication. Baym (2010) identifies seven features which can be used to do just this. They are reach, replicability, storage, mobility, temporal structure, interactivity, and social cues. These provide a useful framework for thinking about the different contextual environments that we encounter online, and for thinking about how the contexts in which we communicate might shape our production and interpretation strategies. Danah boyd (2010) offers an alternative framework, identifying four affordances which she suggests shape users' participation in online communication: persistence, replicability, scalability, and searchability.[2] Boyd's affordances crosscut and overlap with Baym's concepts, and so the two frameworks are presented here together.

REACH

When we communicate face-to-face we can only transmit messages to those people who are physically in the same space as us. While it is possible to mass-produce and distribute offline written language to a wide audience, this is usually only available to professional writers working within the structure of an industry. In contrast, anyone with an internet connection and an email address can post a message on an open social media platform such as Twitter or Instagram. With just a few keystrokes we can create a message that can be seen by millions of people all over the world. As boyd (2010: 54) points out, 'networked media allows anyone to be a media outlet'. Different sites, software, and platforms vary in their reach, and they vary in how much the ordinary user can control the distribution of their post or message. Boyd uses the term *scalability* to capture this aspect of online communication. As she points out, while the potential reach or scalability of a post is enormous, it is far from guaranteed. A post may reach millions or it may be seen by nobody. What is key, from a pragmatic perspective, is the lack of control that a user has over this. As boyd (2010: 48) describes, '[t]he property of scalability does not necessarily scale what individuals want to have scaled or what they think should be scaled, but what the collective chooses to amplify'.

The reach of a platform plays a role in how much control users have over the context in which their posts will be interpreted. There have been several documented and high-profile cases where users have underestimated the reach of their posts, and have lost control of the context in which they are interpreted. Several examples are discussed by author Jon Ronson in his book *So You've Been Publicly Shamed* (2015). We think about just one of those here to illustrate the speed and scale with which online content can spread. In 2012, Lindsey Stone and her colleague Jamie took a photograph that they thought was funny while on a trip to Arlington National Cemetery in Washington DC. Jamie posted the photograph to Facebook, thinking that it would amuse their friends. The photograph showed Lindsey making a vulgar gesture and pretending to shout while standing next to a sign that said, 'Silence and Respect'. This was part of a running joke that the two had where they photographed themselves doing silly things such as pretending to disobey signs and notices. Several weeks later, Lindsey became aware that the photograph had spread beyond her own network, and was generating complaints, threats, and even calls for her to lose her job. The photograph had spread far beyond the audience it was originally intended for, and had been interpreted by people who did not have access to the original context. The consequences of this, and of audience members interpreting the photograph outside of the intended context, had real-world implications for Lindsey. She lost her job and struggled to find a new one. Any Google search for her name inevitably brought up the photograph, and she was judged on that one moment, taken out of context. She was unable to control the spread of the post, and she was also unable to remove all traces of it once it was in the public domain. What she had intended as a silly, if slightly inappropriate joke between friends, had reached an audience who interpreted it as deeply offensive, and there was little she could do to remove the image. This brings us onto the next dimension of online communication identified by both Baym and boyd: storage or persistence.

Storage and persistence

Captured via Baym's concept of storage, boyd identifies the persistence of mediated language as a key affordance in understanding online communication. Spoken language is ephemeral. It happens in a moment and is gone. Of course, we now have the means to record spoken utterances, but as boyd points out, the majority of spoken utterances are not recorded, and the default situation is that speech is ephemeral and transient. The act of writing, whether online or offline, captures and preserves an utterance, making it potentially available to audiences who were not present at the time or place of its production. As boyd (2010) points out, the act of writing an utterance makes it persistent and this changes the nature of the communicative act. The fact that the utterance has an ongoing presence means that it can be accessed and interpreted at a later time and by any number of people. While physical written documents can be destroyed, and online messages can be deleted, as boyd points out, the default with writing is persistence, and, of course, online, a digital trace often remains even after we think we have removed the content by clicking delete.

The persistence of digital content also means that the utterance can be revisited and scrutinised. The writer can be held accountable for the exact wording of her message long after it has been produced, and perhaps long after it was intended to be interpreted. It may be very difficult to reconstruct the exact context in which a writer intended her utterance to be interpreted, and yet the message is there for people to find, read, and react to. This enduring persistence of many digitally mediated utterances is in contrast with a common perception of the online world as fast-moving and transient. Online communication on social media platforms often has the speed and immediacy of speech, and messages and replies may be posted with very little reflection or, indeed, editing. Digital language can be stored in a way that is more typical of written communication, but it is usually not subject to the same editorial, redrafting, or proofreading processes that are associated with traditional, offline written texts.

Shortly after midnight on May 31, 2017, then president of the United States of America, Donald Trump, tweeted the message in (19).

(19)   Despite the constant negative press covfefe.

It is widely assumed that *covfefe* is a typographical error, and that the final word in the tweet should be *coverage*. It is unlikely that such an error would have made it to the public version of a more traditional presidential written message. Had this been a spoken message, a slight mispronunciation would have been immediately corrected and perhaps barely even noticed. However, on Twitter, the error was widely shared, and even though the message was deleted by Trump a few hours later, screenshots persist and allow for ongoing scrutiny and ridicule.

Replicability

Both Baym (2010) and boyd (2010) identify replicability as a key factor to consider when thinking about online communication and interaction. When we move into online contexts the scale and speed with which a message can be reproduced and shared is unprecedented. A message intended to be read by one person at one time may be rebroadcast and shared with any number of people at any time. We consider rebroadcasting as an act of communication in its own right in Chapter 3, and in that discussion we consider the various motivations that users might have for replicating third-party messages online.

Digital media also make it increasingly easy to edit and adapt content as part of the replication process. We will see how this is used to creative effect in meme creation in Chapter 6. However, the fact that content can be manipulated is another way in which users lose control of their messages and of the context in which they may be encountered and interpreted.

Mobility

When writing in 2010, Baym identified mobility as a dimension via which mediated forms of communication may vary. As she pointed out, the extent to which a technology is portable affects both the way we use it and the context in which we encounter messages and posts. At the time of writing this book in 2021, most, if not all, social media platforms are compatible with mobile devices. Indeed, some, such as Instagram, have reduced functionality in their desktop versions and so users must access via a mobile app to make full use of the site. The fact that users can access content anywhere and anytime necessarily affects the context in which communication takes place. However, it does not make that context any less unpredictable.

The mobility of devices also means that more than one screen may easily be used in parallel. In the practice of second screening, users use a smartphone or laptop while watching television 'to obtain more information about or discuss the program they are watching' (Gil de Zúñiga et al. 2015: 793). Users can now interact with media that previously offered only one-way, passive watching or listening experiences. Synchronous, online discourse can take place between physically distanced participants as news or entertainment events unfold live.

Social cues

When we communicate face-to-face we use a variety of non-linguistic or para-linguistic resources and strategies to guide our addressee to our intended meaning. These include facial expressions, tone of voice, and gestures. When we communicate via mediated channels these resources and strategies may be unavailable to us. Media vary as to the degree to which these sort of social cues are afforded. Early online communication was largely text-based, and there are still media, such as email, which predominantly rely on text-based messaging. With voice or video messaging we have access to more social cues. We may be able to hear the speaker's tone of voice and/or see their gestures and facial expressions. However, even online media which use visual channels, such as vlogging, are not equivalent to a face-to-face interaction. As Frobenius (2014: 70) notes in her work on audience design in vlogs on YouTube, the constraints of talking to a camera and watching a fixed screen mean that interlocutors cannot visibly co-orient and 'gestures and gaze behaviour cannot be used by the viewers to negotiate participant status'. In face-to-face interactions, we may use directional gaze to encourage joint attention on a referent, and we have the option to indicate that we are addressing somebody by making eye contact or by gesturing towards them. These discourse and audience management strategies are not available in camera mediated media such as vlogs and video chat.

It is common to talk about online interactions as being lean or impoverished in terms of social cues. After all, online, participants are likely to lack access to the wealth of information that can be gleaned from a speaker's intonation, facial expressions, or gestures. However, in this book, I move away from an approach which considers mediated communication to be impoverished in some way. As humans, we make use of the resources available to us. In face-to-face communication we can augment our messages with these extra-linguistic clues to our intended meaning. When we move online, other resources become available to us. We can include various types of images and graphics in our messages, we can choose to react to something by publicly sharing it or liking it, and we can create a message which includes a link to directly take readers to source materials. None of these possibilities are available offline in exactly the same way. We think of communicators as making use of these affordances, not as a poor substitute for the extra-linguistic cues which guide face-to-face communication, but rather as a means to the same end. The communicator's goal is to successfully communicate her intended message. Indeed, we are starting to see instances where online behaviours and expressions are being used in offline, unmediated contexts, presumably because they solve a communicative problem. The online initialism *lol* has moved into some people's spoken lexicon, and, as we see in Chapter 4, the pragmatic functions of hashtags have proved useful enough to have been co-opted into some speaker's offline repertoires. In Chapter 5, we look more closely at the strategies that users have adopted to communicate non-verbally via digital media.

Interactivity

Mediated forms of communication vary in terms of the interactivity that they afford. An online newspaper article or blog post may offer the audience limited opportunities to interact or respond. There may be a comments section or the option to share or like the content, but these media are largely designed to communicate a one-way message in a format that is similar to traditional newspapers. Social media networks, on the other hand, thrive on interaction, and they often offer a range of options for interacting with other users and with the content. On Facebook, for example, the options for interaction include sending someone a private message, posting on your own profile homepage, posting on somebody else's profile wall, tagging somebody in a post, and creating groups where people interact with each other. Web conferencing platforms like Zoom and Microsoft Teams offer a chat functionality that runs parallel to the video conferencing. Users might interact with some participants via video and audio chat, and others via text-based messages posted in the chat window.

Temporal structure

Face-to-face communication is generally synchronous. It takes place in real time. An addressee hears a spoken utterance as it is produced, and speakers have immediate access to the responses or reactions of their addressees. Written communication was traditionally asynchronous. A text would be written at one point in time and then read at a later point, and we might have to wait a considerable time for a reply, response, or reaction, if indeed we ever got one. These differences in temporal structure have an effect on how we interact and on the messages that we produce. As we saw when thinking about persistence, written texts can be planned, redrafted, and edited, while spoken texts tend to be more spontaneously produced, and may be adapted on-the-fly in response to audience or interlocutor feedback or reaction. Digitally mediated forms of communication tend to fall between these two extremes, and, indeed, we find wide variation across the temporal structures associated with different forms of mediated communication. Emails may be delivered to the recipient's inbox within seconds of being sent, but they may not be read or responded to for days or weeks, if at all. At the other end of the spectrum, video calls and conferencing happen in real time. Interactions on social media sites may take place in near real time, but there may also be a substantial delay between a message being posted and it being seen and responded to.

While so-called instant messaging platforms such as WhatsApp can facilitate near synchronous exchanges, the fact that they are mediated and not face-to-face still impacts on the messages and the interaction in a variety of ways. Messages are composed and received as whole units. It is not possible to interrupt someone as they are composing a message. Messages may, however, overlap with one another. That is, both participants may be composing their messages at the same time. This is in contrast to face-to-face spoken communication where interlocutors generally work towards an ideal of turn taking where one is speaking while the other listens. Of course, interruptions are possible in spoken discourse, and not all turns will necessarily be completed as intended. However, the interaction is negotiated in the moment between the interlocutors.

These near-asynchronous, but remote and written forms of digitally mediated communication often result in discourses that are complex in structure. On instant messaging platforms, users may send a series of messages each initiating the first part of a topic, known as a first pair part or FPP. The replies to those FPPs, known as second pair parts or SPPs, are unlikely to be adjacent to the relevant FPP on the screen. According to Herring (1999: 5), '[v]iolations of sequential coherence are the rule rather than the exception' in digitally mediated communication. Instant messaging platforms have incorporated features which provide the user with information about the status of their message and the activity of their interlocutor. On WhatsApp it is possible to see when a message has been delivered and when it has been read, and it is also possible to see when your interlocutor is typing a message. These features are unavailable when communicating via SMS, and these differences appear to have had an impact on the ways in which the platforms are used. König (2019) compared the features of SMS conversations with conversations on WhatsApp. She found that WhatsApp exchanges were more chat-like than those that took place via SMS. Users would tend to establish that their interlocutor was available to chat before entering into a conversation on WhatsApp. Once the exchange had started, WhatsApp users sent more messages than users of SMS. However, the messages were shorter on WhatsApp. WhatsApp users would also allow topics to emerge gradually over the course of a chat. In comparison, users of SMS tended to raise various topics within the same message by including several FPPs within one text message.

Searchability

Boyd identifies searchability as a key affordance of digital media communication. Not only are our messages stored, but as part of a digital network, they are organised and connected. They can be searched and retrieved in a way not possible in face-to-face communication, and both the coverage and the ease and accessibility of searchable content online is much greater than in offline written texts. In Chapter 4, we discuss the development of hashtags. While they were originally designed to facilitate searching online, their functions have developed beyond this, and we will see how they can be used to guide pragmatic processes. In Chapter 7, when we think about clickbait, we will see how the language that a writer uses might be affected both by the means by which readers are likely to access the post, as well as by the context in which it will be read. Writing a headline that will appear at the top of search engine results requires different techniques to writing a headline that will grab the attention of readers as they scroll through a social media feed.

Baym's and boyd's features provide us with a useful means of thinking about the factors and variables that influence user behaviour in digitally mediated contexts. They allow us to compare different media, and to think in more precise terms about how mediated communication is different to communication that takes place face-to-face.

OVERVIEW OF THE BOOK

As communicative technologies change and develop, users adapt their behaviours to both mitigate the restrictions and exploit the opportunities of digital contexts. Over the course of this book, we look more closely at these adaptations and their consequences from the perspective of pragmatics. We consider how discourse contexts change when we move into digital spaces, and we examine some of the new forms of interaction that online communication makes possible. In each case, we think about how the digital contexts and resources interact with our pragmatic processes and with the production and interpretation of communicative acts.

Understanding context is at the heart of pragmatics. When language use moves online, the context in which we are communicating changes in interesting and new ways. We look at the nature of online contexts in more detail in Chapter 2, and we introduce the notions of context collapse and the imagined audience. Many of the topics in this book focus on the strategies that users have adopted to communicate successfully in these new online contexts. We start in this chapter by exploring some of the ways in which users manage their privacy and navigate collapsed contexts.

In Chapter 3, we look at the practice of sharing content online. Digitally mediated networks make it easier and quicker than ever to share content with an audience, and that audience is potentially larger than ever before. Social media sites depend on the sharing and rebroadcasting of content, and in Chapter 3, we think about the pragmatics of sharing. We will see that users share third-party content for a variety of reasons, and we can understand these in terms of how they achieve relevance. We also briefly consider what it means to react to content via a *like* button on social media sites. Both sharing and liking are discussed as ostensive communicative acts which raise expectations of relevance.

Chapter 4 looks at the pragmatics of tagging. We consider the various ways in which users may employ tagging techniques on social networking sites for communicative purposes. With a focus on Twitter hashtags, we see that a range of pragmatic tagging functions have emerged. These contribute to the relevance of the utterance by guiding readers in their inferential processes. We also briefly look at @mention tags on Twitter, and discuss the various communicative functions that they may serve.

A common observation about online communication is that it is lean in terms of social cues. In Chapter 5, we look at the non-verbal means that users may employ in digital contexts. We think about how users may vary the presentation of text, and how they may use non-standard spelling and punctuation to help them convey their meaning. In the second half of the chapter, we focus specifically on emoticons and emoji, considering the range of communicative functions that they may perform. Reaction GIFs may also be used to communicate a user's emotions and attitudes, and we briefly consider these from a pragmatic perspective at the end of the chapter.

Chapter 6 focuses on memes. We think about the defining characteristics of memes, and discuss various common meme types. Object labelling image memes are a very common and popular category of memes, and in the second half of this chapter, a pragmatic analysis of the so-called *Distracted Boyfriend* meme is presented. We see that these type of memes function as multimodal metaphors, and interpretation of them draws on the same pragmatic processes as the interpretation of verbal metaphors. Also like verbal metaphors, they can be used to communicate a wide array of weak implicatures.

The way that we search and find content online influences the texts that writers create. In the noise of social media feeds it can be hard to get a reader's attention, and yet, that is what the creators of websites need to do if they are to monetise content. In Chapter 7, we take a pragmatic approach to a phenomenon that has emerged in response to the context in which online news content is produced and consumed: clickbait. Clickbait headlines are carefully constructed to attract the attention of readers and to entice them to click. In this chapter, we discuss the linguistic techniques behind a successful clickbait headline, and we see how they exploit our natural tendency to seek out cognitive effects and relevance.

Finally, in Chapter 8, we look more closely at the research that has informed the various discussions from the rest of the book. A range of data collection methods are discussed, and we also consider the role that theories and frameworks play in the development of knowledge. The chapter ends with brief discussions of the complexities of ethics and the importance of diversity when researching online.

The topics covered in this book are by no means an exhaustive list of the ways in which pragmatics interacts with the affordances of online communication. Technology is developing and new practices are emerging all the time. However, the discussions here provide a range of examples of the ways in which users have adapted to online contexts and found new ways to get their intended meaning across.

NOTES

1 In this chapter, and throughout the book, I follow the convention of referring to the speaker as *she* and the hearer as *he*. This is to help distinguish between the roles during discussions of interactions. No further meaning is intended by this use of pronouns.
2 Danah boyd does not capitalise her name. You can read more about her reasons for this on her website: http://www.danah.org/name.html

REFERENCES

Arendholz, J. (2013). *(In)Appropriate Online Behavior: A Pragmatic Analysis of Message Board Relations*. Amsterdam: John Benjamins.
Arielli, E. (2018). Sharing as a speech act. *Versus*, 127(2), 243–258. doi:10.14649/91354
Austin, J. L. (1962). *How to Do Things with Words*. Oxford: Oxford University Press.
Barton, D., & Lee, C. (2013). *Language Online: Investigating Digital Texts and Practices*. Abingdon: Routledge.
Baym, N. K. (2010). *Personal Connections in the Digital Age*. Cambridge: Polity Press.
boyd, d. (2010). Social network sites as networked public: affordances, dynamics and implications. In Z. Papacharissi (Ed.), *Networked Self: Identity, Community and Culture on Social Network Sites* (pp. 39–58). Abingdon: Routledge.

Carston, R. (2002). *Thoughts and Utterances: The Pragmatics of Explicit Communication*. Oxford: Blackwell.

Chapman, S. (2011). *Pragmatics*. Basingstoke: Palgrave Macmillan.

Clark, B. (2013). *Relevance Theory*. Cambridge: Cambridge University Press.

Darics, E. (2010). Politeness in computer-mediated discourse of a virtual team. *Journal of Politeness Research, 6*, 129–150. doi:10.1515/JPLR.2010.007

Frobenius, M. (2014). Audience design in monologues: How vloggers involve their viewers. *Journal of Pragmatics, 72*, 59–72. doi:10.1016/j.pragma.2014.02.008

Gil de Zúñiga, H., Garcia-Perdomo, V., & McGregor, S. C. (2015). What is second screening? Exploring motivations of second screen use and its effect on online policital participation. *Journal of Communication, 65*(5), 793–815. doi:10.1111/jcom.12174

Herring, S. (1999). Interactional coherence in CMC. *Journal of Computer-Mediated Communication, 4*(4). doi:10.1111/j.1083-6101.1999.tb00106.x

Kecskes, I. (2014). *Intercultural Pragmatics*. Oxford: Oxford University Press.

König, K. (2019). Sequential patterns in SMS and WhatsApp dialogues: Practices for coordinating actions and managing topics. *Discourse & Communication, 13*(6), 612–629. doi:10.1177/1750481319868853

Langlotz, A., & Locher, M. A. (2012). Ways of communicating emotional stance in online disagreements. *Journal of Pragmatics, 44*(12), 1591–1606. doi:10.1016/j.pragma.2012.04.002

Locher, M. (2010). Politeness and impoliteness in computer-mediated communication. *Journal of Politeness Research, 6*, 1–5. doi:10.1515/JPLR.2010.001

Locher, M. A., & Graham, S. L. (2010). Introduction to interpersonal pragmatics. In M. A. Locher, & S. L. Graham (Eds.), *Interpersonal Pragmatics* (pp. 1–13). Berlin: Mouton.

Mey, J. L. (2001). *Pragmatics: An Introduction*. Oxford: Blackwell.

Miltner, K. M., & Highfield, T. (2017). Never gonna GIF you up: Analyzing the cultural significance of the animated GIF. *Social Media + Society*, 1–11. doi:10.1177/2056305117725223

Rudolf Von Rohr, M.-T., & Locher, M. A. (2020). The interpersonal effects of complimenting others and self-praise in online health settings. In M. E. Placencia, & Z. R. Eslami (Eds.), *Complimenting Behavior and (Self-) Praise across Social Media: New Contexts and New Insights* (pp. 189–212). Amsterdam: John Benjamins.

Ronson, J. (2015). *So You've Been Publicly Shamed*. Oxford: Picador.

Searle, J. R. (1965). What is a speech act? In M. Black (Ed.), *Philosophy in America* (pp. 221–239). London: Allen and Unwin.

Searle, J. R. (1969). *Speech Acts*. Cambridge: Cambridge University Press.

Shakespeare, W. (1597/1980). *Romeo and Juliet*. London: Methuen & Co. Ltd.

Skovholt, K., Grønning, A., & Kankaanranta, A. (2014). The communicative functions of emoticons in workplace e-mails :-). *Journal of Computer-Mediated Communication, 8*(4), 780–797. doi:10.1111/jcc4.12063

Sperber, D., & Wilson, D. (1986). *Relevance: Communciation and Cognition* (2nd (with postface) ed.). Oxford: Blackwell.

Verschueren, J. (2009). Introduction. The pragmatic perspective. In J. Verschueren, & J. O. Östman (Eds.), *Key Notions for Pragmatics. Handbook of Pragmatics Highlights* (pp. 1–27). Amsterdam: John Benjamins.

Wilson, D., & Sperber, D. (2004). Relevance theory. In L. R. Horn, & G. Ward (Eds.), *The Handbook of Pragmatics* (pp. 607–632). Oxford: Blackwell.

Wilson, D., & Sperber, D. (2012). *Meaning and Relevance*. Cambridge: Cambridge University Press.

Zappavigna, M. (2012). *Discourse of Twitter and Social Media: How We Use Language to Create Affiliation on the Web*. London: Bloomsbury.

Zappavigna, M. (2018). *Searchable Talk: Hashtags and Social Media Metadiscourse*. London: Bloomsbury.

Zhao, S., Grasmuck, S., & Martin, J. (2008). Identity construction on Facebook: Digital empowerment in anchored relationships. *Computers in Human Behavior, 24*(5), 1816–1836. doi:10.1016/j.chb.2008.02.012

2

EXPLORING ONLINE CONTEXTS

On July 5, 1993, *The New Yorker* magazine published a cartoon by Peter Steiner which shows a dog sitting at a computer keyboard. The dog appears to be in conversation with another dog who is sitting on the ground next to him. The caption underneath reads, 'On the internet, nobody knows you're a dog'. In many ways, this one image, now a meme in its own right, encompasses many of the issues that we will be exploring in this chapter. When communication is mediated by a keyboard, a screen, and an internet connection, the options for how we present ourselves to others become very flexible. As Turkle (1995: 184) puts it, when you move online:

> You can be whoever you want to be. You can completely redefine yourself if you want ... You don't have to worry about the slots other people put you in as much. They don't look at your body and make assumptions. They don't hear your accent and make assumptions. All they see is your words.

As we will see in later chapters, our options for how we communicate in digitally mediated contexts have expanded since Turkle's observations, and since Steiner's cartoon was originally published. However, in many ways, these points are just as valid today as they were in the mid-1990s. It is not always possible to have a clear and accurate idea of who we are communicating with in virtual contexts. We can also hide who we are, or control what and how

DOI: 10.4324/9781003254201-2

much about ourselves we reveal when we go online. In this chapter, we think about the pragmatic implications of this. How do we interpret utterances when we do not know who the speaker is? How do we tailor our own utterances for an unknown audience? How do we navigate unpredictable discourse contexts? We will also briefly think about the implications that digital media contexts have for our notions of privacy and anonymity, and we will explore some ways in which users navigate and negotiate these issues online.

CONTEXT COLLAPSE

When we move into digitally mediated spaces, the notion of context becomes complicated in various and interesting ways. Communication that takes place offline is, for the most part, anchored in a specific time and place. This means that we are likely to have a clear idea of the context in which our utterance will be encountered and processed. This contextual information plays a crucial role in the communicative choices that we make when we construct an utterance. It also guides a hearer's interpretation of that utterance. Online, however, we may be communicating with people who are remote in distance and/or in time. We may have very little control over how, when, or where our messages are accessed. As a consequence, we have little control over the discourse context in which our utterances will be interpreted.

Offline communication, for the most part, takes place in a specific discourse context. Speakers and hearers have particular roles and statuses, and their interactions are produced and interpreted relative to the context and to their position in it. Any one individual will inhabit various roles, and will move between different social and cultural contexts regularly. We might, for example, be teachers in one context and students in another; we might play the role of a parent or carer for part of our day, but be a friend, colleague, or partner for another. As we move between these different social contexts, we present ourselves in different ways, and this influences the way in which we interact and the language choices that we make.

Think about the different social contexts and social groups that you move between in your day-to-day life. Perhaps you have a group of work colleagues or school friends that you see regularly. These are likely to be largely separate from your family, at least for some of the time. Your family might also be separate from your close personal friendships, or there might be some overlap between these two social groups. Your personal friendships may also fall into different social groups, and these may or may not overlap and interact. Perhaps some of your friends are old school friends that you have known for years, while others are friends from a sport or social activity in which you participate. As you move between these different social contexts, it is likely that the way in which you communicate will change. You probably use different vocabulary with different groups. You are also likely to vary the formality of your speech, and you will make different assumptions about the knowledge that you share and the perspectives that you take. This can often be difficult to navigate in situations where otherwise separate groups find themselves together in a particular social context. For example, your family, friends, and work colleagues might meet for the first time at a birthday party or wedding. It is on occasions like this that we become acutely aware of how we communicate differently with these different groups of people. As boyd (2010) points out, events such as weddings are usually carefully scripted and choreographed occasions. This provides some structure for the participants and helps to mitigate the awkwardness that comes with this overlapping of social groups.

Now think about the spaces and contexts in which you communicate online. Much like weddings and birthday parties, social networking sites tend to bring people from different social contexts together into one space. You may, for example, be Facebook friends with your colleagues, with your family members, and also with other friends from various different parts of your life. When you post an update on Facebook, the message will usually be available to all of these people. This creates a new and complex social and discourse context that must be navigated and managed. This is known as context collapse. In a collapsed context we might find that we 'must address anybody, everybody, and maybe even nobody all at once' (Wesch 2009: 23). The audience for online posts is potentially 'everyone who has or will have access to the Internet – billions of potential viewers, and your future self among them' (22). As Wesch (2009: 23) discusses, speaking to this 'infinitely ambiguous audience in an undefined context' can often feel overwhelming. In other cases, the collapsed contexts can make us feel awkward and self-conscious. As 17-year-old social media user Carmen describes, 'it's just uncool having your mom all over your [Facebook] wall, that's just lame' (Marwick and boyd 2014: 1058).

Androutsopoulos (2014) takes a sociolinguistic approach to the issue of context collapse. As he explains:

> [t]he notion of context collapse aims to capture what happens when a networked audience comprises "friends" with different socio-demographic features and types of social relationship.
>
> (63)

Building on this and other sociolinguistic work, Tagg et al. (2017) argue that it is useful to think about online interaction in terms of what they call 'context design'. They propose a theoretical model which is designed to examine how participants:

> take on board a range of factors in imagining the various ways in which their online posts may be re-contextualised ... [and] how this awareness both shapes and constrains what they say.
>
> (Tagg et al. 2017: 19)

With a focus on Facebook, Tagg et al. identify seven elements which they argue users take into account when constructing online posts. They organise these into the mnemonic POSTING: Participants, Online media ideologies, Site affordances, Text type, Identification processes, Norms of communication, and Goals (37–39). They claim that Facebook users have a 'semi-conscious awareness of these elements ... and that this awareness influences their behaviour on the site' (39). Context is, they argue, 'actively co-constructed by users in the course of their online interactions' (33), and this approach provides useful insights when considering digitally mediated communication from the perspective of pragmatics. According to relevance theory, constructing a context is part of the interpretation process. It involves accessing contextual assumptions that the hearers use as they form hypotheses about the speaker's intended meaning. Several of Tagg et al.'s seven elements can be understood as categories of contextual assumptions. Interlocutors are likely to hold assumptions about the other participants in the discourse as well as about online ideologies and norms of communication. These contextual assumptions are used by the hearer during the interpretation process, and must be allowed for by the speaker when she constructs her utterance. Recall, from Chapter 1, that speakers will aim to make their utterances as relevant as they can be while allowing for their abilities and preferences. Tagg et al.'s site affordances and text types can be understood as constraints on the online speaker's abilities. The speaker's preferences will determine both the overall communicative goals of the interaction and the identification processes by which the speaker chooses to 'perform and make visible their identity, commonality, connectedness and belonging' (Tagg et al. 2017: 38). Thus, the seven elements which drive Tagg et al.'s notion of context design can be understood in relevance-theoretic pragmatic terms, and are useful for unpacking the various factors which shape utterance production and interpretation in digitally mediated contexts.

Much of the literature on digital contexts and context collapse discusses the choices that users make about the content they post and about the ways in which they self-censor (Marwick and boyd 2011). We will look at some of these strategies later on in this chapter. From a pragmatic perspective, context collapse raises questions about how a speaker achieves their communicative goals while speaking to an audience in which different members bring different contextual assumptions to their interpretations. Many of the discussions and analyses that follow in the rest of this book deal with strategies that users have adopted to navigate and negotiate meaning in a collapsed context.

ONLINE AND IMAGINED AUDIENCES

When communication takes place offline, we usually have a good sense of who we are addressing and who is in our audience. From a pragmatic perspective, communicators tailor their messages based on the context in which they will be interpreted. Who we intend our message to be for, and who we envision as our audience have a significant impact on how we do this. A speaker would usually formulate her utterance for a particular addressee or addressees. This intended audience occupies a privileged position because the utterance has been constructed with their assumptions and perspectives in mind.

Of course, the addressee of an utterance is not necessarily the only person who will hear and interpret a message. However, addressees are the only people who can expect the speaker to have taken their perspective into consideration when the utterance was formulated. In relevance theory, this is captured via the communicative principle of relevance and the special status of ostensive communication. When we communicate, we tailor our utterances based on the intended audience and on our assumptions about what they know, what they do not know, and what information they have access to. For example, when talking to my non-work friend, I am likely to refer to my work colleagues by their roles, rather than by their names. I am assuming that my friend could not possibly know the names of the people I work with, and if I want to be understood I must take my hearer's perspective into consideration. In face-to-face communication, we also have access to information based on the fact that we share a physical space with the addressee. We know where our addressees physically are, what they can see and hear, and this will give us some idea about the knowledge they have and the assumptions that they hold.

In digital contexts, we may have a much less clear sense of who specifically we are addressing, and we often have much less control over who will see and interpret our posts. Furthermore, the boundaries between what is public and what is private can become blurred when we move online (boyd 2010). We might, for example, have a one-to-one conversation in a publicly accessible digital space. Online discourse contexts vary widely, of course, and our sense of who we are addressing with an online utterance is likely to vary from medium to medium. A WhatsApp message may, for example, be directed to one specific individual and to only that one specific individual. At the other end of the spectrum, a tweet on an unprotected Twitter account or a public video post on a YouTube channel can potentially be seen by anyone with an internet connection. There are not, however, two distinct categories of site, private and public. Rather we find a continuum between online communication from closed groups with tightly controlled membership, such as a family WhatsApp group, to sites on which anonymous users can post openly for anyone with an internet browser to see.

Social media sites are what boyd (2010) calls 'networked publics'. The affordances of the sites shape and structure how people engage and interact while using them. Sites such as Facebook, for example, 'tend to give online expression to existing offline communities (Seargeant et al. 2012: 514). Online forums, chats, and blogs, on the other hand, allow anonymous interactions, but may be the catalyst for new, digital communities (Baym 2000). One of the key affordances of Twitter is its reach and the fact that a user can browse a feed of followed accounts or search for a particular term. Users also opt-in as part of a particular audience by following an account or a hashtag. While a tweeter will not know who precisely has read their individual posts, they can see who is following them, and they can see general statistics about how many times a particular tweet has been viewed and engaged with.

Barton and Lee (2013) divide intended audiences online into three broad types: a general 'unknown' audience, an audience of contacts or connections who might broadly be considered 'friends', and an audience of real-life friends. Communicating with an unknown audience might be more common on platforms like Twitter, Instagram, and YouTube, while more closed platforms like WhatsApp are associated with an audience of real-life friends. The notion of a Facebook friend epitomises the audience members in the middle group. These are people that you may or may not have met or have regular contact with in the offline world, but who are named and with whom you have some connection. Barton and Lee focus on ways in which the conceptualisation of an intended audience influences language choice amongst multilingual users. However, the conceptualisation of audience is key from a pragmatic perspective as well. Marwick and boyd (2011: 115) point out that, 'we need a more specific conception of audience than "anyone" to choose the language, cultural references, style and so on that comprise online identity presentation'. We also often need this more specific conception simply to get our message across in a way that is clear and relevant.

How then, do we navigate the potentially unbounded and collapsed contexts in which we find ourselves when we move online? We cannot possibly construct messages that simultaneously communicate the same message to everyone, and, indeed, for the most part this is not our aim. Rather, when we communicate online, we construct messages for what has become known as an 'imagined audience' (Marwick and boyd 2011; Brake 2012; Litt 2012; Litt and Hargittai 2016). In reality, the audience that will actually see what we have posted may be very different to what we have imagined. However, addressing a 'cognitively constructed audience' (Marwick and boyd 2011: 116) provides us with a context in which to construct our utterance. It helps us to determine what information we might include and what we might leave implicit based on how we imagine our audience, and on what intended interpretation we want that imagined audience to reach.

Social media users vary in their conceptions of their imagined audience. Marwick and boyd (2011) conducted a survey to investigate how Twitter users imagine their audience. Their results reveal that different users conceptualise their audience in different and varied ways, and that there is often a complex and multi-layered relationship between those posting on Twitter and their perceived audience(s). Some respondents reported using Twitter as a personal diary or journal for recording their lives and experiences, and, as such, they claimed to be writing either for nobody or for just themselves. As Marwick and boyd point out, these users have nonetheless chosen to perform this act of writing in a public sphere. They are not 'tweeting into a void', and they do not, in fact, lack an audience. Rather, it seems that these users are not comfortable in viewing those who read their tweets as an 'audience', and they are not primarily concerned with the reactions of their readers. At the other end of the spectrum, we find users with large followings on Twitter who are more tactically and strategically aware of their audiences, and who explicitly acknowledge that they tailor their posts with a very specific audience in mind.

A study by Litt and Hargittai (2016) revealed that most users report sometimes writing with a specific target audience in mind while at other times writing with a much more abstract notion of who might be in their audience. When they have an abstract audience in mind, users tend to describe the process of posting content to social media in terms of self-presentation. It is the act of sharing that is the focus of the activity, rather than who may or may not see the content. When they write for a specific target audience, on the other hand, users describe their motivation in terms of the audience's experience. They post something because they think certain groups of people will be interested in it or entertained by it.

The imagined audience is, of course, not a new phenomenon. For as long as it has been possible to communicate with an unseen, mass audience, speakers and writers have had to make assumptions about who that audience is. Journalists and authors, as well as radio and television broadcasters, have always spoken or written for an imagined public, rather than for specific addressees. They have had to predict what assumptions audience members hold and what information they will find interesting and relevant. However, users communicating in online networks are more likely to interact directly with members of their actual audience. While broadcast media may communicate with a large and anonymous audience, social media sites such as Facebook, tend to consist of a more limited, and perhaps less anonymous, audience (Androutsopoulos 2014). The consequences of misjudging what is appropriate are therefore likely to be more serious on social media than in broadcast media contexts. As Marwick and boyd (2011: 129) put it:

> While the broadcast audience is a faceless mass, the networked audience is unidentified but contains familiar faces; it is both potentially public and personal.

While the networked nature of social media sites may give a user some idea of who is in their audience, as Marwick and boyd (2011: 99) note, 'it is virtually impossible for Twitter users to account for their potential audience, let alone actual readers'. In reality, most tweets will be read by relatively few people (Marwick and boyd 2011). However, their significance lies in the 'possibility of tremendous visibility, not the guarantee of it' (boyd 2010: 47).

Imagined audiences and relevance

How might the notion of an imagined audience be allowed for within a pragmatic theory such as relevance theory? As we saw in Chapter 1, the addressee of an utterance occupies a privileged position as far as relevance theory is concerned. It is the addressee who can use the presumption of optimal relevance in his interpretation of the utterance. Of course, people other than the addressee may hear or read an utterance. However, to interpret it, they must view the information from the perspective of the addressee. When we speak or write, we aim at optimal relevance for our addressees, not for eavesdroppers, and it is this which shapes our communicative choices, and, ultimately, our utterance. The addressees of an utterance are 'the individuals whose cognitive environment the communicator is trying to modify' (Sperber and Wilson 1986/95: 158). In face-to-face communication, this is likely to be specific individuals. However, whose cognitive environments are we trying to modify when we share a photograph on Instagram or post a tweet? Imagined audiences, are, as we have seen, nothing new. Sperber and Wilson, writing before the launch of the first social networking sites (boyd and Ellison 2008), describe how the presumption of optimal relevance applies in discourse contexts where there are no definite addressees. As they explain:

> In broadcast communication, a stimulus can even be addressed to whoever finds it relevant. The communicator is then communicating her presumption of relevance to whoever is willing to entertain it.
>
> (Sperber and Wilson 1986/95: 158)

When there is no definite addressee, any readers or hearers who find the message relevant, may envision themselves as part of the intended audience, and may then use the presumption of optimal relevance and the relevance-theoretic comprehension procedure to guide their interpretation. Remember that the definition of optimal relevance makes allowances for the speaker's abilities and preferences. One of the key constraints on users when they communicate in public contexts online is that they do not have complete knowledge of who their audience is. When interpreting public online utterances, users must take this into consideration. They may have to accept that the overall relevance of an utterance may be lower, because it has been written for an imaginary, rather than actual, audience.

We noted above that the boundaries between private and public communication may become blurred online, particularly in collapsed contexts. A user may direct an utterance to a particular addressee but choose to do so in a public forum, for example. Relevance theory offers us a way to think about how such utterances should be interpreted. We can understand the user as performing two ostensive acts. First she is performing an act of *saying* which is directed at a particular addressee. However, by sharing this act of saying on a public forum or platform, the speaker is simultaneously performing an act of *showing*. She is showing her utterance to a wider audience, and this wider audience is entitled to presume that she has done so for a reason. While they must put themselves in the mental shoes of the addressee to interpret the utterance itself, they are entitled to use the relevance-theoretic comprehension procedure in their interpretation of the act of showing.[1] Acts of showing and sharing are discussed in more detail from a relevance-theoretic perspective in Chapter 3.

ONLINE SPEAKERS, IDENTITY, AND (A)NONYMITY

When we communicate with someone in an offline, face-to-face context, we generally have some idea of who is addressing us. Even if they are personally unknown to us, we have access to a wealth of visual and auditory information about what that person might be like and how they might be feeling towards us in that moment. In face-to-face communication we can also respond to our interlocutor's reactions in the moment. We can rephrase or clarify a point if they seem to have misunderstood, or we can apologise there and then, if we seem to have caused offence. As we saw in the last chapter, many of the social cues that we rely on in face-to-face communication are absent or reduced when we move into digital spaces. Furthermore, online contexts afford users a high degree of control over how they present themselves and how much information about themselves they reveal. Indeed, in some cases complete anonymity may be possible. For example, on the discussion site Reddit, users generally post under pseudonyms. They are, to all intents and purposes, anonymous as far as a standard reader is concerned. It is possible to post to many message boards and online forums without revealing any information that might link the message to the identity of the person who has posted it.

The option to remain anonymous appears to have an effect on what and how a user might communicate. In offline contexts, the way we communicate and the things that we say are likely to have a direct effect on the relationships we have with others and on the way others see us. Online communication allows us to separate our offline selves from the messages we send and the opinions that we express. As Widyanto and Griffiths (2011: 15) explain, 'the internet provides anonymity, which removes the threat of confrontation, rejection, and other consequences of behaviour'. Offence can be very easily given or taken online, and as Tagg et al. (2017: 46), discuss, 'affordances such as the possibility of anonymity, the physical distance between interlocutors, and a relative lack of social cues may … encourage repressive and confrontational behaviour'. Anonymity can, according to Hardaker (2010: 224), 'foster a sense of impunity, loss of self-awareness, and a likelihood of acting upon normally inhibited impulses'. That is, we may do and say things online that we would not do or say in other contexts. Hardaker (2010, 2013) particularly focuses on the practice of trolling. Trolling can take various forms, but a troll aims to create 'disruption and/or to trigger or exacerbate conflict for the purposes of their own amusement' (Hardaker 2010: 237). This might, for example, involve expressing deliberately controversial or divisive views or opinions in order to shock others and cause arguments. Like most other activities that take place online, trolling is context-sensitive. What is harmless fun to some, may be cruel and hurtful to others. However, whatever the motive, trolling is made possible because of the affordances of digitally mediated communication. As Hardaker says (2010: 238), 'with the protection of anonymity and distance,… users can exercise aggression against other real humans, with little risk of being identified or held accountable for their actions'.

Of course, the choice to remain anonymous is not only driven by negative and deceptive motives. Anonymous online contexts offer users a space to discuss sensitive topics which they might not feel comfortable addressing offline. De Choudhury and De (2014) studied anonymity and disinhibition in mental health support groups on Reddit. Their findings suggest that anonymity and the use of 'throwaway' accounts encourages participants to express themselves more freely, and leads to more engaged and helpful suggestions and advice.

Most of the popular social media sites require some degree of authentication to create an account. For example, Facebook, Twitter, and Instagram accounts must be linked to an email address or telephone number. In practice, there is nothing to prevent a user from creating a new email account solely for the purpose of creating a new profile. Nevertheless, much of the communication that takes place via social media networking sites takes place in what Zhao et al. (2008) call an 'anchored relationship'. In an anchored relationship, the participants have some sort of offline connection. Their relationship may be anchored via an institution, such as a workplace or school, they may be family members or offline friends, or the relationship may be anchored via mutual friendships. The level of contextual information that a speaker may draw on in an anchored relationship will vary from case to case. Close friends or partners who know a lot about one another may send each other digitally mediated messages. When they do so, they will be able to assume a large number of shared contextual assumptions, and this may affect the communicative choices they make. At the other end of the spectrum, imagine two remote working co-workers communicating via a company intranet. They may never have met or spoken offline, but the fact that their relationship is anchored in the institution of the particular workplace will mean that they can assume certain things about the context in which they are communicating. For example, they may confidently use company-specific vocabulary without providing any further clarification or elaboration.

The issues of who the speaker is and what role their identity contributes to the interpretation of an utterance in online communication is not merely to do with anonymity. Even if a speaker's online presence is anchored in the offline world, the speaker's identity is still mediated through the digital platform and applications. In offline contexts, we perform our identity via the choices that we make, both linguistic and non-linguistic. We choose what to wear, for example, and we also perform our identities via the language choices that we make. Online contexts, and in particular social media sites, afford us even more control over how the outside world sees us. We can carefully curate which aspects of our lives are documented on these sites, and we can edit and filter images to present what Zhao et al. (2008: 1819) refer to as our 'hoped-for possible selves'. In extreme cases this can lead to so-called catfishing. The term *catfishing* was first used in a documentary-style movie which follows the experiences of a young man who falls in love with a woman he has met online (Joost and Schulman 2010). He tracks her down in real life, only to find that her offline life and identity do not match what she presented in her online profiles. The movie spawned a long-running television show in which host presenters investigate online relationships and help bring the participants together in real life. A participant is said to be a catfish if their real-life persona does not match with the persona that they presented online. There is, of course, a blurred line between presenting an idealised version of ourselves and deceiving those people that we interact with. Cases of so-called catfishing often involve using fake photographs or providing misleading information about sex, age, or other personal characteristics. Clearly, the ability to control and curate how we present ourselves online is a key issue for pragmatics. The identity of our interlocutor is very likely to affect both what we say and how we say it. We may, for example, feel comfortable discussing things with a peer group, but would feel very uncomfortable if this information were shared outside of that group. We might only wish to discuss personal matters with someone of the same sex, or, as in the many cases that feature on the *Catfish* television show, we may only be interested in pursuing a romantic or intimate relationship with a person of a certain sex and/or age. By portraying themselves in a particular way, users can influence how a message is received and interpreted, and similarly, users will adapt their messages based on who they think they are speaking to.

A separate, but no less interesting issue relating to the notion of the speaker in online communication arises in cases where communication is a result of collaboration. This is perhaps most obviously evidenced on a site like Wikipedia. There is generally no one author behind any particular Wikipedia page. Rather the content and text are more or less in a constant state of flux, being edited, enhanced, and updated whenever a user sees fit. At the time of writing, for example, the Wikipedia page for hashtags had been edited 1600 times by 914 different people (Xtools, 2019). These collaborative acts of communication raise interesting issues for pragmatic theories. If the aim of the hearer is to identify the speaker's meaning, and this is linked to the speaker's intentions, how do we interpret utterances in cases of collaboratively produced texts?

We also find collaboration in the creation of online memes. To create a new version of a meme, a user will take a photograph, image, or text template created by someone else and adapt it in a new way. As we will see in Chapter 6, memes derive at least part of their meaning from their position as part of a meme family. In such cases, more than one person is involved in creating the message, and so the notion of a speaker again becomes blurred. Pragmatics is about the interpretation of utterances and other acts of communication. The notion of a speaker's intended meaning is at the heart of many pragmatic approaches. The task of forming a hypothesis about the speaker's intended meaning can become difficult and complex in discourse contexts where speakers may choose to remain anonymous, where they may carefully control and curate their identity, or where they may communicate collaboratively.

NAVIGATING ONLINE CONTEXTS

Digitally mediated discourse contexts bring users together in virtual spaces where contexts may be collapsed, audiences are likely to be imagined, and where it may be possible to remain entirely anonymous. Over the course of the rest of this book we will see examples of users adapting and co-opting resources to help them to navigate online contexts. However, the potential for misunderstandings, disagreement, and conflict in these spaces is far greater than in offline contexts. We may, for example, be misunderstood if the audience that we imagine is very different to the actual audience that accesses a message. We must manage without the social cues, such as facial expressions and tone of voice, that can be used to communicate our attitude and to set the tone of a discourse. How then do users navigate the collapsed context in which they find themselves online, and how do they interact with an imagined audience in a meaningful and coherent way? Given the often-ambiguous contexts in which online utterances are produced, speakers and writers have various strategies available to them.

As discussed, Marwick and boyd (2011) found that users conceive of their imagined audience in various different ways. This then directly impacts on the strategies that they use when posting on social media. Some envision what might be thought of as an 'ideal audience' made up of 'ideal people' who are very much like the user themselves. When posting with this imagined audience in mind, users assume shared values, knowledge, and assumptions. Other users assume what we might think of as a worst-case scenario. This is particularly common on sites with potentially large audiences, and users adopting this strategy imagine an audience 'as its most sensitive members: parents, partners, and bosses' (125). This 'lowest-common denominator' (122) strategy leads to some self-censorship as users only post content that they believe a wide audience will appreciate and find appropriate.

From her study of video blogs posted on YouTube, Frobenius (2014) identified various strategies that vloggers use to manage their imagined audience. While they often used the second person pronoun *you* to address their whole audience, vloggers also addressed sub-groups within the audience, based on general characteristics. For example, one vlogger directed messages specifically at 'new people' in contrast to viewers who are part of an established and regular audience. This offers one way to manage the expectations of individual viewers. If they identify as part of the addressed group, they may expect to find that part of the message particularly relevant to them, and if not, they are likely to self-identify as observers, rather than participants, in that part of the discourse. Similarly, Frobenius found that vloggers used if-clauses to 'invite participants to self-select as addressees' (70). By introducing an utterance with a qualifying if-clause, such as 'if you're interested' or 'if you want to read more…', the vlogger is able to address self-identifying sub-groups of the imagined audience. While vloggers and their audience do not share the same physical space, Frobenius suggests that sites such as YouTube are virtual spaces, and 'once a person accesses the shared virtual space, he or she is a participant' (70). Indeed, she found that the vloggers often asked their audience questions and made specific requests for interaction, thereby assigning the viewers an active participant role in the discourse.

Vladimirou et al. (2021) discuss the complexity of addressivity on sites such as Twitter. Their analysis reveals that when complaining, tweeters often post a publicly available message, but within that post they address specific individuals and organisations by tagging or otherwise mentioning them. In public posts with multiple user tags, it is not always clear who the primary addressees for a particular complaint are. The inclusion of multiple addressees introduces an ambiguity over who is to blame, which, Vladimirou et al. suggest, is linked to an escalation of aggression. We return to the pragmatic function of @mentions and other user tags in Chapter 4.

Navigating context collapse and managing the imagined audience is not always a case of making the utterances accessible and interpretable by all. For many users, it is about restricting access to meaning in some way. Ideally, users seek to maintain some degree of privacy whilst still engaging in the networking that social media sites afford. For many users context collapse is experienced as a violation of their privacy, and, in general, they are much more concerned with whether people they know, such as parents or employers, will see their posts, rather than with whether their content will be accessed by strangers (Marwick and boyd 2011; Vitak et al. 2012).

Most social media sites have inbuilt privacy settings which afford users some control over who sees their content. For some sites, privacy settings apply at account level. That is, your account is either public or private. On Twitter and Instagram, a user can choose to lock their account so that only those on a curated follower list have access to the posts (Marwick and boyd 2014). Permission to follow the account has to be explicitly requested and authorised. This does not entirely remove the issues associated with a collapsed context, as a user may still be followed by a wide range of people from different areas of their life. However, it does provide the user with some knowledge about who can and cannot see messages, and it also affords them some degree of control. Facebook allows more fine-grained management of the audience for a particular post. The user can control precisely who can see a message, either via placing their friends into groups and making posts accessible only to certain groups, or by customising visibility at an individual friend level. However, as Marwick and boyd (2014: 1056) point out, these privacy settings are 'complicated and confusing', and there is evidence that they are not widely or consistently used (Sleeper, et al. 2013). According to Remy (2019) only 13% of Twitter accounts are private. It is perhaps therefore not surprising that users have developed a range of other strategies to help them to manage their audience and to navigate context collapse.

Multilingual users may rely on language choice as a key strategy in managing their audience (Androutsopoulos 2014; Tagg and Seargeant 2014; Tagg 2015: 153–162). In a study of multilingual networks on Facebook,

Androutsopoulos identified a range of strategies that users adopted to negotiate the collapsed context. Some users 'partition their networked audiences'
via their language choices. They did this by 'tailoring language style to a particular addressee who is contextualized as such or by tailoring language style
to a specific segment of the network' (Androutsopoulos 2014: 67). In other
instances, users sought to maximise their audience. Strategies to achieve this
included using a common language, replicating messages in different languages, and using non-linguistic resources such as images, emoticons, or
punctuation. Androutsopoulous concludes that 'language style, and more
specifically language choice, [is] a key resource by which to bring together or
separate various parts of the networked audience' (71).

In other cases, users may try to avoid or minimise context collapse by com-
partmentalising their social media presence, and using different sites for different groups of people. For example, some users might choose to use
Facebook to connect with close, named friends with whom they have offline
relationships, while their interactions on Twitter may be more outward-facing
or professionally focused. Other users may create multiple accounts for the
different aspects of their lives, and then post content accordingly (Vitak et al.
2012, 2015).

Marwick and boyd (2014) conducted an ethnographic study of the social
media practices of teenagers. They found that the teenagers in their study use
a variety of strategies to manage who has access to the information they post
and in what context. Hunter, aged 14, describes having a very clear idea of
who each post or status update is intended for, and he expresses frustration
when someone responds to a post that was not intended for them. For him,
users should understand when a post is addressed to them and when it is not.
As he explains:

> I will talk to my sister in a different way than I'll talk to my friends at school...
> I mean, I think you can figure out that I'm not talking to you if I'm talking about a
> certain teacher.
>
> (1057)

The subject matter of the post, along with linguistic cues, should, Hunter
thinks, be sufficient evidence for readers to deduce whether they are part of
his imagined audience or not. However, he also describes other means of
directly managing his audience. For example, he reports using the technological affordances of Facebook to block certain users from seeing particular
posts.

In Chapter 1, we discussed the potential reach of social media posts. While
this is a positive if you are seeking to communicate with a wide audience, the
networked nature of social media sites means that we can easily lose control
over who sees the content that we post. Marwick and boyd (2014) report the
case of high school friends Ramón and Matthew who used Facebook in quite
different ways. Matthew used it to communicate with his peers and to share

silly and sometimes juvenile content. Ramón used it to network with representatives from colleges and universities. Matthew had his privacy settings configured so that friends-of-friends could see his posts. This meant that the college representatives who were friends with Ramón could see Matthew's juvenile posts. This ended up impacting negatively on them both. Ramón and Matthew had different expectations about how the media were used, and Matthew did not know the full context in which he was posting.

Another strategy that emerged from Marwick and boyd's work is what they call 'social steganography'. Different friends or followers have access to different information and assumptions. Social steganography involves posting a message that appears to mean one thing on the surface, but which has hidden, additional meaning for anyone with access to specific assumptions or cultural information. Marwick and boyd describe the example of Carmen who posted a social media update reading 'Always look on the bright side of life'. Carmen's friends recognised this as a reference to the Monty Python film *The Life of Brian*, and, more specifically, to a scene where a character sings this line while being crucified. They realised that all was not well and contacted Carmen to find out why. Carmen knew, however, that her mother would not recognise this reference and would take the message at face value.

Users of online media do not always have to imagine their audience, of course. When messages are sent to WhatsApp groups, for example, users are not only able to see who is in the group, but they can also see who has seen their messages. Knowledge of the potential and actual audience for a message does not, however, completely remove the need to adjust utterances when interacting in mediated contexts. Various studies suggest that users change and adapt their strategies for doing politeness and relational work in asynchronous communicative contexts, and that new norms of appropriateness emerge in new online contexts. Flores-Salgado and Castineira-Benitez (2018) examined the politeness strategies that were used within WhatsApp group chats by speakers of Mexican Spanish when making requests. Their findings suggest that the users' choice of strategies is directly impacted by the properties of the digital context in which they are communicating. In Mexico, politeness has been shown to be associated with involvement strategies such as attending to the hearer, claiming in-group membership, and use of nicknames and informal pronouns (Curcó 2007). However, in the WhatsApp chats, strategies associated with independence, and in particular conventional indirectness strategies, were preferred over those associated with involvement. This, Flores-Salgado and Castineira-Benitez suggest, can, in part, be explained by the asynchronous nature of WhatsApp groups, along with the public and impersonal nature of the specific groups on which their study was focused. Thus, users are adapting their relational strategies as they negotiate the constraints and affordances of the digital context in which they are communicating, and new norms of appropriateness are emerging. In their study on Swiss French chats, Petitjean and Morel (2017) also found a link between the use of politeness strategies and the asynchronicity of WhatsApp conversations.

They found that users employed transcribed laughter ('*hahaha*') to indicate that their message was non-serious. This helped them to navigate potentially delicate actions such as requests and complaints.

Other context-driven differences in the relational work that we see online arise from the lack of social cues. In a study of a Spanish online forum, Landone (2012) found that politeness and relation-oriented discourse markers were used in a way that did not pattern with either spoken language or more traditional forms of written communication. The differences, she suggests, are at least partly due to the lack of non-verbal cues in this communicative medium. Discourse markers were used to mitigate the force of assertives and to negotiate (dis)agreement. According to Landone (2012: 1817), the frequency with which they were used in the forum reflects 'the speaker's urgent need to provide a clear and immediate relational signal' in the absence of social cues. These findings are paralleled in Georgakopoulou's (2011) analysis of relational work in a corpus of private emails in Greek and English. She found that the users compensated for the lack of social cues via 'strategic manipulation of the verbal part of the message'. This served to maintain and enhance alignment between the users, and thus manage their relationship. The specific strategies that Georgakopoulou found in her corpus were 'intimately linked with the linguistic and sociocultural features of the specific discourse communities of email users'. That is, all the speakers were fluent in both Greek and English and so could code-switch between the two, and all had close offline relationships with one another. As Georgakopoulou notes, users with different resources available to them 'would arguably draw upon other, comparable discourse strategies' to achieve the same relational ends. Although not the main focus of this book, work in intercultural pragmatics can help us to understand cross-cultural and cross-linguistic differences in mediated communication. It can both shine a light on the cultural assumptions that underpin the production and interpretation of utterances and reveal how differences in linguistic resources affect the strategies that speakers adopt to achieve their communicative goals.

CONCLUSIONS

Pragmatics is concerned with the interpretation of language and communication in context. Pragmatic analyses seek to uncover how hearers interpret utterances based on the context in which they are produced. When we move into online spaces, issues relating to context become complicated in ways that raise interesting questions from the perspective of pragmatics. In digitally mediated contexts we often find ourselves communicating with people who are remote in distance and/or in time. We may have very little control over how, when, or where our messages are accessed. That is, we have little control over the discourse context in which our utterances will be interpreted. We often cannot know who our actual audience is online, and so we have to construct our utterances for an imagined audience. Furthermore, one message may be accessed by a wide range of different people, all of whom bring different assumptions to their interpretation of it. This collapsing of contexts must be navigated and managed if users are to communicate successfully online. Finally, the line between what is public and what is private is often blurred in digital contexts. Users employ a range of strategies and techniques to both manage their audience and to protect their privacy.

Many users seem to be very aware of the collapsed contexts in which they are communicating, and they are aware of the potential pitfalls that are involved. The intricacies of privacy settings and a loss of control over the context of interpretation and the reach of messages can trip users up. However, users have developed a repertoire of strategies for navigating collapsed contexts and imagining their audiences, appropriate to the social, cultural, and linguistic contexts in which they are communicating. As with many of the discussions in this book, these strategies reveal users to have an adaptability to the online medium, and an ability to turn the affordances of digital media to their advantage. As Marwick and boyd (2014: 1060) summarise, users demonstrate the ability to 'appropriate technical affordances and develop different tactics and strategies to segment audiences, restrict flows of information, and limit who can interpret what'.

As we shall see over the course of this book, users have proved themselves extremely adaptable in their communicative practices, and they are adept at communicating their intended messages within the constraints of a digitally mediated discourse context. Further techniques, devices, and strategies for navigating online contexts and for communicating with an imagined audience will emerge as we explore other aspects of digitally mediated communication throughout this book.

NOTE

1 See Sperber and Wilson (1987), Wilson (2018), and Scott (2019) for discussions of how this combination of saying and showing can be used in the analysis of literary texts.

REFERENCES

Androutsopoulos, J. (2014). Languaging when contexts collapse: Audience design in social networking. *Discourse, Context & Media, 4–5*, 62–73. doi:10.1016/j.dcm.2014.08.006.

Barton, D., & Lee, C. (2013). *Language Online: Investigating Digital Texts and Practices*. Abingdon: Routledge.

Baym, N. K. (2000). *Tune In, Log On: Soaps, Fandom and Online Community*. London: Sage.

boyd, d. (2010). Social network sites as networked public: affordances, dynamics and implications. In Z. Papacharissi (Ed.), *Networked Self: Identity, Community and Culture on Social Network Sites* (pp. 39–58). Abingdon: Routledge.

boyd, d., & Ellison, N. B. (2008). Social network sites: Definitions, history and scholarship. *Journal of Mediated Communication, 13*, 210–230. doi:10.1111/j.1083-6101.2007.00393.x

Brake, D. R. (2012). Who do they think they're talking to? Framings of the audience by social media users. *International Journal of Communication, 6*, 1056–1076.

Curcó, C. (2007). Positive Face, group face, and affiliation: An overview of politeness studies on Mexican Spanish. In M. E. Placencia, & C. García (Eds.), *Research on Politeness in the Spanish Speaking World* (pp. 105–120). Mahwah, NJ: Lawrence Erlbaum.

De Choudhury, M., & De, S. (2014). Mental health discourse on reddit: Self-disclosure, social support, and anonymity. In E. Adar, P. Resnick, M. De Choudhury, & B. Hogan (Eds.), *Proceedings of the Eighth International AAAI Conference on Weblogs and Social Media*. Palo Alto, CA: The AAAI Press.

Flores-Salgado, E., & Castineira-Benitez, T. A. (2018). The use of politeness in WhatsApp discourse and move 'requests'. *Journal of Pragmatics, 133*, 79–92. doi:10.1016/j.pragma.2018.06.009.

Frobenius, M. (2014). Audience design in monologues: How vloggers involve their viewers. *Journal of Pragmatics, 72*, 59–72. doi:10.1016/j.pragma.2014.02.008

Georgakopoulou, A. (2011). "On for drinkies?": Email cues of participant alignments. *Language@Internet, 8*, 4. Retrieved June 15, 2021 from https://www.languageatinternet.org/articles/2011/Georgakopoulou

Hardaker, C. (2010). Trolling in asynchronous computer-mediated communication: From user discussions to academic definitions. *Journal of Politeness Research, 6*(2), 215–242. doi:10.1515/jplr.2010.011

Hardaker, C. (2013). 'Uh...not to be nitpicky, but...the past tense of drag is dragged, not drug.' An overview of trolling strategies. *Journal of Language Agression and Conflict, 1*(1), 58–86. doi:10.1075/jlac.1.1.04har

Joost, H., & Schulman, A. (Directors). (2010). *Catfish* [Motion Picture].

Litt, E. (2012). Knock, Knock. Who's there? The imagined audience. *Journal of Broadcasting & Electronic Media, 56*(3), 330–345. doi:10.1080/08838151.2012.705195

Litt, E., & Hargittai, E. (2016). The imagined audience on social network sites. *Social Media + Society, 2*(1). doi:10.1177/2056305116633482.

Landone, E. (2012). Discourse markers and politeness in a digital forum in Spanish. *Journal of Pragmatics, 44*(13), 1799–1820. doi: 10.1016/j.pragma.2012.09.001

Marwick, A. E., & boyd, d. (2011). I tweet honestly, I tweet passionately: Twitter users, context collapse, and the imagined audience. *New Media and Society, 13*(1), 96–113. doi:10.1177/1461444810365313

Marwick, A. E., & boyd, d. (2014). Networked privacy: How teenagers negotaite context in social media. *New Media and Society, 16*(7), 1051–1067. doi:10.1177/1461444814543995

Petitjean, C., & Morel, E. (2017). "Hahaha": Laughter as a resource to manage WhatsApp conversations. *Journal of Pragmatics 110*, 1–19. doi:10.1016/j.pragma.2017.01.001

Remy, E. (2019). *How public and private Twitter users in the U.S. compare — and why it might matter for your research*. Retrieved April 12, 2021, from Pew Research Center: Decoded: https://medium.com/pew-research-center-decoded/how-public-and-private-twitter-users-in-the-u-s-d536ce2a41b3

Scott, K. (2019). Misleading and relevance in Shakespeare's Twelfth Night. In S. Chapman, & B. Clark (Eds.), *Pragmatics and Literature* (pp. 93–114). Amsterdam: John Benjamins.

Seargeant, P., Tagg, C., & Ngampramuam, W. (2012). Language choice and addressivity strategies in Thai-English social network interactions. *Journal of Sociolinguistics, 16*(4), 510–531.

Sleeper, M., Balebako, R., Das, S., McConahy, A. L., Wiese, J., & Cranor, L. F. (2013). The post that wasn't: Exploring self-censorship on Facebook. *CSCW '13: Proceedings of the 2013 conference on computer supported cooperative work*, (pp. 793–802). doi:10.1145/2441776.2441865

Sperber, D., & Wilson, D. (1986). *Relevance: Communciation and Cognition* (2nd ed. (with postface)). Oxford: Blackwell.

Sperber, D., & Wilson, D. (1987). Précis of Relevance: Communication and Cognition. *Behavioral and Brain Sciences, 10*, 697–754. doi:10.1017/S0140525X00055539

Tagg, C. (2015). *Exploring Digital Communication: Language in Action*. Abingdon: Routledge.

Tagg, C., & Seargeant, P. (2014). Audience design and language choice in the construction and maintenance of translocal communities on social network sites. In P. Seargeant, & C. Tagg (Eds.), *The Language of Social Media: Identity and Community on the Internet* (pp. 161–185). Basingstoke: Palgrave Macmillan.

Tagg, C., Seargeant, P., & Brown, A. A. (2017). *Taking Offence on Social Media: Conviviality and Communication on Facebook*. Cham: Palgrave Macmillan.

Turkle, S. (1995). *Life on Screen*. New York: Touchstone.

Vladimirou, D., House, J., & Kádár, D. Z. (2021). Aggressive complaining on Social Media: The case of #MuckyMerton. *Journal of Pragmatics*, 177, 51–64. doi:10.1016/j.pragma.2021.01.017.

Vitak, J., Blasiola, S., Patil, S., & Litt, E. (2015). Balancing audience and privacy tensions on social network sites. *International Journal of Communication*, 9, 1485–1504.

Vitak, J., Lampe, C., Gray, R., & Ellison, N. (2012). 'Why won't you be my Facebook friend?': Strategies for managing context collapse in the workplace. *Proceedings of the 7th Annual iConference* (pp. 555–557). New York: ACM.

Wesch, M. (2009). YouTube and you: Experiences of self-awareness in the context collapse of the recording webcam. *Explorations in Media Ecology*, 8(2), 19–34.

Widyanto, L., & Griffiths, M. D. (2011). An empirical study of problematic Internet use and self-esteem. *International Journal of Cyber Behaviour*, 1(1), 13–24. doi:10.4018/ijcbpl.2011010102

Wilson, D. (2018). Relevance theory and literary interpretation. In T. Cave, & D. Wilson (Eds.), *Reading Beyond the Code: Literature and Relevance* (pp. 185–204). Oxford: Oxford University Press.

Xtools. (2019). *Xtools: Hashtag*. Retrieved September 18, 2019, from https://xtools.wmflabs.org/articleinfo/en.wikipedia.org/Hashtag

Zhao, S., Grasmuck, S., & Martin, J. (2008). Identity construction on Facebook: Digital empowerment in anchored relationships. *Computers in Human Behavior*, 24(5), 1816–1836. doi:10.1016/j.chb.2008.02.012

3

THE PRAGMATICS OF SHARING ONLINE

The login screen on Facebook invites you to 'connect and share with the people in your life'. On the homepage, the text in the status update box prompts you to tell the world 'What's on your mind?' When we click to create a new tweet on Twitter, we are asked 'What's happening?' Social networking sites rely on their users sharing their images, stories, and experiences. This makes up the vast majority of the content that they host. It is this content that brings users to the site and allows monetisation of the platform, largely via advertising revenue. The companies behind the platforms produce very little of the site content themselves. The success of social media sites depends on the willingness of their users to share, and a focus on user-generated content is a key characteristic of Web 2.0.

In this chapter, we focus on the sharing and resharing of content as particular practices which are afforded by social media networks and other online platforms. We think about how sharing might function as a communicative act and how acts of online sharing are interpreted.

SHARING AND REBROADCASTING

Sharing is at the heart of social media networking sites. According to John (2013: 169), we can think of sharing as encompassing two types of act: acts of distribution and acts of communication. When we upload a photograph or post a link to an interesting article online, we are distributing content to a

DOI: 10.4324/9781003254201-3

networked audience, and this act of distribution is one type of sharing. However, we also find many acts of sharing online that are more about communication than they are about the simple distribution of content. We are not only encouraged to share pictures, files, and links when we go online, but also to share our ideas, feelings, and, indeed, our lives. As John argues, in online spaces, *sharing* has become synonymous with *telling*. He comments on an observed increase in the use of the verb *share* occurring without an object. This suggests, he notes, that we do not need to be told what to share, and, indeed, sharing has become 'shorthand for participating in the site' (John 2013: 169).

Insomuch as every act of posting content online is an act of sharing, this whole book is concerned with the pragmatics of sharing. However, in this chapter, we focus on one particular type of sharing. We will think about those acts of sharing which involve a user distributing, or redistributing content that they have not themselves created. This act will be referred to as *rebroadcasting*. The act of rebroadcasting is the act of sharing existing, usually third-party content with other users in your online social network (Scott, 2021).

Most webpages and apps have an option built in which allows users to rebroadcast content from the site in various ways. Most platforms allow material to be shared across networking sites, so, for example, a user can share a YouTube video to their Facebook or Twitter feed. Indeed, many non-social media websites now also feature share buttons which allow users to post content quickly and easily from those sites to their social media profiles. Some social media sites also have site-internal sharing functionality built into the platform and into individual posts. With just a few clicks, Twitter users can retweet content, Tumblr users can reblog content, and Facebook users can share content publicly via their news feed or privately in a direct message. Should we treat acts of rebroadcasting as communicative, and, if so, how are they interpreted by the intended audience? Why do users choose to rebroadcast third-party content, and how does sharing fit into a more general pragmatic framework for understanding communication? The rest of this chapter will be focused on these questions, and on what pragmatics can tell us about the answers. It will explore the act of rebroadcasting by focusing on the act of retweeting content on the microblogging site Twitter. The general patterns that emerge from this work are, however, applicable in other social media contexts where rebroadcasting is afforded. We also briefly discuss the communicative dimensions of liking content online. We will see that this sometimes involves an indirect act of sharing and it can also be considered as an act of communication.

WHY DO USERS REBROADCAST CONTENT?

What motivates a user to share a piece of third-party content with their connections on social media? Boyd et al. (2010) looked into this question by surveying Twitter users about their reasons for retweeting and their understanding of why other people might choose to retweet content. They did this by posting the question in (1) to Twitter, and then analysing the 99 responses that they received.

(1)   What do you think are the different reasons for why people [retweet] something. (boyd et al. 2010: 4)

Notice that this question asks the participants to think about the different reasons why people might retweet content. As such, it is designed to provide insight into how these users are interpreting others' acts of rebroadcasting, as well as revealing the respondents' own motivations for doing so. Boyd et al. acknowledge that their sample is small and convenience-based, and that it is therefore likely to be biased. However, the responses they received still reveal what they describe as 'diverse motivations' for retweeting. They group their responses into the ten categories given in (a) to (j) below (list adapted from boyd et al. 2010: 6). While the motivations covered by these categories are not claimed to be exhaustive, they do reveal at least some of the reasons why users click on the retweet button and choose to rebroadcast content to their followers on Twitter. We consider them here in turn.

(a)   To save tweets for future personal access.

Some users reported that they retweeted so that they could more easily find the content in the future. With millions of tweets being posted every day (Internet Live Stats n.d.), an individual post can easily become lost in the noise. At the time of boyd et al.'s survey in 2010, there was no specific means of marking or bookmarking a tweet for future reference. Retweeting and/or liking a tweet links the user's profile to the original post. This makes the content easier to find again at a later date. Users reported that they used the retweeting option for this function. They had co-opted the retweet option to create an archive of tweets for future reference. A bookmarking feature was introduced in 2018 giving users an alternative way to do this (Shah 2018).

(b)   To amplify or spread tweets to new audiences.

Users described retweeting content that they thought their followers had not yet, or might not otherwise, come across.

(c)   To entertain or inform a specific audience, or as an act of curation.

This motivation is similar to (b), but is described in terms of curating content for a specific audience of followers. As we saw in Chapter 2, the actual audience for a tweet or retweet may be very different to the audience that the user imagines. However, this motivation reveals that, at least on some occasions, users are imagining an audience for the retweet and that their behaviour is being driven by the assumed interests of that imagined audience.

(d)   To comment on someone's tweet by retweeting and adding new content, often to begin a conversation.

Here users describe retweeting in order to begin a conversation around the topic with their own followers, and to provide their own perspective on the subject of the tweet.

(e)   To make one's presence as a listener visible.

As we have seen, audiences on social media are often invisible, and we may have very little information about who has seen something that we have posted on a social media site. In category (e), users describe using the retweet function to indicate that they have seen the message. One tweeter explained that 'it shows that one is not just talking, but also listening' (boyd et al. 2010: 6).

(f)   To publicly agree with someone.

Here users describe an endorsement motivation for retweeting. Sharing content with your own followers can, it seems, be a way to communicate agreement with the content of the original post.

(g)   To validate others' thoughts.

Category (g) is similar to (f), but focuses on the content that is shared, rather than the act of endorsement. As a respondent put it, they retweet 'because sometimes, someone else just says it better' (boyd et al. 2010: 6).

(h)   As an act of friendship, loyalty, or homage by drawing attention, sometimes via a retweet request.

We see this category evidenced in the retweeting activities of followers of celebrity accounts. They will retweet content as a way of performing their loyalty and demonstrating their support for the celebrity.

(i)   To recognise or refer to less popular people or less visible content.

The motivation described in (i) is similar to (b) in that it is about amplifying content. However, the respondent has framed this in terms of spreading content to a wider audience than it might otherwise reach. Celebrity accounts may choose to retweet a post about an issue or cause that they support, knowing that by doing so the actual audience for the tweet will be increased.

(j)   For self-gain, either to gain followers or reciprocity from more visible participants.

Boyd et al.'s final category captures acts of retweeting that are attempts by the retweeters to increase their own audiences. Others may see the retweet and decide to follow the account as a result, or users may retweet content in the hope that the favour will be returned.

Boyd et al.'s categories are based on self-reported motivations for retweeting, and there is some overlap between the categories. For example, one might retweet as an act of endorsement, (f), while also hoping that the original tweeter might notice the retweet, (e), and perhaps reciprocate, (j). Likewise, we may retweet a post because we think our followers would find it interesting, (b), while also using the retweet to express an opinion about the topic and perhaps encourage further discussion, (d).

In the next section, we reanalyse these motivations in terms of how different acts of retweeting may achieve relevance, drawing on arguments and examples that are explored in Scott (2021).

REBROADCASTING AS SHOWING

When a user retweets on Twitter or shares on Facebook, she causes the content of the original post to appear in her own timeline, making it available for her own followers or friends.[1] They can do this with or without adding an additional comment to the post. How might we characterise such acts of rebroadcasting in pragmatic terms?

In Chapter 1, we defined the domain of pragmatics as being all ostensive acts of communication. That is, our pragmatic interpretation processes are triggered whenever we are the addressee of an intentional act of communication. Rebroadcasting is an intentional act of communication which causes a tweet to appear in the feed of anyone following the retweeter's account. It brings the content of the original tweet to the attention of these other users. That is, by retweeting, we are directing the attention of our followers to the retweeted content. We can understand the act of retweeting as an act of showing, and it may in this way be thought of as similar to directive pointing (Pepp et al. 2019). When a user retweets a post she is showing the tweet to her followers. Relevance theory recognises showing as an ostensive act of communication (Sperber and Wilson 1986/95: 46–54, 2015; Wharton 2009). By showing the tweet to her followers, the retweeter is communicating that it is worth them paying attention to the tweet. As Marsili (2020: 16) says, 'the communicative point of retweeting seems to be rather linked to [the retweet's] ostensive role'. According to Sperber and Wilson (1986/95: 49), there is 'no point in drawing someone's attention to a phenomenon unless it will seem relevant enough to him to be worth his attention'. By requesting someone's attention you are communicating that you think that 'by paying attention, [the addressee] will gain some relevant information' (49). Therefore, by retweeting a post, a retweeter is signalling that the content of the post will be relevant in some way. How do these acts of showing achieve relevance? To answer this question and to understand the pragmatic motivation behind the reasons for retweeting that boyd et al. identified, we will draw on another key distinction from relevance theory pragmatics. The distinction between descriptive and attributive uses of language.

RETWEETING AS ATTRIBUTIVE USE

Retweets and quotations

When a user retweets content she performs an act of rebroadcasting in which she shows third-party content to her users. We might then start from the assumption that retweeting is an act of quotation. After all, the retweeter is reproducing somebody else's words for a new audience.

Marsili (2020) suggests that retweets cannot simply be understood as quotations because a retweet includes an identical copy of the original post. We would, he says, not be expected to mimic the gestures, tone of voice, accent or facial expressions of the original speaker when quoting them. Nor would we be expected to reproduce the typeface, font, or handwriting style of an original text when we provide a written quotation. However, according to relevance theory, a speaker or writer is aiming to make her utterance optimally relevant. That is, her utterance should be the most relevant it can be allowing for her abilities and preferences, and the hearer or reader should not be put to any unrewarded effort. Therefore, relevance theory predicts that when quoting we would only reproduce the aspects of the original utterance that contribute to the relevance of the message that we are intending to convey. A speaker will only reproduce tone of voice or accent, for example, if these are relevant to her message. I might recreate an angry tone of voice when quoting someone if the fact that the original speaker was angry is relevant. However, I will not recreate these extra and paralinguistic elements of the original utterance if they are not relevant. If, for example, nothing follows from the fact that the angry speaker has a Welsh accent, then drawing attention to it by mimicking it in my quotation would put the hearer to unrewarded effort. When we speak or when we write by hand, we can choose which features to include in our quotations and which to leave out. However, when we retweet content we are constrained by the affordances of Twitter. Retweeting reproduces the tweet exactly. The hearer knows this, and so will not infer any additional meaning from the fact that the retweet is an exact replica of the original. Remember that readers only expect the stimulus to be as relevant as is compatible with the communicator's abilities and preferences. They will not look for further effects but rather will accept that the form of the message is constrained by the functionality of the interface and by the retweeter's inability to change that functionality.

Descriptive and attributive uses of language

We can understand how retweets and other acts of rebroadcasting achieve relevance if we think about the broader category of language use into which quotations fall. According to Sperber and Wilson and relevance theory, quotations are a type of attributive use (Wilson 2000). Rather than describing the world from the speaker's perspective, attributive uses of language are a representation of some other utterance or thought. This may be something that the speaker has said or thought at a previous moment in time, or it may be something that another speaker has said, or, indeed, thought. To illustrate this contrast between descriptive uses of language and attributive uses of language, consider how we might understand Mel's reply to Esam's question in (2).

(2)   Esam: What did Lee say when you asked him to come next week?
      Mel: I'm not talking to you.

Without further information we do not know if Mel is intending her reply to be descriptive or attributive. If Mel is using her utterance to describe the world as she sees it, then she is communicating that she (Mel) is not talking to you (Esam), and we might then infer that she is refusing to answer his question. However, there is another possibility. She could be quoting Lee's reply. If she is quoting Lee, Mel's words do not describe the world as she sees it, but rather they represent Lee's utterance. On this interpretation she is communicating that Lee told her that he (Lee) was not talking to her (Mel). This is an attributive use of language. As Sperber and Wilson explain, '[d]irect quotations are the most obvious examples of utterances used to represent not what they describe but what they resemble' (Sperber and Wilson 1986/95: 228).

Descriptive uses of language achieve relevance because the description of the world (as the speaker sees it) provides information which leads to some cognitive effects for the addressee. For example, on the descriptive interpretation of Mel's utterance in (2), Esam is likely to update his assumption about whether Mel is currently talking to him. Attributive uses of language, on the other hand, achieve relevance 'by informing the hearer of the fact that so-and-so has said something or thinks something' (Sperber and Wilson 1986/95: 238). This can, as we shall see, play out in at least three different ways.

Some attributive uses achieve relevance by informing the audience of the content of the attributed thought (Wilson and Sperber 2012: 128). This is the most likely way in which the attributive interpretation of Mel's utterance in (2) would achieve relevance. The fact that Lee told Mel that he is not talking to her will be relevant in its own right to Esam. The speaker must believe that the contents of the attributed utterance or thought will be relevant to the addressee(s). As Wilson (2000: 424) explains, these uses have been the main focus of existing literature on quotation. I will refer to such uses as *informative attributive uses*, as they are 'are primarily intended to inform the audience about the content of an attributed thought' (Wilson and Sperber 2012: 129).

Some attributive utterances are produced, not (only) to communicate new information, but to communicate the speaker's attitude towards the thought or utterance that is being attributed. In relevance-theoretic terms these are referred to as *echoic uses*. Wilson and Sperber (2012: 128–129) define echoic use as:

> a subtype of attributive use in which the speaker's primary intention is not to provide information about the content of an attributed thought, but to convey her own attitude or reaction to that thought.

The relevance lies not in the content, but in the attitude. The attitude may be positive or negative and 'the speaker may indicate that she agrees or disagrees with the original, is puzzled, angry, amused, intrigued, sceptical, etc., or any combination of these' (Wilson 2000: 432). This notion of echoic attributive use of language is central to the relevance-theoretic account of irony. To illustrate, consider the following example, adapted from Sperber and Wilson (1987: 708). Imagine that Donnacha utters (3) to Olivia in the morning as they are discussing how to spend their day.

(3)   It's a great day to drive to the beach!

They decide to drive to the beach, but end up spending all day in a traffic jam. As they sit in their stifling hot car, Olivia utters (4) to Donnacha.

(4)   It's a great day to drive to the beach indeed!

Here she is quoting Donnacha's words back to him. However, the relevance of her utterance lies in the mocking, dissociative attitude that she is communicating. This is a typical example of verbal irony.

Finally, a speaker's motivation for an attributive utterance might be to show the addressee that she has heard the original utterance, or to manage the social interaction in some other way. We might, for example, repeat somebody's words back to them to show that we are listening and thinking about what they have said. We can see this in action in example (5).

(5)   Clare: When he shouted at me it made me feel really upset.
       Paula: hmm, it made you feel upset.

The informational content of Paula's utterance in (5) will not be relevant to Clare in its own right. She already knows that she felt upset, so this information will not directly lead to cognitive effects for her. Paula is not communicating a particular attitude towards Clare's utterance, and so this is not an echoic attributive use. Rather, Paula is communicating that she has heard what Clare has said and is thinking about it, and it is this itself that leads to cognitive effects. It may, for example, strengthen Clare's assumption that Paula is an attentive listener and a good friend. It may lead Clare to derive the assumption that Paula is open to discussing the subject further and that she will be sympathetic. The relevance of such uses lies in the effects they have on social relationships and social interactions (Malinowski 1923; Žegarac and Clark 1999; Padilla Cruz 2004, 2005), and, as such, we can think of these as *phatic attributive uses*.

Having outlined these three varieties of attributive use, we can now use them to reanalyse the motivations for retweeting that were identified by boyd et al. (2010) in their user survey. As with any act of communication, rebroadcasting is context-sensitive. As we shall see, sometimes it is simply about redistribution of the content, and we can understand it as an informative attributive use. If the simple redistribution of content does not lead to an optimally relevant interpretation, then we will look for additional cognitive effects. They may be found in the attitude that the retweeter conveys (echoic attributive uses), and/or they may relate to the impact that the act has on the interaction and the social relationships involved (phatic attributive uses). Forming a hypothesis about how an act of retweeting is relevant is an inferential process and will be guided by pragmatics.

UNDERSTANDING REBROADCASTING ON TWITTER

Informative attributive uses

Informative attributive acts of rebroadcasting will be relevant if cognitive effects arise from the dissemination of the content of the tweet. This is captured in categories (b) ('To amplify or spread tweets to new audiences') and (c) ('To entertain or inform a specific audience, or as an act of curation'). By retweeting, the user intends to spread the propositional content of the original tweet to a wider audience. The user descriptions captured in (b) and (c) differ slightly in terms of how the motivation for retweeting is framed. Description (b) is focused on spreading the content to new audiences and amplifying the content as much as possible. We see this occurring when a high-profile news story breaks. Consider the tweet in (6), which was posted by the BBC Breaking News Twitter account (@BBCBreaking) on April 21, 2016.

(6)   The musician Prince has died at his Paisley Park estate aged 57, his publicist tells.

This tweet announcing the death of the singer Prince was retweeted by thousands of users. These users were, we assume, treating this as news that would be highly relevant to many people, and they were using the retweet function to spread this information as widely as possible.

The motivation described in (c) focuses on retweeting as an act of curation. Twitter users with a following focused around a particular topic may retweet content that they think is likely to be relevant to their particular followers. For example, the @gatewaywomen account focuses on supporting childless women, and on March 31, 2020 retweeted the tweet in (7), which was originally posted by the @ChildlessWeek account.

(7) There are many aspects to being childless; as there are to being a parent. Self isolation can be hard on many of us for numerous varied reasons. Please note these scenarios can apply equally to men #COVID19 #Selfisolation #workingfromhome #childless

The retweeting account has rebroadcast content from another account which addresses the same issues. The retweeted content has been shared as it is likely to be relevant to those already following the retweeting account.

The motivation described in category (a) ('To save tweets for personal future access') appears to be non-communicative. However, we might think of this use of retweeting as a form of notetaking. The act of writing something down as a memory aid could be interpreted as a self-addressed utterance which carries with it the presumption that it will be relevant to the writer at some future point. On this analysis, retweets that arise from motivation (a) are relevant because of their informational content. The motivation behind such retweets will not, of course, be apparent to the users who see the retweet. They will still search for relevance as normal, and they are still entitled to form relevance-guided hypotheses about the intentions behind the act of retweeting.

Echoic attributive uses

If we class rebroadcasting as attributive use, we might expect to find instances of retweeting where the relevance lies, not solely in the content of the tweet itself, but in the attitude that the retweeter conveys as part of her act of rebroadcasting. Categories (d) ('To comment on someone's tweet by retweeting and adding new content, often to begin a conversation'), (f) ('To publicly agree with someone'), and (g) ('To validate others' thoughts') describe acts of retweeting driven by this motivation. In (d), the user describes retweeting for the purpose of commenting on the original content, and categories (f) and (g) also focus on the communication of the retweeter's attitude. Of course, the information in these retweets may be relevant to some readers in its own right, but the relevance of the retweet lies, at least partly, in the communication of the retweeter's agreement or validation of the original message. Therefore, they are considered echoic. In echoic uses of language, the attitude communicated towards the original utterance can be positive or negative, and it can be explicitly signalled or left unspoken. We might therefore expect to see both positive and negative attitudes communicated by the attributive act of retweeting, and we might expect to see cases where the attitude is left unspoken for the readers to infer, alongside cases where the attitude or reaction is explicitly signalled.

When users click the retweet icon on a tweet, they are given the option to add their own comment to the message. This then appears along with the original retweeted post in the feeds of their followers. Cases where users choose this option and include a comment offer perhaps the most obvious cases of echoic retweets. On March 4, 2016, the Voice of Researcher (@ Research_Voice) posted the message in (8) which also included a link to an associated article. This was then retweeted by IoPPN PostDocs account (@ IoPPN-postdocs) with the comment in (9).

(8)   'The voices of #postdoc organizations are growing stronger …'.

(9)   Good!!

In this case, the retweeting account appears to be explicitly endorsing the content of the embedded tweet. The owners of the account have retweeted, not just to spread the content to a wider audience, but also to communicate their endorsement of that content.

We also find cases where the 'add comment' function has been used to communicate a negative attitude towards the embedded content. Following terrorist attacks in Brussels in March 2015, president of the United States of America Donald Trump (@realDonaldTrump) posted the tweet in (10).

(10)   Do you all remember how beautiful and safe a place Brussels was. Not anymore, it is from a different world. U.S must be vigilant and smart.

This was retweeted by one user with the (paraphrased) comment in (11) added.

(11)   The fool Donald Trump wants us to think he knows what a place other than America is actually like!

This user is using the retweet to communicate a clearly dissociative attitude towards the original post and towards its author.

However, just as a speaker can leave her attitude tacit when producing an attributive spoken utterance, so a retweeter can choose to leave her attitude towards the retweeted content tacit, for the readers to infer. Consider the tweet in (12). On March 19, 2016, the official Twitter account of Chelsea Football Club (@ChelseaFC) posted the tweet in (12) as part of their live Twitter commentary during a football match.

(12)   GOAL!!! 2-2 Fabregas!!! #CFCLive.

This tweet is reporting that a goal has been scored. It was retweeted almost 2000 times. Many of these retweets were posted without any further comment attached. At first it may seem reasonable to conclude that the users chose to retweet this post to spread the information to a wider audience. However, when we consider the context of the retweet and if we take a closer look at the functionality of Twitter, this motivation seems less central. First, we might reasonably assume that anyone who is interested in the live football match would be following the commentary themselves. They would see the goal announcement by following the original feed or the *#CFCLive* hashtag.

Furthermore, a retweet (without comment) only appears in the timelines of people who do not follow the original account. Therefore the only people who would have seen the retweet are those who are not actively following the match already. The information in the tweet is also time-sensitive. It is only relevant at that point in the game, and there is no guarantee that the score will remain as it is or, indeed, that this will be the final score. Anyone who is not following but who might find the final score relevant would have to check elsewhere anyway. Why then have so many people clicked on the button to retweet this announcement? The key to understanding what motivated nearly 2000 people to retweet this information lies, I suggest, in accepting that some attributive acts achieve relevance by communicating an attitude, and that this attitude is not always explicitly communicated. The retweeters of (12) have rebroadcast the content to communicate their reaction, presumably positive in most cases, to the information in the embedded tweet. They are happy that the player Fabregas has scored an equalising goal and they want all of their followers to know how they feel about it. Thus these retweets are echoic uses.

Echoic uses and (non)endorsement

It is notable that the results of boyd et al.'s survey do not include any explicit reports of users retweeting for the purpose of dissociating themselves from the original tweet. While such uses may be covered by category (d) ('To comment on someone's tweet by retweeting and adding new content, often to begin a conversation'), retweeting seems to be strongly associated with endorsement. When the attitude of the retweeter is left implicit, it must be inferred by the readers. According to the relevance-theoretic comprehension procedure, the readers will follow a path of least effort and test interpretive hypotheses in order of accessibility. Crucially, they will also stop when they have reached an optimally relevant interpretation and they will accept this as the intended interpretation. Therefore, as with other inferential processes, inferring the motivation and, if relevant, the attitude behind a retweet, will be context sensitive. It may be that on very many occasions, the most accessible hypothesis to explain an act of retweeting is that the user approves and endorses the content of the tweet. After all, by retweeting content, a user is rebroadcasting it to her audience from her account, and a highly accessible assumption is that she does so because she agrees and wants to be associated with that content in some way. If this interpretation satisfies the reader's expectations of optimal relevance, then an endorsement interpretation will be accepted.

However, this is not to say that endorsement is the default interpretation of the act of retweeting. If the context of retweeting makes a non-endorsement interpretation more accessible, then that will be the first to be tested by the reader and will be accepted if it yields an optimally relevant overall interpretation. After all, users do not only share content that they approve of. They may share content that they think is ridiculous or outrageous. They may share a post with the motive of shaming the creator of the original content

(Pepp et al. 2019). Recall the infamous *covfefe* tweet by Donald Trump that was discussed in Chapter 1. This was retweeted thousands of times before it was deleted. Also consider the following attested case of retweeting. British political commentator and journalist Owen Jones (@OwenJones84) posted a tweet suggesting that some people use Twitter to be unpleasant to others under the guise of making a political point. Jones received an insulting reply to this tweet. The reply called him an idiot. However, he retweeted the reply to his followers, and he did so without comment. Given that the retweeted content openly insulted him, it seems unlikely that Jones intended to endorse the sentiments that it expressed. Rather, the most accessible interpretation is that Jones wanted to bring this tweet to the attention of a wider audience and communicate his dissociative attitude to the reply and to the replier. This is an example of a retweet without comment that is clearly not endorsing the original post.

Metaxas et al. (2014) consider the disclaimer that some users put in their profile summary that states that 'retweets are not endorsements'. They found that most users who include this disclaimer are journalists, reporters, and media producers, along with some politicians. As they discuss, the very fact that some users feel that they need to explicitly state this 'is an implicit admission … [that] for most people retweeting is endorsement'. Overall, they conclude that 'retweeting indicates, not only interest in a message, but also trust in the message and the originator, and agreement with the message content'. However, the Owen Jones retweet of the insulting reply, along with examples such as the mass retweeting of the Trump *covfefe* tweet cast doubt on this conclusion. Interpretation of retweets is context-dependent and is inferred based on the assumptions of the readers and their expectations of relevance.

A relevance-theoretic analysis also helps us to understand why general claims that 'retweets are not endorsements' are often looked upon with scepticism. If an attitude of endorsement is the optimally relevant interpretation in the discourse context, then the reader is entitled to take it as the intended interpretation. Objections from the retweeter that that is not what she meant, seem rather hollow and insincere. The retweeter should have anticipated that this is how it would be interpreted and she should have added a comment to clarify her position.

Phatic attributive uses

Boyd et al.'s categories of motivations for retweeting suggest that some users knowingly use the retweet option to manage social interactions and social relationships. Category (d), while mainly focusing on echoic motivations, also describes using a retweet as a conversation starter. In category (e) ('To make one's presence as a listener visible'), users describe retweeting as a way to show their presence as a reader. As discussed in Chapter 2, the non-face-to-face, asynchronous nature of Twitter means the tweeter is writing for an imagined audience. A Twitter user will not normally be aware of who has seen a particular tweet. Retweeting, however, triggers a notification to the original poster, and is also recorded on the retweet count below the original post. Users can easily see who has retweeted their content. Those users who described retweeting in terms of (h) ('As an act of friendship, loyalty, or homage by drawing attention, sometimes via a retweet request') are also acknowledging a phatic motivation behind some retweets. Retweeting content may be relevant not just because it rebroadcasts the content to a wider audience but also because by doing so it signals affiliation and association with the original poster.

On March 2, 2016, the Chelsea FC account (@ChelseaFC) tweeted a photograph of their men's team captain along with the message in (13).

(13)   Good morning!

While the tweet itself is perhaps unremarkable, it was retweeted by over 500 people almost immediately. The informational content of the original post is minimal. It is a greeting from the club account to the followers of that account. It is therefore perhaps hard to see what relevant effects could follow from the spreading of this information by a third party. However, the retweeters are showing that they have seen the message and that they wish to be associated with the account. The relevance lies in the affinity that the retweeters are claiming with the post and with the account behind the post.

Perlocutionary acts

Finally, some of the motivations that emerged from boyd et al.'s survey describe the decision to retweet in terms of the perlocutionary effects that may follow from the act. Recall, from Chapter 1, that perlocutionary effects are those that follow as a result of a speech act being performed. They are the effects of the act on the participants involved (Austin 1962; Searle 1969). Category (i) captures retweets that are motivated by the urge 'to recognise or refer to less popular people or less visible content'. On the surface, this category is about disseminating the information in the tweet more widely. However, the retweeter intends that by doing so, the value of the content and the contribution of the original tweet and its author should be more widely recognised and appreciated. Category (j) ('For self-gain, either to gain followers or reciprocity from more visible participants') also describes the act of retweeting in terms of the perlocutionary effects that the retweeter intends to produce. In this case, the retweeter is hoping that by sharing the content more widely, and presumably by communicating her endorsement of it, she will gain followers, and that the author of the original tweet might help raise the retweeter's profile by reciprocating the attention. Finally, category (c), while mostly focused on informative attributive motives, also notes that retweets may be intended 'to entertain' a specific audience. Again, this is a perlocutionary act which follows from the wider sharing of the information in the original tweet.

As these perlocutionary examples illustrate, motivations for retweeting are, of course, complex. Some acts of retweeting achieve relevance in more than one way. For example, users might take the opportunity to express their attitude towards a tweet while also wanting to share the content with a wider audience. If that attitude is positive it may signal loyalty or friendship. If it is negative, it may be designed to start a conversation or even an argument. The relevance-theoretic notion of attributive use and the acknowledgment that attributive acts of communication may achieve relevance in different and overlapping ways provides us with a framework for understanding the pragmatic processes that lie behind acts of retweeting as described by boyd et al.'s participants.

LIKING (AND OTHER REACTIONS)

Most social media sites offer a range of means by which a user can publicly interact with previously posted content. So far in this chapter, we have focused on acts of rebroadcasting in which the user chooses to share third-party content on their own newsfeed. Most sites also include the option to leave a comment, along with some sort of built-in reaction or 'like' button. The Facebook 'like' button was introduced in 2009 and takes the form of a thumbs up icon. A wider range of reactions was introduced for Facebook users in May 2016, and they can now choose between *Like*, *Love*, *Haha*, *Wow*, *Sad*, and *Angry* buttons, each with an accompanying emoji. YouTube offers users the option to like or dislike content. Posts on Instagram and TikTok include heart-shaped 'like' buttons, as do current Twitter posts.

Reaction interactions, along with comments and replies, are public. A record of them is appended to the original post, usually via a counter of some sort underneath the main message. The act of liking or commenting on a YouTube video or Instagram post creates an annotation that is stored with the post itself for other users to see. The same is true when a user comments on or likes content on Facebook or Twitter, subject to individual privacy settings. These interactions also generate notifications which are sent to the creator of the original post. However, on Facebook and Twitter, when users like something or when they post a response as a comment or reply, the content will also appear in the newsfeed of their friends or followers. Liking and commenting/replying on these platforms therefore also have an indirect sharing function. Interacting with third-party content publicly is an ostensive act of communication, whether it involves the production of new utterances (in the form of comments) or not. Clicking on a 'like' button is not just a personal reaction to third-party content. We can, after all, react to something without communicating our reaction to anyone. Reacting via a reaction button is also an act of showing. When we click a 'like' button we are showing our response to the creator of the original post and to other members of our network.

When Twitter was first launched, users had the option to 'favorite' a tweet by clicking on the star icon below the post. In 2015, this was changed to a heart-shaped icon and rebranded as a 'like'. In a press release, the motivation behind the change was explained as follows:

> You might like a lot of things, but not everything can be your favorite. The heart, in contrast, is a universal symbol that resonates across languages, cultures, and time zones. The heart is more expressive, enabling you to convey a range of emotions and easily connect with people.
>
> (Kumar 2015)

This was little more than a rebranding exercise, and the functionality of the button stayed the same. 'Likes', like favourites, are recorded on the tweet itself and they also facilitate retrieval at a later date by adding the tweet to a 'likes' list (formally a 'favorites' list). However, the change perhaps reflects an understanding from the developers that users wanted to do more than simply endorse or show appreciation for the content. To think of the reaction as marking something as a 'favorite' foregrounds the curation motivation for doing so and the idea that users are creating lists that they can return to. The rebrand to a 'like', on the other hand, foregrounds the communicative aspect of liking. It is an 'expressive' act by which you can 'convey a range of emotions' and 'connect with people'. The heart icon, like the thumbs up icon on Facebook, is compatible with a range of reactions and emotions. The tweet from the BBC Breaking News account announcing the death of the singer Prince, given in (6) above, has been liked 2455 times. We can presume that most of the users who clicked the 'like' button on this tweet were not pleased that someone had died, but were using the button to record some other sort of response or reaction to the news. Barton and Lee (2013: 89) identify the following range of pragmatic uses associated with the Facebook 'like':

- To express positive stance … but not want to leave a written comment.
- To express interest in the post or the content of it.
- To show support to the content poster.
- To agree or align with the stance of the status poster.
- To answer 'yes' to a question raised in the post.
- To indicate that the post has been read.

Levorashka et al. (2016) identified a similar range of motivations. In their study, users reported liking content not only to literally indicate that they appreciated the content, but also to show support, to maintain the social relationship and to acknowledge that they had seen the content. Just as acts of rebroadcasting are context-dependent, so too are reaction responses. We may take the icon and the name of the reaction button as a clue to the user's intention, but, ultimately, we have to judge the act relative to the discourse context. The wider range of options now available on Facebook may allow users to send more specific clues as to their reaction. However, we can be sad or angry to various degrees and we can laugh for many different reasons. The six options now available clearly do not individually align exactly with the full range of emotions and attitudes that they may be used to communicate. Spottswood and Wohn (2019) suggest that clicking on the 'like' reaction button on Facebook may have become a habit for some users in a way that is not yet the case for the other options. Liking has been an option for longer, and a 'like' can be posted with just one click. To choose another option, users must hover over the reaction menu and make a more deliberate choice. This takes slightly longer and involves more clicks. Therefore, use of one of the alternative buttons may, Spottswood and Wohn suggest, be a signal of a more mindful interaction and specific reaction.

As we saw in the discussion of rebroadcasting earlier in this chapter, there is often an assumption that sharing is an act of endorsement. While we have seen that this is context-sensitive and by no means the only interpretation, the act of liking is also strongly associated with endorsement. Meanwhile, commenting on a post is a more neutral activity, and, indeed, on some platforms is associated with disagreement and debate. We finish this chapter with a brief discussion of a user-led, albeit completely unscientific, interpretation of these patterns of interaction on Twitter: the so-called 'Twitter Ratio'. This is an emergent phenomenon first noticed in March 2017 by user @85mf, and it captures the relation between the success (or otherwise) of a tweet and the relative number of likes, comments, and retweets that the tweet receives. A user and their post is said to have been 'ratio'd' when a tweet receives many more (usually negative) comments than it does 'likes' and retweets. While, of course, individual retweets may be dissociative, and comments may easily be positive and supportive, the Twitter ratio taps into a general assumption that there are patterns in the way that people behave and interact online. The potential reach and associated audience size that Twitter makes possible allows these patterns to emerge. According to the Twitter ratio, when people agree with content, they tend to either share it more widely by retweeting or they associate themselves with it via a 'like'. However, when they disagree, they tend to post comments articulating their disagreement. As O'Neil (2017) explains, '[i]f the number of replies to a tweet vastly outpaces its engagement in terms of likes and retweets, then something has gone horribly wrong'. The Twitter ratio, therefore, is used as an informal measure of the success or otherwise of a tweet, and along with other patterns of interaction that emerge on social media, is a topic that is ripe for further study and investigation.

CONCLUSIONS

Rebroadcasting material on social media is an ostensive act. When users retweet, reblog, or share third-party material in some other way, they highlight the rebroadcast content on their timelines. By doing so, they draw it to the attention of their followers or friends. Rebroadcasting is an act of showing and it is an act of attributive use. Attributive uses of language can be relevant in at least three ways. First, attributive utterances may be relevant because of the information that they communicate. Second, it may be that the relevance lies in the attitude that the speaker communicates towards the rebroadcast content. Finally, attributive uses of language may achieve relevance because the fact that they have been produced provides social information or helps manage the interlocutors' relationship in some way. All three of these routes to relevance are apparent in the self-described motives for retweeting identified by boyd et al. (2010). The examples discussed in this chapter demonstrate that all three routes to relevance are also represented in attested tweets on Twitter. They are not, however, mutually exclusive, and one retweet may achieve relevance via more than one route. Liking, and other reactions on social media sites are also acts of showing. They are public responses to content. As with acts of rebroadcasting, they are context-sensitive, and their interpretation is a matter of inference.

NOTE

1 In line with the convention of referring to the speaker as *she* and the hearer as *he*, I will refer to the user who retweets the content as *she*. The user who interprets the act of retweeting will be referred to as *he*. This is to facilitate ease of discussion of individual cases and no further significance is intended.

REFERENCES

Austin, J. L. (1962). *How to Do Things with Words*. Oxford: Oxford University Press.

Barton, D., & Lee, C. (2013). *Language Online: Investigating Digital Texts and Practices*. Abingdon: Routledge.

boyd, d., Golder, S., & Lotan, G. (2010). Tweet, tweet, retweet: Conversational aspects of retweeting on Twitter. In *Proceedings of the 43rd Hawaii International Conference on System Sciences* (pp. 1–10). Honolulu, HI: IEEE.

Internet Live Stats. (n.d.). *Twitter Usage Statistics*. Retrieved April 2, 2021, from Live Internet Stats: https://www.internetlivestats.com/twitter-statistics/

John, N. A. (2013). Sharing and web 2.0: The Emergence of a keyword. *New Media and Society*, 15(2), 167–182. doi:10.1177/1461444812450684

Kumar, A. (2015). *Hearts on Twitter*. Retrieved November 17, 2019, from https://blog.twitter.com/official/en_us/a/2015/hearts-on-twitter.html

Levorashka, A., Utz, S., & Ambros, R. (2016). What's in a like? Motivations for pressing the like button. In *Proceedings of the Tenth International AAAI Conference on Web and Social Media*, pp. 623–626. California: The AAAI Press.

Malinowski, B. (1923). The problem of meaning in primative languages. In C. K. Ogden, & I. A. Richards (Eds.), *The Meaning of Meaning* (pp. 146–152). London: Routledge.

Marsili, N. (2020). Retweeting: Its linguistic and epistemic value. *Synthese*. doi:10.1007/s11229-020-02731-y

Metaxas, P., Mustafaraj, E., Wong, K., Zeng, L., & O'Keefe, M. (2014). Do retweets indicate interest, trust, agreement? *CoRR arXiv preprint arXiv. 1411.3555*.

O'Neil, L. (2017). *How to Know if You've Sent a Horrible Tweet: A Deep Dive into the Ratio*. Retrieved April 15, 2021, from esquire.com: https://www.esquire.com/news-politics/news/a54440/twitter-ratio-reply/

Padilla Cruz, M. (2004). On the social importance of phatic uttearnces: Some considerations for a relevance-theoretic approach. In P. Garcés Conejos, R. Gómez Morón, L. Fernández Amaya, &

M. Padilla Cruz (Eds.), *Current Trends in Intercultural, Cognitive and Social Pragmatics* (pp. 199–216). Seville: Intercultural Pragmatics Research Group.

Padilla Cruz, M. (2005). On the phatic interpretation of utterances: A complementary relevance-theoretic approach. *Revista Alicantina de Estudiso Ingleses, 18*, 227–246.

Pepp, J., Michaelson, E., & Sterken, R. K. (2019). What's new about fake news? *Journal of Ethics and Social Philosophy, 16*(2). doi:10.26556/jesp.v16i2.629

Scott, K. (2021). The pragmatics of rebroadcasting content on Twitter: How is retweeting relevant? *Journal of Pragmatics, 184*, 52–60. doi: 10.1016/j.pragma.2021.07.022

Searle, J. R. (1969). *Speech Acts*. Cambridge: Cambridge University Press.

Shah, J. (2018). *An Easier Way to Save and Share Tweets*. Retrieved March 7, 2021, from https://blog.twitter.com/; https://blog.twitter.com/en_us/topics/product/2018/an-easier-way-to-save-and-share-tweets.html

Sperber, D., & Wilson, D. (1986). *Relevance: Communciation and Cognition* (2nd (with postface) ed.). Oxford: Blackwell.

Sperber, D., & Wilson, D. (1987). Précis of Relevance: Communication and Cognition. *Behavioral and Brain Sciences, 10*, 697–754.

Sperber, D., & Wilson, D. (2015). Beyond speaker's meaning. *Croatian Journal of Philosophy, 15*(44), 117–149.

Spottswood, E., & Wohn, D. Y. (2019). Beyond the 'like': How people respond to negative posts on Facebook. *Journal of Broadcasting & Electronic Media, 63*(2), 250–267. doi:10.1080/08838151.2019.1622936

Wharton, T. (2009). *Pragmatics and Non-Verbal Communication*. Cambridge: Cambridge University Press.

Wilson, D. (2000). Metarepresentation in linguistic communication. In D. Sperber (Ed.), *Metarepresentations: A Multidisciplinary Perspective* (pp. 411–448). Oxford: Oxford University Press.

Wilson, D., & Sperber, D. (2012). *Meaning and Relevance*. Cambridge: Cambridge University Press.

Žegarac, V., & Clark, B. (1999). Phatic interpretations and phatic communication. *Journal of Linguistics, 35*(2), 321–346.

4

THE PRAGMATICS OF TAGGING

The following (slightly abridged) exchange took place in the comments section of the Guardian Online newspaper on January 6, 2013.

(1) User1: Where are the hover boards I was promised for the millennium in the decades before #stillwaitingstillwaiting #nonsensepredictions
       User2: @User1 You're not on Twitter – hashtags don't work here
       User1: @User2 – hashtags work everywhere

In this chapter we explore how hashtags work both within digitally mediated communication and beyond. We will think about the various roles that they might play and the various motivations that might lead a user to include one in a message. What will emerge is a picture of hashtags as a user-driven innovation that has been developed, adapted, and co-opted to help navigate and negotiate the discourse contexts in which we find ourselves online. The main focus of the discussion here will be the ways in which hashtags contribute to the meaning that is conveyed by a message, and in particular how they guide the inferences that readers make. We also discuss how these uses of hashtags help users to navigate and negotiate online contexts, and how the pragmatic functionality of hashtags has proved to have a communicative role in other, offline contexts.

DOI: 10.4324/9781003254201-4

THE EMERGENCE AND EVOLUTION OF THE HASHTAG

Hashtags were not part of Twitter in its original conception. They grew out of a proposal by Chris Messina to introduce a system to tag and track content on the site. In 2007, he posted the tweet in (2), proposing that the # symbol be used to categorise content and link it together.

(2) How do you feel about using # (pound) for groups. As in #barcamp [msg]?

Messina discussed his proposal in more detail on his blog (2007), and explained that it was driven by the aim of 'improving *contextualization*, *content filtering* and *exploratory serendipity* within Twitter'. Originally, he called the system 'channel tags'. It was designed, not only to help users find and follow content, but also to tell users about the topic of the post and to allow others to 'eavesdrop on the context of it'. Thus, from their original conception, hashtags were envisioned as tools to help users to navigate online contexts. Their invention and adoption were driven by the communicative needs of the users. As we will see, this drive has continued to be instrumental in their use and development.

Although Messina is credited as the inventor of the hashtag, the term itself was coined by Stowe Boyd (@Stoweboyd) in a response to Messina's tweet, given in (3).

(3) I support the hash tag convention: http://tinyurl.com/2qttlb #hashtag #factoryjoe #twitter.

Two years later, in 2009, hashtags were formally adopted as a feature of Twitter. The interface was developed so that any string of characters which is preceded by a hash symbol becomes a hyperlink. This allows users to search for any content that includes the same tag simply by clicking on the hyperlink. If a large number of people post tweets containing the same hashtag within a short space of time, that hashtag will be said to be trending, and current trends are available for users to browse and view in real time. As Messina points out, an important part of the motivation behind the hashtag was that it would be easy to use without any technical knowledge of coding or expertise in search functionality. As he says, hashtags allow users to 'track content and updates more relevant and interesting to them without exerting a great deal of extra effort or learning any kind of extraneous … syntax' (Messina 2007). Now a fully integrated part of the Twitter interface, hashtags have their own section in the online support pages (Twitter.com n.d.), where the following definition is given:

> A hashtag – written with # symbol – is used to index keywords or topics on Twitter. This function was created on Twitter, and allows people to easily follow topics they are interested in.

Users may incorporate hashtags into the body of a tweet by tagging a word in the main message, as illustrated in (4) or the tags may be structurally separated from the main message, as illustrated in (5). Both examples are taken from the BBC Sport Twitter feed (@BBCSport).

(4) If you missed today's action from Augusta, we've got #TheMasters highlights starting right now.

(5) After victory over Derby, Championship leaders Norwich are now on the verge of securing promotion back to the Premier League. #bbcfootball

The original and perhaps most straightforward function of hashtags is to make the content in tweets searchable and findable. Interested users can click on the hashtag to access other tweets on the same subject. Some examples of hashtags used for this purpose are given in (6) to (8).

(6) If you don't want to know what happens in #Sherlock, avoid spoilers. If you want to know what happens in #RipperStreet fight for its return

(7) VienettaIce #Failed90sRappers

(8) So it's 2014. A brand new year. How can we make a difference to the care of our patients? Keep your ideas for #hellomynameis coming …

In (6), a hash symbol has been added to the names of the television programmes *Sherlock* and *Ripper Street*. This turns them into hyperlinked hashtags which a user can click on to access other content that contains the same tag. This is a fairly common practice and many television shows will promote a particular hashtag to encourage participation in online discussions around the programme. In example (7) the user is contributing to a hashtag meme (Zappavigna 2018: 172–173). In this case, users are playing with the names of '90s rap acts to create funny alternative names. We will return to look more closely at hashtag memes in Chapter 6. Finally, the tweet in (8) contains the hashtag associated with a campaign to improve doctor–patient relations and was posted by a user encouraging people to engage with the campaign. It has become very common for social movements and political activists to use hashtags in their campaigning activities. Indeed, so-called hashtag activism has been central to campaigns such as the #MeToo (Clark-Parsons 2019) and the Black Lives Matter (Ince et al. 2017) movements.

While search functionality and content linking are key and enduring functions of hashtags, we find many cases where the hashtags that have been added to a tweet do not appear to be performing (or not only performing) these functions of 'discovery' and/or 'navigation' (Zappavigna 2018). Consider, for example, the tweet in (9).

(9)   I think all drs should be made to lie in a hospital bed wearing PJs & be stood over. See what it feels like. #vulnerability #powerbalance

In (9), the user is reflecting on the experience of being in hospital and is commenting on the patient–doctor relationship. She includes two hashtags, set out separately from the main body of the message: *#vulnerability* and *#powerbalance*. While it is possible that someone might search Twitter looking for posts about hospital experiences, it seems unlikely that anyone would use these hashtags to do so. Furthermore, users who see the tweet in (9) and want to read more about the subject are likely to be disappointed if they click on the hashtags in the tweet. These search terms are neither an efficient nor an effective way to access further content on the subject of hospital experiences. Rather, the hashtags in (9) appear to be performing a function above and beyond discovery and navigation. They give us clues about how we should interpret the rest of the message. The tweeter is implying that the situation described creates a feeling of vulnerability and that it illustrates an issue in the balance of power inherent in the patient–doctor relationship. The hashtags are contributing to the meaning of the tweet and guiding the readers in how the message should be interpreted. As such, these hashtags, and many more like them, have a pragmatic function.

A METAFUNCTIONAL ANALYSIS OF TWITTER HASHTAGS

The non-search-oriented uses of hashtags fall broadly into two, non-mutually exclusive categories. They can be used to either mark the topic of the tweet and/or they may communicate something about the tweeter's attitude or emotions. As such, they align with the experiential and interpersonal metafunctions recognised in Systemic Functional Linguistics (Halliday 1978). Systemic Functional Linguistics (SFL) places the functions for which language is used at its core, and it is focused on language as a resource for making meaning. It developed from the observation that when speakers use language they make choices and it is via these choices that meaning is made (Halliday 2013). According to Halliday and Matthiessen (2004: 60), '[l]anguage is as it is because of the function in which it has evolved in the human species'. SFL recognises three metafunctions which represent 'three kinds of meaning [which] run through the whole of language' (60). These are the ideational metafunction, the interpersonal metafunction, and the textual metafunction. The ideational function is about 'making sense of our experiences' (29), and has two components: the experiential metafunction and the logical metafunction. The interpersonal metafunction is about 'acting out our social relationships' (29). Finally, SFL recognises a third textual metafunction. This metafunction is about the construction of the text itself. It includes all of the resources that speakers use to organise the discourse and to produce texts that are both cohesive and coherent in the discourse context.

Zappavigna (2015, 2018) adopts the SFL approach and uses this to categorise and analyse hashtags in terms of the experiential and interpersonal
functions they perform. This analysis forms part of her broader work on
online language as 'searchable talk'. Online discourse is searchable 'in a
way and to an extent that has never been seen in history' (Zappavigna 2012:
6). Zappavigna explores how the searchable nature of online discourse
'opens up a new kind of sociality, where [users] engage in ambient affiliation' (96). While users may not always interact directly with one another,
the affordances of social media allow social groups and communities to
form, however momentarily, around aligned values and shared experiences.
The next two sections provide a brief overview of Zappavigna's work on
hashtags, focusing on how SFL can be used to understand the different
functions that hashtags perform on Twitter. While we discuss these functions separately here, they are not mutually exclusive. One hashtag can, and
often does, perform more than one of these functions simultaneously
(Zappavigna 2018: 43).

The experiential function of hashtags

Hashtags which perform an experiential function provide the user with some
details of what the tweet is about. They often situate a post as part of an
ongoing conversation and they may also perform a cataloguing function,
linking together all tweets on a particular topic (Zappavigna 2018: 43–46). We
can see this illustrated by the hashtags in examples (10) to (12).

(10)   That was the perf ending to what has been a chaotic but really cute and
        fun series, the winner has been legit one of my favs for so so long and
        they're just wonderful. And I am so happy for them! #MaskedSingerUK

(11)   Boom 3 out of 3 correct (yes I did do a last minute change for Sausage)
        #MaskedSingerUK

(12)   Gutted it's over now!!!! Frowning face that was my lockdown week-
        end!!!!! #MaskedSingerUK

The hashtag *#MaskedSingerUK* is used in each of these examples, and it
trended in early 2021 in the United Kingdom during the airing of a television
series called *The Masked Singer*. In each episode of the programme, celebrities performed a song while disguised in elaborate costumes with the weakest
performer being unmasked at the end of each show. While purported to be a
singing competition, a key component of the show was that viewers should
try to guess who was in each costume. Discussion of the show was facilitated
online by the use of the hashtag *#MaskedSingerUK*, and viewers used this to
join and track the ongoing conversation about who the singers could be.

Notice, however, that while the hashtags in examples (10) to (12) perform the experiential function of marking the topic and telling the readers what the tweet is about, this does not only serve to facilitate searching or linking tweets together. As Zappavigna (2015: 9) points out, tweets such as these 'would be relatively opaque or bizarre without the hashtags indicating the semantic field evoked'. In each case, the hashtag provides contextual information to aid in the interpretation of the tweet. This contextualising function plays an important role on Twitter, and on social networking sites more generally, where, as we have seen, the audience for a tweet may be largely 'imagined' (Marwick and boyd 2011; Litt 2012) and the context largely collapsed (Wesch 2009; Marwick and boyd 2011). Topic-marking hashtags may therefore perform the dual functions of labelling a tweet for searching purposes and providing contextual information to aid interpretation. Zappavigna (2015) goes on to claim that this 'type of contextualizing relation between the post and the tag is how hashtags have been popularly conceived' (9) and she claims that it is their most commonly found function (6).

The interpersonal function of hashtags

While these searching and contextualising functions of hashtags were envisioned in Messina's original conception of the tagging system, new functions have emerged alongside them. We find many examples where hashtags communicate information about the speaker's attitude, emotions, and relationship with the audience. Zappavigna (2018) describes such uses as providing an 'evaluative metacommentary' on the post and they are central to the interpersonal metafunction of hashtags. As she describes, when used in this way, the hashtag functions as a 'conversational aside in which a speaker reveals their true feelings' (2018: 66). In SFL terms, these hashtags perform an interpersonal function. They have 'little to do with aggregating posts into searchable sets and much more to do with adopting particular attitudinal dispositions' (Zappavigna 2018: 49). The information in the tag can interact with the information in the main tweet in several ways. Evaluative hashtags may be used to supply information about the tweeter's attitude that is not available in the body of the text. We can see this in the example in (13).

(13)   11 more days until Trump is President #overjoyed ☺ (Zappavigna 2018: 67).

The tweeter's attitude is not clear without the additional information provided in the hashtag (and the accompanying emoji). In other cases, the tweeter's evaluation may be evident from the main message, but the hashtag supplements this by either augmenting it, as in (14) or disrupting it, as in (15).

(14)   I feel angry about this all the time #angry

(15)   Is it just me or has everyone suddenly stopped tweeting photos of their
       pets? #justkidding

Disruptive evaluative comments may be used to invoke humour or mark sarcasm (Zappavigna 2018: 68).

Other work suggests that this interpersonal function of hashtags extends beyond Twitter. Bourlai (2018) identifies a similar function for tagging content on the blogging site Tumblr. She claims that comment tags on posts perform three main functions. They may express a user's opinion, they may express a user's reaction, or they may be used to give an indirect statement in the form of an aside. Matley's (2018) analysis of the #sorrynotsorry hashtag on Instagram also suggests that users are employing this tag for an interpersonal, rather than experiential function.

In her study on Twitter, Page (2012) also considers the different functions of hashtags and she divides her data into two categories which broadly parallel Zappavigna's experiential/interpersonal distinction. Page labels these as 'topic-based' and 'evaluative' respectively. According to Page, 'hashtags are primarily used to make the topic of a tweet visible, rather than to emphasize stance', and she notes that 'expressive uses of hashtags do occur, but that these examples are by far in the minority' (187).

A key issue to take from the examples in this section is that the emergence of these experiential and interpersonal functions has been driven by use. The function of hashtags has evolved from a need to communicate, and the affordances of the hashtag have been co-opted by users to facilitate this. In the next section we look more closely at how this plays out in action, and we think about the pragmatic processes involved in interpreting these uses.

HASHTAGS AS GUIDES TO INFERENTIAL PROCESSES

We have seen that hashtags can perform experiential and interpersonal functions alongside their discovery and navigation functions. Now we turn our focus to how this is achieved. That is, we think about how marking a topic or providing an evaluative comment contributes to the communication of the speaker's meaning. To do this, we will consider the role that hashtags play in pragmatic interpretation processes.

When a tweeter adds a hash symbol to a word or phrase on Twitter, thereby creating a hashtag, that tag becomes a hyperlink. A reader clicking on that link will have access to any other tweets which feature the same tag. Therefore, by creating a hashtag, tweeters are signalling that they consider the tagged word or phrase to be a topic and to be related to, or representative of, the tweet's content. In its original functionality, this enabled a reader to find related content amidst the noise of Twitter (Page 2014), and indeed, as we have seen, this remains a key function. However, many of the examples that we have looked at so far, including those which may contribute to an experiential and interpersonal function, suggest that users now treat the hashtag as a general means by which they can highlight a topic or theme for the tweet, irrespective of the tag's potential for retrieving related content. The hash symbol appears therefore to have become a highlighting device. Wilson and Wharton (2006) and Wharton (2009) propose that in face-to-face communication, contrastive stress and pointing or ostensive gazing may be used to 'draw attention to a particular constituent in an utterance' (Wharton 2009: 142). That is, they can be used as highlighting devices. Hashtags can be used on Twitter to achieve a similar effect. By highlighting a constituent that might otherwise not have been highlighted, or, indeed, by including an extra, highlighted word at the end of the message, the tweeter is drawing the reader's attention towards that constituent and making it more salient in the reader's cognitive environment. Readers can expect to find relevance in having their attention drawn to a particular constituent in this way. By drawing attention to the tagged content, the tweeter can guide the overall interpretation of the utterance by making certain inferential routes more accessible.

As we saw in Chapter 1, to work out what a speaker is intending to communicate, we must form hypotheses about what the speaker is explicitly communicating (the explicature) as well as what she is implying or implicating (the implicatures). Inferential processes are involved at both these levels, and in offline contexts speakers have various resources available to them to guide hearers in these processes. Here we discuss a range of examples where the content in hashtags appears to be contributing to meaning-making in this way. The hashtagged content provides clues to the speaker's intended meaning and guides the hearer's inferential processes.

As we have seen, in the collapsed contexts we encounter online, the context of interpretation may be impoverished or ambiguous. Furthermore, on Twitter, users have a restricted character limit. Individual tweets have a limit of 280 characters (increased from 140 in 2017). The tweeter must therefore rely on the reader accessing certain contextual assumptions in order to draw inferences and, if all goes well, reach the intended interpretation. As discussed in Chapter 1, online platforms are often lean in terms of social cues, and they provide very little control as to when or by whom a message will be read. As a consequence, the tweeter is unlikely to be able to predict which contextual assumptions, if any, will be accessible to the, potentially many, readers of the tweet when they come across it on their feeds. However, the inclusion of a hashtag provides the tweeter with a means to raise the accessibility of certain contextual assumptions without including extra content in the main body of the utterance itself. In the next sections we look at examples of hashtags used in this way and discuss the various inferential processes that they may be used to guide. Many of the examples discussed here were first presented in my analysis of hashtag use and conversational tone on Twitter (Scott 2015).

Constructing a proposition expressed

To work out what a speaker is explicitly communicating, a hearer must construct a truth-evaluable proposition from the clues provided in the speaker's utterance. This will often involve disambiguation, enrichment of vague terms, and reference assignment. These tasks are inferential in nature, and hearers or readers will draw on a wide range of contextual information to guide their inferences. We find examples on Twitter where the user has included hashtags which guide the readers in these inferential processes. The example in (16) illustrates how hashtags can guide the process of assigning reference to referring expressions.[1]

(16)   She's done it! An amazing amazing effort. #davina #windermere

This tweet was posted by the Twitter account of a sport-related charity fundraising campaign (@sportrelief) on February 10, 2014. This was a week in which British television presenter Davina McCall was taking part in a high-profile charity endurance challenge to swim across Lake Windermere. The full challenge lasted a week, and the hashtag #davina allowed Twitter users to follow the presenter's progress online. In this respect, the hashtag performed a traditional search function, linking together tweets about the challenge. However, for anyone not actively following the topic or not aware of the context in which the tweet was posted, the message in (16) would be uninterpretable without the inclusion of the hashtags. Any number of people might come across the message via retweets and promotions, and they could do so days, weeks, or months after the tweet was originally posted. To derive the proposition that is expressed by the first part of the tweet, repeated here as (17), the reader must infer who *she* refers to and what *it* is that she has done. That is, the reader must assign reference to the two pronouns in the tweet: *she* and *it*.

(17)   She's done it!

Setting the hashtags aside for a moment, the textual content of the tweets tells us that some female person has done something amazing. The text in the tweet was accompanied by a photograph of a number of unidentifiable people in wetsuits standing in shallow water, and this might provide us with further clues as to the intended meaning. Perhaps we might infer that the amazing thing is something to do with water, for example. If we recognise that the tweeting account is the charity Sport Relief, this might give us access to further assumptions that could guide our interpretation. We might, for example, be aware that celebrities often take on high-profile challenges to raise money for charity. However, these clues still do not provide enough information to construct a truth-evaluable proposition expressed.

The writer of the tweet could, of course, have made the utterance more explicit, by tweeting something like (18).

(18)   British television presenter Davina McCall has finished her swim across
        Lake Windermere to raise money for charity.

This strategy would have reduced the inferential processing load required of
the reader and lowered the risk of misunderstanding. However, it requires the
reader to process more linguistic information, and it has stylistic implications.
The more information that is left implicit, the more the speaker indicates that
she assumes a mutual understanding with the intended audience. The inverse
is also true. The fewer the assumptions that are shared between the speaker
and hearer, the more the speaker will have to spell out in her message. Use of
a more explicit utterance therefore carries with it a suggestion that shared
assumptions cannot be presumed. This results in a tone that is less casual, less
personal, and less conversational.

The hashtag offers an alternative solution. By including the intended referent in the hashtag, the tweeter is able to make the referent highly accessible. In
this example, it performs the role that may be played by demonstrative pointing gestures in face-to-face communication. That is, it highlights the referent,
bringing them into focus, and making it more likely that the reader will test
this as the intended interpretation first. In this example, the hashtag #*davina*
originally and primarily functions as a search term, connecting all of the
tweets relating to the challenge. Indeed, many users may have come across the
tweet via a hashtag search. However, the fact that it is included, allows the
tweeter to assume that Davina will be a highly, if not the most, accessible
candidate referent for the pronoun *she*. This frees the tweeter up to use a stylistically preferable pronoun, without risking miscommunication or interrupting or disturbing the casual, personal tone of the utterance.

We can see a further example of experiential hashtags guiding inferential
processes which contribute to the proposition expressed in the tweet in (19).

(19)   Get your snacks and sit down… #cinema[2]

Whereas (18) related to a topical event and included other contextual clues,
the tweet in (19) was posted with no additional information to guide the
reader. The hashtag seems to have very little practical value in terms of search
functionality. It is hard to imagine why anyone would search on Twitter using
the general term #*cinema*. As with (18), without any further contextual information, readers might find it difficult to construct a hypothesis about the
intended interpretation of (19), and, indeed, they might eventually give up,
perhaps assuming that they are not part of the intended audience. A more
explicit version, for example (20), would solve this problem, but would, again,
have stylistic implications.

(20)   When you are at the cinema, get your snacks and sit down…

Part of the expressive force of (19) comes from the fact that the tweeter is
pretending to be addressing her fellow cinemagoers directly and in the

moment. This is lost in the version in (20). Again, the hashtag offers the tweeter an alternative. The inclusion of the hashtag *#cinema* immediately activates encyclopaedic information associated with a visit to the cinema and makes that information available for use in the interpretation. According to Wilson and Sperber (2012: 181), encyclopaedic entries are likely to contain 'ready-made chunks or schemas describing often-encountered sequences of actions or events'. Schemas about a trip to the cinema are likely to include information about buying a ticket, and perhaps buying some snacks to eat during the movie before taking your seat. Once this schema has been activated, the reader has access to certain assumptions about the sort of snacks the addressee is likely to be eating, the sort of seat they will be sitting in, and so on. The reader is also likely to assume that the pronoun *you* refers to other people in the cinema. Using the hashtag is an effective and efficient way of guiding readers to the contextual assumptions that they should use in their inferences and thereby guiding them to the intended interpretation.

Finally, while the search functionality may not be central to these pragmatic uses of hashtags, the fact that adding a hashtag to a word or phrase turns it into a hyperlink means that they can be used to provide access to extra contextual information for readers who might need it. Consider the tweet in (21).

(21)   Sending positive vibes. Positive vibes. Positive vibes. #mcfc

The main content of this tweet is fragmentary, and readers must enrich it into a fully propositional explicature. To be able to evaluate the truth of the utterance, readers must infer who is sending the positive vibes and to whom. The writer of the tweet is very likely to be the most accessible potential referent for the missing subject pronoun.[3] However, without the information in the hashtag it is impossible to know who the intended recipient of the positive vibes might be. Readers who know the tweeter well and who access the tweet in real time may be able to infer this information. However, as we have seen, social media posts may be accessed at any time and by virtually anyone. The inclusion of the hashtag in this example, allows the tweeter to include information that contextualises the tweet for a wider audience, while not interrupting the conversational tone and air of spontaneity of the message. For a subset of readers, the initials in the hashtag *#mcfc* will be immediately recognisable as referring to Manchester City Football Club. This information will activate a range of assumptions and guide those readers to the intended interpretation, which is that the tweeter is sending positive vibes to her favourite football club. The readers will derive the proposition expressed in (22).

(22)   The tweeter is sending positive vibes to Manchester City Football Club.

However, the inclusion of the hashtag also provides access to contextualising information for any readers who are not familiar with the initialisation *mcfc*.

If they click on the hyperlink, they will be taken to a search screen displaying other tweets that contain the same hashtag. Even years after the original tweet was posted, a search on the hashtag brings up information which very quickly makes it obvious that this is a sports related tweet. This will guide readers to the proposition in (23).

(23)   The tweeter is sending positive vibes to a sports club.

For readers who are not interested in sports, this may be enough information. They will hold general assumptions about sports teams and their supporters, and the explicature in (23) will combine with these to guide them to an interpretation that is relevant for them. Other readers may be more interested or may recognise that the hashtag relates specifically to a football team. This will guide them to the more specific proposition in (24).

(24)   The tweeter is sending positive vibes to a football team.

This proposition is likely to combine with different assumptions about football teams and their supporters to yield a different relevant interpretation. Finally, there are likely to be readers who hold a wider range of assumptions about different football clubs and their supporters. These readers can use the information provided by the hashtag search to construct the proposition expressed given in (22), and, again, this may combine with assumptions that those readers hold about Manchester City Football Club to yield further implicatures. Thus, different members of the Twitter audience bring different assumptions to their interpretations, and this guides them to different explicatures. The information provided by the hashtag and by the hyperlink search results can be used as needed in this interpretation process. The search functionality afforded by the hyperlink in the hashtag means that it is a highly efficient way to make the tweet accessible and interpretable by a wide audience.

In examples (16), (19) and (21), the tweeter has used hashtags to provide contextual information which contributes to the proposition that is expressed by the utterance. As we have seen, hashtags can also be used to communicate information about the speaker's attitude or emotions. In the relevance theory framework, this information is captured via the notion of higher-level explicatures. We now turn our attention to this part of the speaker's meaning, and to the role that hashtags may play in communicating it.

Constructing higher-level explicatures

As Zappavigna's (2015, 2018) metafunctional analysis of hashtags reveals, we find users employing hashtags to communicate interpersonal meaning relating to their attitudes and emotions. In terms of the speaker's overall intended meaning, we understand such uses as contributing to the construction of higher-level explicatures. In these cases, the content of the hashtag does not seem to play an obvious role in the derivation of the proposition expressed. Consider the role that the hashtags play in examples (25) to (27).

(25)   Finally got my MacBook setup how I like it. All my bookmarks and favorites ready to go #excited

(26)   It's only Wednesday and it feels like Monday #exhausted

(27)   i ALWAYS manage to ruin my nails everytime i paint them #angry

In each of these examples, the explicature of the utterance is unaffected by the content in the hashtag. We can derive a truth-evaluable proposition expressed without reference to the information in the hashtags. For example, the tweeter of (27) will have said something true, if and only if she always manages to ruin her nails every time she paints them. However, in each case the tweeter has chosen to include additional information by adding a hashtag. This content is part of the utterance and so readers will assume that it is relevant in some way. When the hashtag describes an emotion, attitude, or feeling, a highly accessible interpretation is that this relates to the tweeter's current experience in some way. Readers will then use this assumption in the construction of higher-level explicatures, in much the same way as facial expression, gesture, or tone of voice might be used in face-to-face communication. In the case of (27), the hashtag communicates that the tweeter is angry about the fact that she always manages to ruin her nails every time she paints them. We can represent this as the higher-level explicature in (28).

(28)   The tweeter is angry that [she always manages to ruin her nails every time she paints them].

Of course, it is possible that a reader might have inferred that the tweeter was angry even if the tweet had not included the hashtag. However, inclusion of the hashtag indicates to the reader that the higher-level explicature in (28) is to be taken as part of her intended meaning. The tweeter is not just accidentally transmitting information about her emotional state, she is doing so intentionally.

Deriving implicatures

Working out what a speaker or writer intends to communicate is not just a matter of working out the explicit meaning of an utterance. We must also construct a hypothesis about the speaker's implicated meaning. Derivation of implicatures is an inferential process. Given that an emergent function of hashtags is to guide inferential processes, we might expect to find cases where they are used to guide readers in their implicature formation processes. Consider the example in (29), where this indeed appears to be the case. This message was posted as a status update on Facebook.

(29)   I feel like I am falling over on the inside. #winehangover

As with the examples in (25) to (27), the hashtag used here does not contribute to the derivation of the proposition expressed. We can construct a truth-evaluable proposition based on the main message alone simply by assigning reference to the pronouns. Given that we assume the writer to be referring to herself, we are likely to take the basic explicature of the utterance to be something like (30).

(30)   The user feels like she (the user) is falling over on the inside.

Furthermore, the hashtag does not tell us about how the writer is feeling, nor does it communicate her attitude. It does, however, provide background contextual information which, we assume, is intended for use in the overall interpretation of the utterance. Without the hashtag, we know that the user feels as though she is 'falling over on the inside', but we do not know what precisely she means by this. She could be referring to a physical, emotional, or mental falling over, and the feelings being described could be fairly trivial or incredibly significant. Inclusion of the hashtag, however, makes certain contextual assumptions accessible, and readers are entitled to presume that they will contribute to the overall meaning of the utterance in some way. The tweeter has not explicitly stated that she has a hangover caused by drinking wine. However, the inclusion of the hashtag #winehangover makes that highly accessible as a contextual assumption for use in the interpretation of the post. Had the tweeter not intended readers to follow this inferential path, then she would have been misleading them by including the hashtag. Readers access this assumption as an implicated premise, as given in (31).

(31)   The user is suffering from a wine hangover.

This implicated premise now forms part of the context of interpretation, and from this, a range of implicated conclusions become available to the readers. The precise nature of these will depend on the particular assumptions that each reader holds at the time of reading, but could, for example, include those in (32) to (34).

(32)   The user's suffering is not serious or life threatening.

(33)   The user is likely to feel better within a short period of time.

(34)   The user does not deserve sympathy as her suffering is self-inflicted.

Of course, the writer could have made this information available explicitly to the readers by posting the alternative version in (35).

(35)   I drank too much wine last night and have a hangover this morning. I feel like I am falling over on the inside.

However, the hashtag version allows her to foreground the description of her feelings rather than simply give a description of facts. It is her feelings rather than the cause of them that are relevant. Providing the backstory in the alternative version in (35) reduces the force of the emotions and they are no longer the main focus of the utterance. Compared with the more explicit version in (35), the utterance in (29) results in more stylistic or poetic effects. In (29) the cause, type, and extent of the 'falling over' must be inferred on the basis of the hashtag, rather than it being explicitly stated. The readers are left largely unconstrained by explicitly communicated content. They are 'encouraged to be more imaginative and to take a large share of responsibility in imagining' (Sperber and Wilson 1986/95: 221) what it may be like for the tweeter to be 'falling over on the inside'. As Sperber and Wilson (1986/95: 224) put it, such poetic effects 'create common impressions rather than common knowledge'. The hashtag version of the utterance encourages the readers to derive a wide range of weak implicatures, rather than one or two strong implications.

In example (29), the hashtag functions to make certain contextual assumptions highly accessible and in doing so guides the readers to the assumptions that they should use in their interpretations. However, we might also expect to find cases where hashtags are used to guide readers to the implicated conclusions that they should draw. We can see how a tweeter does just this in (36), which was posted during an international tennis tournament.

(36)   Azarenka in shorts. Venus in a dress. #Contrast.

Once again, the hashtag in this example does not contribute to the truth-evaluable content in the main body of the tweet. Neither does it directly express the tweeter's attitude or emotion towards the content. Rather, it seems to be instructing the readers to draw a contrast between the two propositions that have been expressed in the tweet. That is, it prompts the readers to look for relevance in a contrast between the facts that [Victoria] Azarenka is wearing shorts while Venus [Williams] is wearing a dress. As such, it seems to be performing a very similar role to discourse connectives *but* and *however* (Blakemore 2002; Iten 2005; Hall 2007). It guides the readers by indicating that they should find meaning and relevance in a contrast between the two propositions.[4]

As a final example, consider the contribution that the information in the hashtag makes in example (37).

(37)   Note that no homeopaths representative organisation will take a stand on use of homeopathy for dangerous diseases like Ebola. #complicit.

As with examples (29) and (36), the explicit content of the tweet can be fully evaluated in its own right, and the hashtag does not contribute to the proposition that is expressed. However, the tweeter is clearly directing the readers as to how they should find the proposition expressed relevant. By using the hashtag *#complicit*, the readers are prompted to look for who might be complicit and in what. Given the content of the main body of the tweet, it is reasonable to assume that the tweeter intends us to infer that homeopaths who do not comment on the use of homeopathy for dangerous diseases should be considered complicit in any resulting deaths. Further implicatures might also follow, including, for example, the inference that the tweeter believes that the homeopaths' lack of a stand is irresponsible, and that homeopathy generally should not be supported or promoted. The tweeter has not stated any of these explicitly. However, she uses the hashtag to make certain assumptions highly accessible for use in the interpretation of the overall message. If we take the tweet in (37) to be no more than an instruction to take note of a fact, then we have missed a key part of the intended message.

These examples demonstrate that hashtags can be used to guide inferential processes across the different components of speaker's meaning. Inference is involved in the construction of hypotheses about the intended explicatures (basic and higher-level) and implicatures of an utterance. Highlighting a word or phrase with a hashtag and thus drawing attention to it as relevant, is a strategy that users have adopted and put to use to guide any and all of these inferential processes.

HASHTAGS IN OFFLINE CONTEXTS

There is perhaps no better evidence of the emergent pragmatic function of hashtags than their use in offline contexts. As we have seen, the content in hashtags can be co-opted to help negotiate the text-based, collapsed contexts in which users find themselves online. While these pragmatic functions of hashtags may have developed online, they, unlike the search functions of hashtags, do not depend on the technological affordances of an online mediated discourse context. Providing clues to the context for interpretation and/or the attitude of the speaker may prove useful and relevant in offline contexts as well. If this is the case, we might expect those elements from mediated communication which provide these clues to cross over into spoken or written offline contexts, if doing so is likely to be communicatively advantageous. We see this happening with hashtags. In a study into hashtag use in offline contexts, I collected examples of hashtags produced in spoken utterances, and examined the functions that they perform (Scott 2018). All examples in this section are taken from that dataset. Spoken examples of hashtags are difficult to collect as they are, by definition, only found in spoken discourse, and they are a fairly recent phenomenon. As yet, they are also only used by a minority of speakers, their use is often stigmatised (as the context of these examples demonstrates), and they tend to be confined to fairly specific informal discourse contexts. However, the fact that spoken hashtags are infrequently used does not mean that they are not used systematically, and we can see from attested examples how they have been put to use in offline contexts. Some illustrative examples are given in (38) to (40). These are taken from the reader comments section of an article from the Guardian Online called 'How to say "hashtag" with your fingers' (Meltzer 2012). The contributors are describing uses of spoken hashtags that they have witnessed.

(38)   Two young girls were sat at the bar talking to each other about some or other tripe and I kid you not one turned to the other and said 'He was so fit! hashtag i definitely would'

(39)   I'm afraid I recently sat on a train from Manchester to London in the same carriage as a group of middle-class 20-year-old girls (loudly sharing tales of their 'gap yahs' in South America) who constantly interrupted each other with things like 'hashtag OMG!' and 'hashtag awkward' and 'hashtag pissed' in every other sentence.

(40)   My brother heard someone shout 'Hashtag; Banter!' in a pub in London this year. I can only hope that he drank up and left immediately.

Page (2012) and Zappavigna (2015) found the interpersonal function of hashtags to be in the minority online, with the experiential function dominating. However, offline, the reverse appears to be the case. Offline hashtags often perform an interpersonal function, communicating the speaker's attitude, or providing an evaluation or comment on the main utterance or stimulus. We can understand why they might be performing this function if we think again about the discourse contexts in which the hashtags are being used.

As we saw in the previous section, hashtags in online posts offer an effective way for users to communicate to an imagined audience and to navigate the constraints of context collapse by indicating the topic of the tweet. We can explain these uses in terms of constraints on the speaker's abilities in a mediated context. Once hashtags move to an offline, spoken context, those constraints will largely disappear. The utterances which feature spoken hashtags are part of a synchronous discourse, and they are both produced and interpreted in the same discourse context. They are part of an utterance that is said by a particular speaker to a specific audience in a known discourse context. It is therefore much less likely that the speaker will feel the need to indicate the topic of the utterance. Furthermore, there are no character limits or length constraints in offline spoken contexts, and the speaker has access to immediate feedback on whether her utterance has been understood as she intended. Therefore, there is simply less need to use hashtags to communicate contextual information. We do, however, find a wide range of interpersonal uses in the examples of spoken hashtags.

In some cases the interpersonal spoken hashtags are used to describe the attitude or emotions of the speaker, and they therefore contribute to relevance by guiding the derivation of higher-level explicatures. We see this in (39) with

#awkward and *#OMG* ('*oh my god*'). Further examples of spoken hashtags are given in (41) and (42), and the associated higher-level explicatures are given in (43) and (44).

(41)   #blessed

(42)   #proud

(43)   The speaker is blessed that [...]

(44)   The speaker is proud that [...]

Whereas in these examples the hashtag explicitly describes the speaker's emotions, in other cases, such as (45) and (46), the specific attitude or emotion must be inferred from the content of the hashtag.

(45)   #are you kidding me

(46)   #did that just happen

In these cases the speaker uses a rhetorical question in the tag to communicate surprise or disbelief. The relevance lies in the fact that the questions have been asked and in the associated attitude, rather than in any real interest in receiving an answer.

Other interpersonal hashtags are used to provide some sort of comment on or evaluation of the proposition expressed in the main utterance. For example, in (40), the speaker describes someone using the label 'banter' to signal that the associated utterance (or behaviour) should not be taken too seriously. In (47), the speaker indicates that she is being sarcastic and in (48), the speaker explicitly labels the content of the main utterance as the 'truth', communicating her epistemic stance.

(47)   #sarcasm

(48)   #truth

In several cases the attitude or evaluation is achieved via the use of an established, formulaic meme hashtag, as in examples (49) to (51).

(49)   #sorry not sorry

(50)   #first world problems

(51)   #YOLO (you only live once)

These are the most commonly occurring examples in my dataset, with (50) and (51) reported in several different sources and by various informants.

Of course, many of these interpersonal functions could be communicated in face-to-face discourse via non-verbal means such as facial expressions, gesture, or affective prosody (Wharton 2009). While these non-verbal means are available to speakers in the spoken contexts, the use of a verbal hashtag allows the speaker to both explicitly foreground this aspect of the communicated message, and, as examples in (49) to (51), present the utterance as part of a group of utterances that might be so tagged. Hashtag memes such as these will be discussed further in Chapter 6.

It remains to be seen whether hashtags in spoken language will become more established and more widely accepted. History would suggest that this would only be the case if they continue to serve a different or additional function which contributes to the speaker's communicative purpose. However, even with the limited examples discussed here, we see how speakers adapt their use of the hashtag relative to the discourse context and to make their utterance relevant. The development and adaptation in use and function that these examples demonstrate is evidence that speakers are as linguistically innovative and pragmatically sensitive as ever. Speakers are adapting their use to fit with the affordances and constraints of the discourse context, and offline uses reflect the pragmatically motivated online functions more closely than they reflect the online uses linked to searching functionality and content retrieval. Even with a limited set of examples, a pattern of use emerges. Experiential, topic-based pragmatic uses dominate in the lean, collapsed, and imagined contexts online, but interpersonal uses linked to attitudes and emotions are becoming more prominent in the offline, spoken uses.

USER TAGS

Twitter, and other social networking sites, allow not only the tagging of topics and content, but also the tagging of people. On Twitter this is known as mentioning and is achieved by including the user's Twitter handle, preceded by the @ sign. On Facebook, a user will be prompted with the option to tag a friend if they type the first three letters of a friend's name with initial capitalisation. On both sites, the act of tagging creates a hyperlink to the profile of the tagged user and generates a notification to that user telling them that they have been tagged/mentioned.

As with many of the features and functions that we are exploring in this book, mention tags are used for a range of communicative and pragmatic purposes. First we find examples where mention tags are used to refer to another user. Consider the example in (52), which is an edited version of a tweet posted by a journalist underneath a link to an online article and which @mentions another journalist from the same newspaper.

(52)   Another great interview by @User1

In this case, the @mention is a referring expression. The tag forms a part of the main sentence in place of the user's name. The notification functionality of Twitter means, however, that @User1's attention is likely to be drawn to the tweet, even though the message is not explicitly directed at that user. The act of tagging someone in a tweet is the virtual equivalent of openly gesturing towards someone when speaking about them. It differs from an offline act of referring, of course, in that mentioning someone on Twitter generates a referring expression which is also a link through to their account. If a third party does not have much information about the user, they can follow the link to find out more. Referring to someone on Twitter without tagging them is known as subtweeting (Marwick and boyd 2014; Cheplygina et al. 2020), and is considered to be the equivalent of talking about someone behind their back. Journalist Hannah Jane Parkinson (2014) provides the example in (53) which she posted on Twitter and which refers to fellow journalist Susanna Reid without tagging her.

(53)   Susanna Reid might be at ITV now but she's still a Breaking News reporter at heart ♡

This example includes Reid's name, but not her @Twitter handle, and so it is considered a subtweet. However, it is also possible to subtweet without including a name at all. Often in these cases the tweet will appear on the surface to be a general observation or comment. However, for anyone familiar with the context of interpretation, it will be understood to be about a specific person. A constructed example is given in (54).

(54)   Wow, some people really need to check their spelling before they post nasty comments about my hair.

A related phenomenon on Facebook is known as vaguebooking (Child and Starcher 2016). Vaguebooking is generally considered to be an attention-seeking behaviour where a user posts a very vague, generally emotional message with the intention that it will prompt replies and questions from other users. Typical examples are given in (55) to (57).

(55)   I'm so angry right now!

(56)   How could this happen to me?

(57)   Best day of my life!

Notice that these messages are designed to make the readers curious. Why is she so angry? What has happened to her? Why is this the best day of her life?

In Chapter 7, we will see that similar techniques are used in clickbait, and like clickbait, vaguebooking is generally considered to be manipulative and deceptive.

Mention tags can also be used as an audience management strategy. A user might explicitly define her audience by indicating who the intended addressee is by adding an @tag. Consider the example in (58), which is adapted from a real tweet posted in March 2021.

(58)   Hi @Company. I have a new boiler. The instructions are impossible to understand. Please can you help me?

Here the user has tagged the Twitter account of the boiler company in the message. This both triggers an alert to the company account and acts as a vocative, indicating to whom the message is addressed. Vladimirou et al. (2021) further analyse the role played by addressivity in social media complaints. As discussed in Chapter 2, the fact that this message has been posted on a public timeline rather than sent via a direct message, suggests that the user intended it to be seen by people other than just the company. The user has chosen to say the message to the company but to simultaneously show the message to a wider audience. Both saying and showing are ostensive acts of communication and trigger the pragmatic interpretation processes of the addressees.

CONCLUSIONS

In this chapter we have looked at the various ways in which tagging may be used in digitally mediated communication. Both #hashtags and @mention tags perform a range of functions, and many of these have been co-opted and adapted by users for pragmatic purposes. It is in a communicator's interests to guide her addressee(s) to her overall intended meaning. When we communicate via digital media we are often producing utterances with little knowledge of who will read them or when they might be read. As such, it can be very difficult to predict which contextual assumptions readers might have access to when they interpret an utterance. Hashtags provide an efficient, effective, and stylistically unobtrusive way to highlight words or phrases. Drawing attention to expressions in this way, makes associated schemas and assumptions accessible to the readers, and they will look for ways in which they might be relevant as part of the overall interpretation. We have seen examples of hashtags guiding various inferential processes, including reference assignment and the derivation of higher-level explicatures and implicatures. We have also seen that some of these functions can be useful in offline contexts, and that, again, users have been adept at using the resources available to them to achieve their communicative goals.

NOTES

1 Text of tweet edited to remove telephone number.
2 Original tweet edited to remove expletives.
3 See Scott (2013, 2020) for further discussion of subjectless sentences in English.
4 On the surface, *but* appears to prompt up to three different interpretations: denial of expectation, contrast and correction. Blakemore (2002) and Iten (2005), amongst others, argue against there being a specific 'contrast' *but*, and instead propose that all uses of *but* activate 'an inferential process which results in the contradiction and elimination of an assumption' (Blakemore 2002: 107).

REFERENCES

Blakemore, D. (2002). *Relevance and Linguistic Meaning: The Semantics and Pragmatics of Discourse Markers*. Cambridge: Cambridge University Press.

Bourlai, E. E. (2018). 'Comments in Tags, Please!': Tagging practices on Tumblr. *Discourse, Context and Media*, 22, 46–56. doi:10.1016/j.dcm.2017.08.003

Cheplygina, V., Hermans, F., Albers, C., Bielczyk, N., & Smeets, I. (2020). Ten simple rules for getting started on Twitter as a scientist. *PLoS Computational Biology*, 16(2). doi:10.1371/journal.pcbi.1007513

Child, J. T., & Starcher, S. C. (2016). Fuzzy Facebook privacy boundaries: Exploring mediated lurking, vague-booking and Facebook privacy management. *Computers in Human Behavior*, 54, 483–490. doi:https://doi.org/10.1016/j.chb.2015.08.035

Clark-Parsons, R. (2019). "I SEE YOU, I BELIEVE YOU, I STAND WITH YOU": #MeToo and the performance of networked feminist visibility. *Feminst Media Studies*. doi:10.1080/14680777.2019.1628797

Hall, A. (2007). Do discourse markers encode concepts or procedures? *Lingua*, 111(1), 149–174. doi:10.1016/j.lingua.2005.10.003

Halliday, M. (1978). *Language as Social Semiotic: The Social Interpretation of Language and Meaning*. London: Edward Arnold.

Halliday, M. (2013). Meaning as choice. In L. Fontaine, T. Bartlett, & G. O'Grady (Eds.), *Systemic Functional Linguistics: Exploring Choice* (pp. 15–36). Cambridge: Cambridge University Press.

Halliday, M., & Matthiessen, C. M. (2004). *An Introduction to Functional Grammar*. London: Arnold.

Ince, J., Rojas, F., & Davis, C. A. (2017). The social media response to Black Lives Matter: How Twitter users interact with Black Lives Matter through hashtag use,. *Ethnic and Racial Studies*, 40(11), 1814–1830. doi:10.1080/01419870.2017.1334931

Iten, C. (2005). *Linguistic Meaning, Truth Conditions and Relevance: The Case of Concessives* (Vol. 10). Basingstoke: Palgrave.

Litt, E. (2012). Knock, Knock. Who's there? The imagined audience. *Journal of Broadcasting & Electronic Media*, 56(3), 330–345. doi:10.1080/08838151.2012.705195

Marwick, A. E., & boyd, d. (2011). I tweet honestly, I tweet passionately: Twitter users, context collapse, and the imagined audience. *New Media and Society*, 13, 114–133. doi:10.1177/1461444810365313

Marwick, A. E., & boyd, d. (2014). Networked privacy: How teenagers negotaite context in social media. *New Media and Society*, 16(7), 1051–1067. doi:10.1177/1461444814543995

Matley, D. (2018). "Let's see how many of you mother fuckers unfollow me for this": The pragmatic function of the hashtag #sorrynotsorry in non-apologetic Instagram posts. *Journal of Pragmatics*, 133, 66–78. doi:10.1016/j.pragma.2018.06.003

Meltzer, T. (2012). *How to say 'hashtag' with your fingers: So addicted to Twitter you need to tag your every spoken word? Here's how to add the social media equivalent of air quotes to your conversation*. Retrieved March 24, 2016, from The Guardian: http://www.theguardian.com/technology/shortcuts/2012/aug/01/how-to-say-hashtag-fingers?CMP=twt_fd

Messina, C. (2007). *Groups for Twitter; or a proposal for Twitter tag channels*. Retrieved July 30, 2014, from FactoryCity: http://factoryjoe.com/blog/2007/08/25/groups-for-twitter-or-a-proposal-for-twitter-tag-channels/

Page, R. (2012). The linguistics of self-branding and micro-celebrity in Twitter: The role of hashtags. *Discourse and Communication*, 6(2), 181–201. doi:10.1177/1750481312437441

Page, R. (2014). Saying 'sorry': corporate apologies posted on Twitter. *Journal of Pragmatics*, 62, 30–45. doi:10.1016/j.pragma.2013.12.003

Parkinson, H. J. (2014). *Subtweeting: what is it, and how to do it well*. Retrieved April 01, 2021, from The Guardian: https://www.theguardian.com/technology/blog/2014/jul/23/subtweeting-what-is-it-and-how-to-do-it-well

Scott, K. (2013). Pragmatically motivated null subjects in English: A relevance theory perspective. *Journal of Pragmatics*, 53, 68–83. doi:10.1016/j.pragma.2013.04.001

Scott, K. (2015). The pragmatics of hashtags: Inference and conversational style on Twitter. *Journal of Pragmatics*, 81, 8–20. doi:10.1016/j.pragma.2015.03.015

Scott, K. (2018). "Hashtags Work Everywhere": The Pragmatic Functions of Spoken Hashtags. *Discourse, Context and Media*, 22, 57–64. doi:10.1016/j.dcm.2017.07.002

Scott, K. (2020). *Referring Expressions, Pragmatics, and Style: Reference and Beyond*. Cambridge: Cambridge University Press.

Sperber, D., & Wilson, D. (1986). *Relevance: Communciation and Cognition* (2nd (with postface) ed.). Oxford: Blackwell.

Twitter.com. (n.d.). *How to use hashtags*. Retrieved February 8, 2021, from Twitter Help Center: https://help.twitter.com/en/using-twitter/how-to-use-hashtags

Vladimirou, D., House, J. & Kádár, D. Z. (2021). Aggressive complaining on Social Media: The case of #MuckyMerton. *Journal of Pragmatics*, 177, 51–64. doi:10.1016/j.pragma.2021.01.017.

Wesch, M. (2009). Youtube and you: Experiences of self-awareness in the context collapse of the recording webcam. *Explorations in Media Ecology*, 8(2), 19–34.

Wharton, T. (2009). *Pragmatics and Non-Verbal Communication*. Cambridge: Cambridge University Press.

Wilson, D., & Sperber, D. (2012). *Meaning and Relevance*. Cambridge: Cambridge University Press.

Wilson, D., & Wharton, T. (2006). Relevance and prosody. *Journal of Pragmatics*, 38(10), 1559–1579. doi:10.1016/j.pragma.2005.04.012

Zappavigna, M. (2012). *Discourse of Twitter and Social Media: How We Use Language to Create Affiliation on the Web*. London: Bloomsbury.

Zappavigna, M. (2015). Seachable talk: The linguistic functions of hashtags. *Social Semiotics*, 25(3), 274–291. doi:10.1080/10350330.2014.996948

Zappavigna, M. (2018). *Searchable Talk: Hashtags and Social Media Metadiscourse*. London: Bloomsbury.

5

NON-VERBAL COMMUNICATION ONLINE

NON-VERBAL COMMUNICATION

The way speakers sound and the expressions and gestures that they use undoubtably have an effect on the way their utterances are interpreted. Imagine someone tells you they are fine with a broad smile on their face. Now think about the same verbal message delivered in a mumble with a shrug and a frown. In face-to-face spoken interaction speakers may use gestures, body language, and facial expressions to communicate their attitudes or emotions as they speak. Speakers can also vary their tone of voice to affect the overall message that they convey. They might, for example, shout or whisper to communicate an attitude or emotion. Intonation can also affect utterance meaning by conveying contrast or focusing attention on a particular part of an utterance (House 2006; Wilson and Wharton 2006; Wharton 2009; Scott 2017).

The lack of visual, social, and prosodic cues in digital contexts is often assumed to make online communication less effective and more likely to go wrong than face-to-face interactions. Online communication is often viewed as an impoverished medium in which misunderstandings are inevitable. This has become known as the 'cues filtered out' approach (Kiesler et al. 1984; Walther 1992). It was particularly prevalent in the early years of computer-mediated communication when most online discourse was purely text-based. A leanness of social cues is, of course, not specific to mediated written communication. Typographical features, including letterform and punctuation,

DOI: 10.4324/9781003254201-5

have long been used to perform at least some of the same functions in written offline language as tone of voice performs in spoken communication. However, as we discussed in Chapter 2, digitally mediated writing does not align exactly with traditional offline writing. Online writing has the potential for much greater reach and interactivity than offline texts, and it often displays features more associated with spoken language, such as synchronicity, spontaneity, and informality. Furthermore, as technology has developed, a broader range of additional resources has become available to be used as part of a message. We can now add images, videos, and audio files to messages, and manipulating the appearance of text is very easy on most digital devices. This has led to an alternative approach to studying non-verbal communication online. More recent work in the area has focused, not on the poverty of mediated contexts, but on the strategies and techniques that users employ to achieve their communicative aims. The focus here is not on trying to find textual equivalents to facial expressions, intonation etc., but rather to investigate how users perform the same relational and pragmatic tasks in online mediated contexts (Vandergriff 2013). As we have seen already with hashtags, online users often drive innovation and adapt their practices to the resources available. In this chapter, we focus on non-verbal communication and on how the affordances of online platforms have been co-opted and adapted for pragmatic purposes.

We begin by looking briefly at how typography, punctuation, and spelling are employed by users to communicate their meanings. We will then move on to consider image-based resources in the form of emoticons, emoji, and reaction GIFs. We will see that, while emoticons and emoji may have originally emerged as an attempt to render facial expressions in text and then later in graphic form, their use and functionality have evolved beyond that.

TEXT PRESENTATION AND PRAGMATICS ONLINE

When we produce a written text, whether online or offline, we make decisions about how that text will look. We can choose the size and style of the letterforms, we can choose what punctuation to use or not use, and we can choose whether to employ additional features such as underlining, bolding, or italicisation. Even minor changes to the presentation of the text on the page can affect how readers understand the message and how they perceive of the writer (Lea and Spears 1992). Writers can use typography and text presentation to guide readers to the intended meaning of the utterance. That is, they can use the way the text looks to guide the readers in the inferences that they make. In the example in (1), taken from Scott and Jackson (2020: 168), italicisation changes the way in which reference is resolved. Without the italics, it is Andrew who throws to Matthew. However, when *he* is italicised, we take the pronoun to refer to Patrick or perhaps to some other salient male in the discourse context. In this way, typography can affect the propositional content of a written utterance.

(1)   Andrew threw to Patrick and then *he* threw to Matthew.

The presentation of the text on the page can also affect the attitudes or emotions that the writer communicates. This is illustrated in an example from the novel *American Psycho* (Ellis 1991: 162), given in (2), and again, discussed by Scott and Jackson (2020: 168).

(2)   …there was a private sale at the boutique on Madison…*two weeks ago!*
       and though I figured out that one of the doormen probably withheld the
       card to piss me off, it still doesn't erase the fact that *I missed the fucking*
       sale…

By placing certain words in italics the writer draws attention to them, and they stand out from the rest of the text. In the case of (2), the most accessible hypothesis for why the writer has done this is that the change in typeface is intended to mimic a change in intonation. It gives us clues to how the utterance would sound were it to be spoken aloud. The reader can use this information along with information from the context to infer that the narrator is angry and that the italicised words would have been shouted.

Digital communication affords us a wide range of options when it comes to text presentation on the virtual page. With relative ease we can change the size, colour, and typeface of online text. Riordan and Kreuz (2010) conducted a corpus analysis of non-verbal cues in computer-mediated communication. They looked at capitalised words, vocal spelling, repeated punctuation, emoticons, and other non-standard uses of punctuation. They found that use of such cues was either associated with indicating emotion or it was used to clarify meaning in some other way. Riordan and Kreuz's corpus analysis revealed capitalisation to be the most widely used non-verbal cue.[1] Capitalisation has been linked to the expression of stance and to the intensification of emotions (Langlotz and Locher 2012). Using all capitals is often assumed to indicate that the writer is shouting, and the assumption that to do so is rude persists in popular media discourse (Tschabitscher 2021). Byron and Baldridge (2007) found that when work emails were typed in all capitals, the sender was perceived more negatively than when standard capitalisation was used. Fleuriet et al. (2014), on the other hand, found that readers of posts on Facebook walls did not view a message in all capitals as being any more negative than one with standard use of capitals. We can better understand these seemingly contradictory findings if we examine more closely the context in which the test utterances were interpreted in each study. As with all of the non-verbal cues that we will look at in this chapter, and as with the italicisation discussed above, the interpretation of capitalisation appears to be context-sensitive. Using non-standard typography, whether that be italics, capitals, or bold facing, puts the reader to more effort. It is more effortful because it deviates from conventions and from what the reader is expecting (Scott and Jackson 2020). The writers of the emails in Byron and Baldridge's study may have been perceived negatively, not because they were perceived to be angry or shouting, but because the non-standard capitalisation signalled a lack of knowledge of, or perhaps a lack of respect for, the normal conventions of work emails. Participants in Fleuriet et al.'s study were asked to interpret a Facebook wall post. There is likely to be more acceptance of deviation from usual written standards in social media posts than there is in work emails. The use of all capitals, in this case, could as easily have been intended as a sign of excitement or enthusiasm as of anger or negativity. Not all digitally mediated communication is alike, and the context in which online utterances are produced must be considered if we are to understand the behaviours that we see and the interpretations that we find.

When individual words or phrases are capitalised, as in examples (3) and (4), the most accessible interpretation is that the writer is emphasising the capitalised part of the utterance, and that some extra meaning should be deduced from that emphasis.

(3) I have SO much reading to do.

(4) It took me ALL DAY.

What that extra meaning is, is a matter of inference and will depend on the discourse context. In (3), for example, we might reasonably take the writer to be focusing the reader's attention on just how much reading she had to do, and in (4), perhaps the extra effects from the capitalisation derive from the writer's, presumably negative, attitude about something taking all day.[2] If, however, a whole sentence or even a whole text is presented in capital letters, the inferences that we draw are likely to be about how the writer is feeling generally in relation to the whole message. Just as both excitement and anger might result in a speaker producing an utterance that is louder and higher pitch than normal, so various emotions can be implied by capitalising a whole text, as in (5) or (6).

(5) I AM SO EXCITED FOR TONIGHT!

(6) I WILL NOT DO IT AND YOU CAN NOT MAKE ME!

Capitalisation does not encode shouting. Readers must pragmatically infer why a text has been presented in capitals, just as they must infer why a speaker has produced a spoken utterance in a louder voice than usual.

Another common feature of text presentation in digitally mediated writing is non-standard or eccentric spelling. This is sometimes referred to as 'vocal spelling' (Riordan and Kreuz 2010: 1809), and often involves the use of repeated letters. However, as we shall see, the connection between the representation on the screen and the vocalisation of an equivalent spoken word or expression is perhaps not as clear cut as it might at first appear. Kalman and

Gergle (2014) studied the use of letter repetitions in email communication. Some examples from their corpus are given in (7) and (8).

(7)   It is sweeeeeeet

(8)   Soooo

They conclude that this use of non-standard spelling is often, but not always, used to emulate a stretched-out syllable in spoken communication. They view the spelling as a cue to how the word would sound if it were spoken, rather than as an emphasis marker or other visual clue to interpretation. Riordan and Kreuz (2010) observed a similar pattern, and they note that the letters which are most frequently repeated (H, M, O, and S) are those which can be elongated when spoken. In their data, repeated letters were most commonly found in words used to strengthen the content of the message, including swear words and words such as *never* and *always*. They conclude that letter repetitions appear, therefore, to be linked to emphasis and to the communication of emotion.

In her study of workplace instant message communication, Darics (2013) also found examples of repeated letters that appear to be a signal of how the writer is feeling. She provides the example in (9) as an illustration of this technique in use in a non-task-oriented workplace message between colleagues.

(9)   IIIIITTTTTTTT'SSSSSS THEWEEEEEKEND BAAAAAAAAAAA ABBBBBYYYYYYYYY!!!!!!!

Here the repetition of letters mimics the sound of someone shouting or screaming with excitement. While the spellings evoke this sound effect, they do not constitute a replication of the oral sound on the screen. Most of the letters in (9) are repeated, even though not all could be elongated in speech. Darics provides other examples in which the repetitions appear to be performing the phatic function of helping the participants to manage the social interaction and to set the tone of the discourse. Consider the examples in (10) and (11) taken from Darics' examples (145). Notice that the letter repetitions here cannot be intended to correspond to elongated sounds in a spoken utterance.

(10)   hello, good morninggggg

(11)   hello thereeee

The sound at the end of *morning* is a stop, and the orthographic <e> at the end of *there* is silent. Daric observes that in these cases the letter repetitions and non-standard spelling appear to be used to contextualise the discourse by signalling informality and friendliness. She argues that the use of letter repetitions and non-standard orthography can be used by a writer to contextualise her written messages and to provide an indication of how they should be interpreted. Similarly, in her study of relational work and politeness strategies in workplace instant messaging conversations amongst a virtual team, Darics (2010: 137), suggests that 'orthographic representation of intonation ... serves as a means to express emotional involvement, and consequently as a means of constructing friendly, informal communication'. Such uses are, however, highly context-sensitive and they depend on there being a shared understanding of communicative norms between the interlocutors. Rudolf von Rohr and Locher (2020: 204) also found that non-standard orthography could have a 'face-enhancing effect' as it helped to 'boost compliments and self-praise'.

Whether it is non-standard spelling or non-standard use of capitalisation, we can see that users online are making use of the resources available to them to communicate their messages. In each of the examples above, the writers are breaking with convention and doing something unexpected. This draws attention to the relevant part of the text and prompts the reader to look for some meaning in the decisions that the writer has made. That meaning must be inferred, and while we see that it is often related to emotions, attitudes, and management of social relationships, it is ultimately dependent on the context, and is a matter of pragmatics. We see the same general pattern emerging in the non-standard use of punctuation online, and we consider some examples of this next.

PUNCTUATION ONLINE

Speakers and writers have a repertoire of devices that they can use to guide an addressee to the intended meaning of an utterance (Wilson 2011). This includes prosody and intonation in spoken utterances, and punctuation in written utterances. Non-standard punctuation has long been associated with digitally mediated communication (Danet 2001), and in particular with the communication of emotions and stance (Langlotz and Locher 2012). In this section we consider some examples of how the rules of punctuation have been adapted and exploited to help users convey their meaning in online discourse contexts.

In offline written language, full stops (referred to as *periods* in American English) mark the boundary between one sentence and the next. In online contexts, however, they appear to have taken on a new function, at least for some users. According to David Crystal (2015), full stops can now be used to mark emotion, and a sentence that ends with a full stop is considered to convey annoyance or anger. Journalist Ben Crair (2013) describes the use of full stops in text messages as communicating 'I am not happy about the sentence I just concluded'. Gunraj et al. (2016) found that text messages that ended with a full stop were indeed rated as less sincere than those that did not. Crucially, they found no such difference when full stops were used in handwritten notes. This suggests that the users are taking the medium and context into consideration in their interpretation, and that new, context-sensitive conventions around the use of punctuation are emerging in digitally mediated channels. Why might this new association between full stops and negative emotion have emerged and how can we understand it in pragmatic terms?

In offline writing, full stops serve a very clear and practical purpose. Without them it would be harder to process a text as it would be unclear where one sentence ends and another begins. However, in synchronous forms of digitally mediated communication such as instant messaging and chatting, line breaks now serve this purpose. Text message exchanges tend to be shorter than offline written texts (Baron 2010), and users can easily send a sequence of messages, one for each sentence. With the key offline function of full stops largely redundant in instant messaging, a pragmatic perspective can help us to understand why this new, negative association may have arisen in certain contexts. According to relevance theory, we should not make our addressees do any unnecessary processing. If a writer puts a reader to extra effort, then the reader will look for extra meaning. Readers will infer what this extra meaning is by following the relevance-theoretic comprehension procedure. As line breaks are doing the old work of full stops in synchronous online discourse, a reader might well look for extra meaning in a writer's decision to include an unnecessary full stop. Given that full stops are associated with endings and finality, a highly accessible interpretation may well be that the writer is emphasising the end of the message and perhaps the end of the exchange. We saw in Chapter 4 that the term *hashtag* has migrated from online contexts to spoken contexts in cases where it served a communicative purpose. Likewise, we find the phrase 'full stop' or 'period' occurring in spoken language. It is often used to emphasise the end of a point or the end of an exchange (Scott 2018; Scott and Jackson 2020). It is perhaps then not surprising that some readers interpret full stops in instant messaging as an indication that the writer is finished with the conversation.

Of course, a reader must take the writer's abilities and preferences into consideration when interpreting an utterance. Feelings often run high over what is considered correct or acceptable in terms of punctuation, and, indeed, in terms of language use generally. Some writers may choose to punctuate their synchronous, informal messages in a way more associated with asynchronous or formal texts simply because they believe it is the correct and proper way to behave. Other users may simply include full stops out of habit and perhaps are unaware of emerging conventions, practices, and associations. This can, of course, lead to misunderstandings if a reader's assumptions about the writer's abilities, preferences, and intentions are incorrect.

The full stop is not the only punctuation mark that appears to be evolving in terms of its functionality online. Simpson (2005) identifies three functions for the ellipsis marks ('...') in text-based online communication. While they can be used in online texts to indicate a textual omission in the same way they may be used in offline writing, there are, claims Simpson, two other uses for this punctuation mark. These additional uses emulate features of spoken discourse. They are illustrated here with examples from my own WhatsApp message history. First, in (12), the ellipsis is used to indicate a pause, and second, in (13), it is used to indicate that the writer has trailed off (aposiopesis).

(12)   Haha…Ok message later

(13)   Yeah, I did wonder about that…

According to Vandergriff (2013: 8) when used turn-finally, an ellipsis indicates an openness to 'dialogic expansion' and is associated with 'unassertiveness'. Thompson and Filik (2016) found ellipsis to be associated with the softening of negative comments, again because it signalled an openness to the exchange continuing or to further discussion of the point. In many ways, the function of ellipsis in asynchronous digital communication appears to be the opposite of the full stop that we discussed above. Offline, speakers may use various non-verbal cues to indicate that they have not finished their turn or that they are unsure, unassertive, or perhaps open to further discussion. These may include facial expressions, gestures, and intonation patterns. Online, an ellipsis can be used to indicate that the writer is silent, but not absent, and that she is still engaged with the discourse in some way. The reader must then infer why the writer has chosen to indicate this explicitly via the use of ellipsis, and these inferences, as always, will depend on the discourse context. A study by Ong (2011) focused on conversational turns that consisted of only an ellipsis. He found this usage to be associated with a range of emotions, including disagreement, confusion, and disapproval. However, he also found that ellipsis was used for discourse management purposes to elicit further responses and to hold the floor. Whereas the full stop signals completeness, an ellipsis appears to signal incompleteness. The reason for the incompleteness must be inferred and so is a matter of pragmatics.

EMOTICONS AND EMOJI

In 2015, Oxford Dictionaries announced that their *Word of The Year* was not a word at all, but an emoji. Officially called *Face with tears of joy*, the emoji, shown in (14) was selected to reflect the 'ethos, mood, and preoccupations of 2015' (Oxford Dictionaries 2015).

(14)   😂

This high-profile acknowledgement of the popularity and pervasiveness of emoji reflects the key role they now play in much of our digitally mediated communication. Emoji and emoticons are associated with informal and playful language use (Danet 2001; Derks et al. 2007; Dresner and Herring 2010) and are often assumed to be a substitute for facial expressions, gestures, and other non-verbal cues. As we shall see, however, their functions have developed beyond providing a mere representation of a communicator's face, gestures, or body language. Their contribution is highly context sensitive and users employ them for a range of pragmatic reasons.

History and development

While emoji were publicly recognised by Oxford Dictionaries in 2015, their beginnings were somewhat more humble, and the roots of the present-day emoji can be traced back over thirty years. As we have seen with tagging and with text presentation and punctuation, the communicative needs of users have been the driving force behind the development of many emerging digital practices. Users are adept at repurposing the resources available to them in order to get their message across. The issue of how to express emotions and tone of voice in written text is nothing new. There have long been reported, and sometimes disputed, cases of writers producing something like the modern-day emoticon to indicate a smile or a wink in a written text. Indeed, claims of this sort are even made about the work of a 17th-century poet (Madrigal 2014) and the speeches of Abraham Lincoln (Fitzgerald 2012).

The invention of the emoticon is, however, generally credited to computer scientist Scott Fahlman. Fahlman made the suggestion in (15) on a bulletin board in 1982. The suggestion was prompted by the misinterpretation of a message that was intended as a joke.[3]

(15)   I propose that [sic] the following character sequence for joke markers: :-)

Read it sideways. Actually, it is probably more economical to mark things that are NOT jokes, given current trends. For this, use :-(

As discussed in Chapter 2, the potential reach of digitally mediated communication is large, and many platforms allow for synchronous, multiuser interactivity. Fahlman explicitly links emoticon use with these features of digital communication. Explicit markers of jokes or sarcasm may not be needed, he points out, by skilled, professional writers who are experienced at carefully composing and editing their work. However, anyone can post a message online. Further devices and resources to clarify and disambiguate meaning may, therefore, be useful for many, and may play a role in avoiding misunderstandings. Furthermore, the reach and immediacy of digitally mediated communication means that the consequences of misunderstandings and misinterpretations online are likely to be more significant than they are for offline written texts. As Fahlman (n.d.) points out on his blog:

If 100,000 copies of a novel or an essay were distributed in printed form, and if 1% of the readers didn't get the joke and were outraged at what they had read, there was nothing these clueless readers could do to spoil the enjoyment of the other 99%.

Thus, from their first inception, emoticons were conceived of as a means of navigating the specific contextual conditions in which we find ourselves when we communicate via digitally mediated channels. Their development was initiated by users and driven by communicative needs.

Emoticons use characters (letters, numbers, and punctuation marks) to create representations of facial expressions when viewed sideways. A typical smiley face is illustrated in (16). Graphical equivalents were then developed and incorporated into software so that now, for example, typing a colon followed by a closed parenthesis mark in Microsoft Word produces the graphic in (17).

(16) :)

(17) 😊

Although similar to emoticons in appearance, emoji are pictograms which can be inserted into messages and documents as a single character. They are typically selected from an emoji keyboard available on devices and built into apps. Emoji sets include various representations of facial expressions and gestures, along with a large and ever-growing array of other pictograms including animals, objects, flags, and symbols. Some examples are given in (18).

(18)   🦐🐱⚽🀄⚙♡

As social media users adopt emoji, they reduce their use of emoticons. This suggests not only that emoticons and emoji perform the same paralinguistic functions, but that emoji are gradually displacing emoticons (Pavalanathan and Eisenstein 2016; Herring and Dainas 2017; Konrad, Herring, and Choi 2020). Prada et al. (2018) found that users had more positive attitudes towards emoji than emoticons, and reported using them more often.

Stickers, like emoji and emoticons, are graphical representations that are shared via social media apps. They take the form of 'illustrations or animations of characters to which words or phrases are sometimes attached' (Konrad et al. 2020: 222). Konrad et al. (2020) discuss the rising popularity of stickers on social media platforms and report their finding that there is a 'functional overlap between emoji and stickers, with differences being mainly ones of degrees' (232). As they suggest, we might expect to eventually see stickers displace emoji, following the same 'evolutionary trajectory' (217) as emoji. While I do not focus on stickers here, many of the claims and analyses made about emoticons and emoji may be extended to or adapted for stickers as well. Research into the communicative and pragmatic function of stickers looks to be a fruitful area for the future.

Many of the studies referred to in this section were written before emoji became widespread and easily accessible via mobile apps and keyboards. In discussion of the various studies into their meaning and pragmatic roles, I use the terminology of the original research in each case. However, many of the observations, conclusions, and analyses drawn about emoticon use can be extended to the corresponding emoji, and vice versa.

Emoticons, emoji, and facial expressions

Emoticons and face emoji portray a range of facial expressions, behaviours, and gestures. Some face emoji represent characters wearing different clothes and accessories such as sunglasses, hats, and surgical masks, and emoji sets now include characters performing a range of different activities from juggling to gymnastics. How do these pictograms relate to offline non-verbal communication? Do they serve the same functions and are they interpreted in the same way?

Some emoji portray facial expressions that are classified as natural signals (Hauser 1996; Wharton 2009).[4] These include emoji that show smiling, laughing, blushing, and frowning faces, and these are amongst the most frequently used emoji on platforms such as Twitter (emojitracker.com). While the equivalent offline expressions evolved for the purposes of communication, they do not encode meaning in the way that linguistic expressions do. What they do convey is context-dependent and often vague. A smile might mean joy, embarrassment, or amusement. A frown might indicate sadness, disapproval, disappointment, or confusion. Smiles, frowns, and other natural signals may be produced involuntarily and spontaneously, and the information that they convey may not always be intentionally communicated. However, they can still be used intentionally and as ostensive stimuli. As Wharton (2009) discusses, natural signals can be deliberately shown to an audience. Matt's broad smile in (19), for example, might be exaggerated beyond a spontaneous, involuntary expression. He may openly and deliberately let his interlocutor see that he is smiling as he speaks in order to communicate his attitude and emotions.

(19)   Matt: (smiling broadly) Today is Friday.

If this is the case, the smile becomes an ostensive act of showing and is therefore considered an intentional act of communication. Of course, emoticons and emoji which represent these natural signals are only ever used intentionally. Mistyping aside, it is not possible to accidentally smile or frown by using an emoji. When someone sends us a smile or frown emoji, we do not necessarily know how they are feeling, but we know what they want us to think they are feeling.

Other face emoji represent natural behaviours such as sweating, shivering, and vomiting. Offline, these behaviours are not communicative in the way that a smile or frown is. They evolved for physical reasons: cooling us down, warming us up, or expelling an unwanted substance from the body. If we see someone shivering, we do not automatically assume that they are doing so to communicate to us that they are cold. However, as with natural signals, these natural behaviours can be intentionally shown to someone else. We might draw attention to the fact that we are shivering for example, perhaps exaggerating the behaviour. By deliberately showing the behaviour, we create an ostensive stimulus which triggers the same pragmatic interpretation processes as other intentional acts of communication. Alternatively, we may produce an exaggerated or stylised mime of the natural behaviour. Perhaps we are not cold enough to actually shiver, but we produce a performed shiver to communicate that we are feeling cold. Similarly someone might mime vomiting or wiping the sweat from their brow to communicate how they are feeling. Notice that as the behaviour becomes more stylised and less natural, the role of the communicator's intentions becomes more important in the interpretation process. We do not have to think about the intentions of someone who is actually shivering, sweating, or vomiting. Their natural behaviours transmit information to us. However, when some element of showing or deliberate production becomes involved, intentions come into play. We must infer the intention behind the acts in order to work out what the communicator meant when she performed them. Again, when emoji representing these natural behaviours are used, they can only be used intentionally. As Yus (2011: 165–171) and Riordan (2017a) discuss, there can be no unintentional non-verbal behaviour in text-only online contexts. That is, it is not possible to accidentally convey information via text-based interfaces in the way that it would be in face-to-face, video, or audio communication. Genuine facial expressions provide direct evidence of the communicator's emotional state. It is often assumed that emoji are a direct replacement for facial expressions and other non-verbal clues to the writer's meaning. However, the use of a smile emoji, for example, provides no direct evidence of the emotion that the communicator is experiencing as she writes the message. As Dresner and Herring (2010) point out, the unintentional expressions of emotion that we find in non-mediated communication are likely to be valued more highly as an indicator of how someone is feeling than intentionally performed expressions. In contrast, the addressee of a mediated message knows that the writer has consciously chosen to include the emoji in her message. While this will prompt the reader to infer why she has done so, it does not follow that he will automatically assume that the emotion is genuine or to be trusted. Likewise, there is no assumption that the emoji used in a message necessarily mirror the facial expressions, gestures, or behaviours of the writer as she sends the message. They are clues to her intended meaning, and the addressee's task is to infer what that intended meaning is.

Finally, while emoticons are largely representations of facial expressions, current emoji sets go far beyond this, and include a wide array of pictograms featuring non-human subjects. Stickers are even more 'elaborate and character-driven' and they portray 'body language and facial expressions more explicitly than emoji' (Konrad et al. 2020: 222). If we are to understand what these contribute to digitally mediated communication, it is crucial that we move away from an approach where we assume that online resources are a direct replacement for offline non-verbal cues. Instead we should consider the ways in which users employ the resources available to them, including emoticons and emoji, to communicate their meaning.

Functions of emoticons and emoji

Attitudes, emotions and tone

Emoticons and emoji can undoubtedly change the interpretation of a message. They are often associated with relational work and politeness (Arendholz 2013), and are perhaps most commonly assumed to be linked to the communication of attitudes and emotions. This is certainly one of their functions, and, according to Danesi (2017: 100), they can be used to 'add emotional tone and to emphasize certain phatic aspects of communication'. Consider the difference in the interpretation of examples (20) and (21), discussed by Pohl et al. (2017: 38).[5]

(20)   Susan's coming over later 😍

(21)   Susan's coming over later 🙁

From a pragmatic perspective, we can understand the difference in terms of the higher-level explicatures that the reader is encouraged to derive. The precise nature of the propositional attitude that the writer is communicating will depend on the context and on the assumptions that the interlocutors share about Susan and one another. However, (20) could communicate the higher-level explicature in (22), and (21) could communicate the higher-level explicature in (23).

(22)   The reader is excited that [Susan's coming over later].

(23)   The reader is upset that [Susan's coming over later].

In their study of emoticons in Nordic workplace emails, Skovholt et al. (2014) found that emoticons were used to convey a positive attitude, particularly when used as part of an email signoff or signature. They suggest that in these cases, the emoticon 'has an iconic function, signalling aspects of the sender's identity and her positive attitude towards the recipient' (788).

Derks et al. (2008) found that emoticons could be used to strengthen the intensity of a message. If a smiling emoticon was added to a positive message, the message was rated more positively than the equivalent message without an emoticon. Similarly, when a frowning emoticon was added to a negative message, the message was perceived as more negative than the text-only message. According to this study, however, it does not seem possible to reverse the positivity or negativity of a message simply by adding an emoticon. Riordan (2017a: 52) reaches a similar conclusion, explaining that 'emoticons are intended to convey affective information – not enough to alter the valence of the message itself, but enough to alter the intensity of the affect'.

Yus (2014) examined the use of emoticons in Spanish WhatsApp conversations. Amongst the uses he identified, Yus found that emoticons were used to signal a propositional attitude, and to strengthen an attitude that is already indicated in the words of the message itself. His examples (in translation from Spanish) are given here in (24) and (25).

(24)   I have no time to get bored, nor to read :(((

(25)   I hope you'll always remember my Spanish lessons :-)

Notice that the propositional attitude of the writer in (24) is unclear without the emoticon. The utterance is compatible with two possible interpretations depending on whether we take the writer to be holding an assumption along the lines of (26) or along the lines of (27).

(26)   People who have no time to get bored or read are living exciting lives.

(27)   People who have no time to get bored or read are overly busy and stressed.

Processing the post in the context of (26) leads to an interpretation on which we take the writer to be feeling positive. Processing it in the context of (27), on the other hand, leads to an interpretation on which the writer is feeling negative. The use of the emoticon indicates that the former is the intended interpretation. The post in (25) is more clearly positive in nature, but, according to Yus, the use of the emoticon serves to intensify this emotion.

   In other examples, a smiling face emoticon or emoji may be used to mitigate the seriousness of a message. Consider the example in (28), taken from my own WhatsApp message history.

(28)   I bet they will end up using the photograph where I am cleaning the lipstick off my teeth 😂

This was posted in a WhatsApp group chat after the participants had taken part in a group photo shoot to publicise an event they were involved in. The writer is complaining that one of the photographs is not flattering, and is worrying that this is the one that will be used in the final publicity. However, the use of the *face with tears of joy* emoji indicates that this is not a serious complaint or worry, and that, indeed, it would perhaps be quite funny if it were to turn out to be the case.

   A range of studies have found that users employ emoticons and emoji to negotiate relationships and perform other relational work (Locher and Watts 2005). Skovholt et al. (2014) found that in workplace emails emoticons were used to manage the tone of the message in a way that contributed to the politeness of the exchange. They found emoticons used as hedges to soften requests, rejections, corrections, and complaints, and to strengthen compliments, thanks, and positive appraisals. In these cases, the emoticons were used to help manage, maintain, and enhance interpersonal relationships whilst performing certain speech acts. Darics (2010: 141) also found that smiley emoticons were an 'essential element of relational work at the workplace', and that they can function as a 'positive politeness strategy for creating a collaborative work environment'. In their work on relational work and politeness on an online health forum, Rudolf von Rohr and Locher (2020: 203) found that emoji were used to 'underline the positive, face-enhancing stance the respondent has adopted'. In her study of relational work on online message boards, Arendholz (2013) found emoticons used to communicate the user's attitude and emotional stance, and she suggests that they have 'a unique way of establishing contact on an interpersonal plane between online interlocutors' (150–151). Arendholz also discusses cases where emoticons are used to mitigate the force of a directive speech act. We think more about the relation between emoticons, emoji, and speech acts in the next section as we consider cases where an emoticon or emoji has been used as an illocutionary force indicator to guide the reader's inferences about which speech act is being performed.

Illocutionary force indicators

While we find a range of cases where emoticons and emoji are used to convey emotion, it is limiting to assume that this is their only function (Dresner and Herring 2010). The primary function of emoticons and emoji is to convey pragmatic meaning, and this can contribute to the overall message in a number of different ways. We find examples of emoticons and emoji used to guide other pragmatic processes, including inference of the intended illocutionary force of the associated message. As we saw in Chapter 1, working out which speech act a communicator is intending to perform is a key part of the interpretation process. Emoticons and emoji can be used to guide this process. In these uses, the emoji and emoticons do not communicate information about the writer's emotional state, and neither do they alter the propositional content of the message. Rather, they indicate which speech act the writer is intending to perform.

Dresner and Herring (2010) discuss examples where a wink face emoticon may be used to indicate that the writer is joking. Joking is not an emotion, and, indeed, we might joke while in any number of emotional states. The emoticon does not tell us about the emotional state of the writer and, indeed, it does not necessarily communicate that the writer is winking as she writes, or that she would necessarily perform an actual wink if the utterance were spoken. Rather the use of the wink emoticon can be used to indicate that the writer does not intend the associated message to be taken seriously. The *face with tears of joy* emoji seems to fulfil this same function along with the corresponding wink emoji. Consider the example in (29).

(29)   I knew you wouldn't be able to resist reminding me

This message was sent by a user to a friend, in response to a reminder about something the user had agreed to do. The emoji faces at the end of the message may suggest that the writer finds the situation amusing, but more likely they are intended to indicate that the message is meant as a joke. That is, the user is communicating that the message is not intended as a complaint or rebuke, but as a gentle tease. Dresner and Herring (2010) discuss the example in (30).

(30)   I would like a noncircumventing solution ;->

Here, the user adds a wink face emoticon to the end of a message to indicate that it is intended as a suggestion, rather than as a demand. Yus (2014: 520) provides the example in (31), translated from the original Spanish.

(31)   Those interested send me a private message first ;-)

The wink face emoticon indicates that the message is intended as a friendly invitation rather than as a command or demand. As with the hedging function discussed in the previous section, these uses contribute to the politeness of the utterance. However, in these cases they do so, not by indicating the tone or attitude behind the speech act, but by changing the illocutionary force of the speech act itself.

Propositional meaning

In this section, we look at some examples where emoticons and emoji contribute to the propositional meaning of a message. They can be used to replace lexical items, either singularly or in combination (Herring 2018), and they can also be used to guide the reader in the inferential processes that contribute to explicature derivation. As the number of emoji available has expanded, it has become possible to represent more and more objects and activities in emoji form. Given the propensity for playfulness and creativity of many users in online spaces, it is perhaps not surprising that emoji are sometimes used as lexical replacements. The example in (32) is taken from Dürscheid and Siever (2017), and (33) is from my own WhatsApp files.

(32)   This time with 🌑 screen 👍 😊

(33)   You're a ☆

In these examples, there is a fairly clear connection between the target word that would otherwise complete the sentence and the concept associated with the emoji. The writer could, of course, have just typed the corresponding word. However, as Pohl et al. (2017: 6.2), suggest, using 'a visual icon instead of a word enables users to introduce ambiguity and playfulness where they see fit'. Sasamoto (forthcoming) analyses emoji as ostensive visual stimuli and argues that the perceptual resemblance between the appearance of the emoji and what it is used to communicate can give rise to a range of weak implicatures and non-propositional (affective) effects. Although Sasamoto focuses on face emoji, we can imagine how use of a colourful representation of a sun or star might make a range of impressions more accessible to the reader for use in onward inferencing compared with use of the corresponding word. In (33), for example, the emoji makes visual impressions of a star more salient, and assumptions about stars as being bright, shining, and visually striking will be accessible for use in the interpretation of the metaphor.

There is evidence that users may employ emoji to guide the reader in disambiguating or refining the meaning that is communicated by the message. Riordan (2017b) found that users rated the message in (34) as less ambiguous than the version in (35).

(34)   Got a shot 🏆

(35)   Got a shot at the bar

In a further study, Riordan (2017a) suggests that readers were more confident in their interpretation of the message in (36) than they were in the interpretation of the same message without any emoji, as shown in (37).

(36)   Party time 🎉🎉🎉

(37)   Party time

They suggest that this may be because the emoji help to narrow the meaning of the word *party*. The word *party* might be used to describe a wide range of events, from a formal dinner party to a riotous celebration. The emoji helps establish that it is the sort of party at which a celebration party horn or party popper would be appropriate or expected.

As we saw in Chapter 2, interactions on instant messaging services such as WhatsApp often feature overlapping topics, and this can lead to a lack of coherence in the discourse structure. Users may introduce more than one point in a single message and responses will not necessarily appear adjacent to the corresponding original message. Emoji can be used to indicate which topic a message belongs with or is responding to. Consider the exchange in (38), from my own WhatsApp files.

(38)   User1: Bought thick white sliced bread last night so we can have toast
               with no nutritional value 😋. If I've got no side effects tomor-
               row I'll message you about a walk.
        User2: Good plan! 🍞🍞🍞

User1 is due to have the Covid-19 vaccination injection that day and is explaining how she has bought comfort food in anticipation of suffering side-effects. However, in the same message she says she will be in contact to arrange a walk the next day. There are two key points in this message, both of which could reasonably be described as a plan. One is a plan to eat toast as comfort food and the other is a plan to message User2 the next day about the possibility of going for a walk. User2 responds, and uses the bread emoji to playfully indicate that 'Good plan!' refers to the comfort eating preparations. In face-to-face communication User1's two points would be likely to be in different turns and so the need for this sort of specification would not arise.

Irony and sarcasm

Emoticons and emoji are strongly associated with jokes and informal discourse. Skovholt et al. (2014) found that emoticons could be used in workplace emails as markers of humour, and we saw above that wink face emoticons can be used to indicate that an utterance is intended to be a joke. There is also evidence that users employ emoticons to indicate that they are being sarcastic. Sarcasm, and verbal irony more generally, depend heavily on context and they always involve inference (Wilson and Sperber 2012; Wilson 2017). Imagine that Rosa produces the utterance in (39) when she hears a loud party starting next door as she is getting ready for bed.

(39)   That is brilliant. Just what I needed right now!

Given the discourse context in which she has uttered these words, we infer that she is being ironic. She does not think the situation is brilliant, and a loud party keeping her awake is not what she needs right now. We reach this interpretation based on contextual assumptions. We may also be guided by certain non-verbal cues such as exaggerated facial expressions and tone of voice (Kreuz and Roberts 1995; Bryant and Fox Tree 2002). It is, of course, possible to be ironic in writing, and various studies suggest that contextual information is far more important than non-verbal cues when it comes to detecting irony (Bryant and Fox Tree 2005; Deliens et al. 2018). However, when we move into online discourse contexts we find ourselves communicating in a collapsed context and to an imagined audience. We are likely to have fewer visual and auditory social cues at our disposal. It is therefore perhaps not surprising that users have developed means of indicating that they are being ironic, particularly as the risks of misinterpreted irony or sarcasm can be high (Hancock 2004). Several studies suggest that emoticons and emoji are one means by which online users indicate that they are being ironic when they communicate in digitally mediated contexts.

Thompson and Filik (2016) found that emoticons were more likely to be used in sarcastic contexts, compared with literal contexts. In particular, they found that use of the tongue face (40) and wink face (41) emoticons were used by participants in production tasks to indicate sarcasm, even when those participants were given the option to add linguistic content to the message.

(40)   😊

(41)   😉

Derks et al. (2008) found that incongruence between the message and the emoticon can be a cue for sarcasm. When a positive emoticon was included in a negative message or vice versa, the message was rated as more sarcastic than when the emoticon and message agreed or when no emoticon was included. This aligns with work on face-to-face irony comprehension, which indicates that contextual incongruence is a more reliable cue for irony than facial expression or tone of voice (Deliens et al. 2018). It is the contrast between the emoji and the message, which cues an ironic interpretation rather than the emoji itself. Indeed, Dresner and Herring (2010: 253) note that emoticons that we might think of as being 'sarcastic', such as the wink face, 'seem to have no self-standing content on their own, but rather contribute to – indeed, provide a vital cue as to how to interpret – the linguistic content of messages'.

From this range of examples and studies we can see that emoticons and emoji are employed by users to guide the interpretation of utterances in a wide variety of ways. They provide clues to the intended meaning of the utterance, but cannot be interpreted without reference to the discourse context in which they are produced.

REACTION GIFS

A GIF (graphic interchange format) is a short, silent, animated image, usually clipped from a longer source video, which plays on a loop. The option to attach a GIF to a post or message is integrated into many social media interfaces, including Twitter, WhatsApp, and even the chat function on web conferencing tools such as Microsoft Teams. While emoji may be integrated into a longer message or sent in isolation, reaction GIFs are usually sent as a complete turn. They may have a message appended to them, and they often include a text annotation over the image as part of the GIF itself. The subject matter for GIFs is often content from popular culture, and many are edited clips of television shows, pop videos, or movies. Notable examples of GIFs include clips of Barack Obama performing a mic drop, Homer Simpson slowly backing away into a bush, and Leonardo DiCaprio in his role as Jay Gatsby raising a glass of champagne towards the camera as if making a toast.

GIFs are very popular and they are another example of user-driven innovation in which a digital resource is adapted and developed to help users achieve their communicative aims. In a study into Tumblr use, Bakhshi et al. (2016) found that GIFs were liked and reblogged more often than text, images, or video posts, and they also found that GIFs which featured faces prompted more engagement than those which did not. Possible reasons for this popularity were then explored via interviews, and users provided a range of answers. GIFs were felt to be more attention-grabbing than static posts, but they require less attention and time commitment than videos. They are silent and so can be watched anywhere, and they function across various devices without being dependent on particular operating systems or software. Users in Bakhshi et al.'s survey also described using GIFs to function in lieu of facial expressions and gestures. One described GIFs as a 'place holder for your own personal reaction' which then 'illustrates the way a person feels when they're reacting' (583). In short, GIFs seem to fall into a communicative sweet spot. They enable the visual expression of gestures, but they do so without putting unnecessary time or technical demands on the user.

This association between use of GIFs and the communication of attitude and emotions is found across the existing research into their use. Tolins and Samermit (2016: 83) analyse them as a 'visual depiction of affect', and Miltner and Highfield, describe the 'performance of affect' as a key function of GIFs (2017: 4). As they go on to explain, GIFs allow 'the user to provide a visual representation of how they are feeling, or how they act in a particular situation' (5). Veszelszki (2015: 139–140) interviewed Hungarian users about their use and interpretation of GIFs, and concluded that they 'express emotion but in a more intensive way than emoticons'.

Emoticons and emoji offer a wide range of options to a user. However, GIFs can be easily created by users themselves in just a few moments. This means that the library of available reaction GIFs is continually growing, and if the user does not find something that fits their taste ready-made, they can create it. Reaction GIFs also draw on and reference cultural media, and individual GIFs can become extremely popular and strongly associated with a particular reaction. As such, they can become a digital shorthand which not only expresses an emotion or reaction but also demonstrates the cultural knowledge and digital literacy of the user.

Most reaction GIFs can be interpreted without specific cultural knowledge, but users who are familiar with the source of the GIF may derive further effects. For example, even someone who does not recognise Leonardo DiCaprio or does not know that the champagne toasting GIF is taken from the movie *The Great Gatsby*, will still be able to infer some meaning from the image of a man toasting towards the camera with a champagne glass. However, recognising the source of the original image may guide a viewer to further weak implicatures. The user might be implying, for example, that they believe an extravagant and decadent celebration worthy of Gatsby himself would be appropriate. Use of intertextual references can also be a way to signal in-group membership. Recognising the source of the GIF may make users aware of the assumptions and cultural knowledge that they share with others who also recognise the source. Thus, use of GIFs can contribute to the 'ambient affiliation' in which social media users engage (Zappavigna 2012, 2015, 2018).

GIFs can communicate different messages and meanings to different audiences. This polysemic quality of GIFs is discussed by Miltner and Highfield (2017), and they note that it can be used as a form of social steganography. In Chapter 2, we saw how users report that they construct messages to have extra or hidden meanings that will only be available to certain members of the audience. This is one way in which users navigate collapsed contexts. The layered meanings in GIFs make them a particularly rich resource in this respect. A reaction GIF might simply be a representation of a gesture or facial expression for some viewers, while others might understand the user to be alluding to certain cultural references, or social and political viewpoints. As an example, Miltner and Highfield discuss the so-called *Hillary Shimmer* GIF. In this GIF, Hillary Clinton is shown smiling and shaking her shoulders slightly in response to a comment by Donald Trump during an election debate. This could be interpreted as representing the user simply smiling to themselves. However, depending on the context in which it is used and the assumptions of the viewers, it could also be used to imply a particular political, social, or critical stance, or to communicate political affiliation. As with *The Great Gatsby* GIF mentioned above, the viewer of the *Hillary Shimmer* GIF need not recognise the person featured, but if they do, this is likely to give them access to a wider range of assumptions and implicatures. Other users might recognise Hillary Clinton, but not be aware of the full context in which the original gesture was produced. Finally, there will be users for whom the GIF activates not only assumptions about Clinton, but also about Donald Trump and the 2016 election campaign. The more assumptions that are activated by the GIF, the wider the range of implicatures that are likely to follow. Notice that users might post the *Hillary Shimmer* GIF to signal affiliation with Clinton, but they might just as easily use it to poke fun at Clinton's reaction. GIFs, like the other non-verbal devices we have discussed in this chapter, are highly context-sensitive, and their interpretation can vary widely depending on the assumptions of the audience and the discourse context in which they are used. As Tolins and Samermit (2016: 81) explain, GIFs are 'responsive in nature, acquiring meaning through contextualization of the embodied actions displayed following the interlocutor's prior talk'. Just as a smile, a frown, or a thumbs up gesture may mean different things in different discourse contexts, so any one GIF may be used to communicate a range of different emotions, attitudes, and reactions.

From a pragmatic perspective, we can understand the act of posting a GIF as an act of showing. The user is showing the clip to her addressees and they will interpret that act of showing by looking for how it might be relevant. As with the use of emoji discussed earlier in this chapter, using a GIF cannot be an accidental act of communication. The facial expression or the gesture depicted in the GIF might not have been produced as a communicative act originally. The GIF may capture a spontaneous, non-communicative reaction or accidental emotional leakage. However, by showing a representation of this to the addressee, the user of the GIF performs an ostensive act. The addressee will infer that something relevant follows from the gestures, action, or expression depicted in the GIF. What is inferred will, of course, depend on the discourse context in which the GIF has been used and the intentions of the user who has posted it. According to Sasamoto (forthcoming), these inferences will emerge from the viewer identifying a resemblance between the visual information in the GIF and the experience that is being communicated. They will tend to lead to 'a range of extremely weakly communicated (or non-propositional) assumptions that form expressive meaning, including attitude and impressions' (25). In the next chapter, we will see how resemblance can be used for communicative purposes as we turn our attention to the analysis of internet memes. Similar analyses might well be useful in developing our understanding of reaction GIFs. What is clear is that interpreting a GIF is an inferential act and as such draws on our pragmatic processing abilities.

CONCLUSIONS

In this chapter we have looked at a range of non-verbal cues that users may employ to communicate their messages in digitally mediated contexts. In each case, we have seen how users have adapted and co-opted the resources that are available to them and that are afforded by the technology and platforms that they are using. What all of these non-verbal resources have in common is their sensitivity to context. The *face with tears of joy* emoji might be used to indicate a joke or sarcasm, to mitigate the force of a complaint, or to simply indicate that a humorous message has been received and appreciated. We would not want to say that any of these functions are encoded by the emoji. The emoji is a clue to the writer's meaning, and the reader must process that clue relative to the discourse context when inferring the intended overall meaning of the message. We see a similar pattern with the use of non-standard spelling, punctuation, and typography, as well as with reaction GIFs. Capital letters do not mean shouting and full stops do not mean anger or frustration. However, both may lead to those inferences, if that is the most accessible interpretation of their use in the discourse context. Ultimately, as in offline communication, non-verbal cues are a clue to the speaker's meaning and guide the hearer in his inferential processes as he forms a hypothesis about what the speaker's intended meaning is.

NOTES

1 The widespread use of emoji did not become common until after the time span covered by Riordan and Kreuz's corpus. This caveat on the interpretation of their findings is discussed further in Chapter 8.

2 Again, I follow the convention of referring to the speaker or writer as *she* and the hearer or reader as *he*.

3 Fahlman acknowledges that this combination of symbols may have been used for this purpose prior to his post. He explains, 'the smiley idea may have appeared and

disappeared a few times before my 1982 post. I probably was not the first person ever to type these three letters in sequence, perhaps even with the meaning of "I'm just kidding" and perhaps even online. But I do believe that my 1982 suggestion was the one that finally took hold, spread around the world, and spawned thousands of variations'.

4 The term natural signal is used here in contrast to sign. Natural signals may also convey information, but their purpose is not to do so. Footprints in the mud are a sign that someone has walked that way recently, but footprints are not inherently communicative. See Wharton (2009) for a full discussion of this distinction.

5 This is to my knowledge the first academic publication to include emoji as part of its title.

REFERENCES

Arendholz, J. (2013). *(In)Appropriate Online Behavior: A Pragmatic Analysis of Message Board Relations.* Amsterdam: John Benjamins.

Bakhshi, S., Shamma, D. A., Kennedy, L., Song, Y., de Juan, P., & Kaye, J. (2016). Fast, cheap, and good: Why animated GIFS engage us. *CHI '16: Proceedings of the 2016 CHI Conference on Human Factors in Computing Systems,* (pp. 575–586). doi:10.1145/2858036.2858532

Baron, N. S. (2010). *Always On: Language in an Online and Mobile World.* Oxford: Oxford University Press.

Bryant, G. A., & Fox Tree, J. E. (2002). Recognizing Verbal Irony in Spontaneous Speech. *Metaphor and Symbol,* 17(2), 99–119. doi:10.1207/S15327868MS1702_2

Bryant, G. A., & Fox Tree, J. E. (2005). Is there an ironic tone of voice? *Language and Speech,* 48(3), 257–277. doi:10.1177/00238309050480030101

Byron, K., & Baldridge, D. C. (2007). E-mail recipients' impressions of senders' likability: The interactive effect of nonverbal cues and recipients' personality. *Journal of Business Communication,* 44(2), 137–160. doi:10.1177/0021943606297902

Crair, B. (2013). *The period is pissed: When did our plainest punctuation mark become so aggressive?* Retrieved April 3, 2021, from New Republic: https://newrepublic.com/article/115726/period-our-simplest-punctuation-mark-has-become-sign-anger

Crystal, D. (2015). *Making a Point: The Pernickety Story of English Punctuation.* London: Profile Books.

Danet, B. (2001). *Cyberpl@y: Communicating Online.* Oxford: Berg.

Danesi, M. (2017). *The Semiotics of Emoji: The Rise of Visual Language in the Age of the Internet.* London: Bloomsbury.

Darics, E. (2010). Politeness in computer-mediated discourse of a virtual team. *Journal of Politeness Research* 6 129–150 doi:10.1515/JPLR.2010.007

Darics, E. (2013). Non-verbal signalling in digital discourse: The case of letter repetition. *Discourse, Context and Media,* 2, 141–148. doi:10.1016/j.dcm.2013.07.002

Deliens, G., Antoniou, K., Clin, E., Ostashchenko, E., & Kissine, M. (2018). Context, facial expression and prosody in irony processing. *Journal of Memory and Language,* 99, 35–48. doi:10.1016/j.jml.2017.10.001

Derks, D., Bos, A. E., & von Grumbkow, J. (2007). Emoticons and social interaction on the Internet: The importance of social context. *Computers in Human Behavior,* 23, 842–849. doi:10.1016/j.chb.2004.11.013

Derks, D., Bos, A. E., & von Grumbkow, J. (2008). Emoticons and online message interpretation. *Social Science Computer Review,* 26(3), 379–388. doi:10.1177/0894439307311611

Dresner, E., & Herring, S. (2010). Functions of the nonverbal in CMC: Emoticons and illocutionary force. *Communication Theory,* 20(3), 249–268. doi:10.1111/j.1468-2885.2010.01362.x

Dürscheid, C., & Siever, C. M. (2017). Beyond the alphabet - Communicating with emojis. *Kurzfassung eines (auf Deutsch) zur Publikation eingereichten Manuskripts.* Retrieved April 4, 2021, from https://www.academia.edu/download/52363872/Beyond_the_Alphabet.pdf

Ellis, B. E. (1991). *American Psycho*. London: Picador.

emojitracker.com. (n.d.). *emojitracker: realtime emoji tracker on Twitter*. Retrieved April 10, 2021, from https://emojitracker.com/

Fahlman, S. E. (n.d.). *Smiley Lore :-)*. Retrieved March 27, 2021, from https://www.cs.cmu.edu/~sef/sefSmiley.htm

Fitzgerald, B. (2012). *Did Abraham Lincoln Pioneer Emoticons? 1862 Speech May Offer Clues*. Retrieved March 26, 2021, from HuffPost: https://www.huffingtonpost.co.uk/entry/abraham-lincoln-emoticons_n_1893411?ri18n=true

Fleuriet, C., Cole, M., & Guerrero, L. K. (2014). Exploring Facebook: Attachment style and nonverbal message characteristics as predictors of anticipated emotional reactions to Facebook postings. *Journal of Nonverbal Behavior, 38*, 429–450. doi:10.1007/s10919-014-0189-x

Gunraj, D. N., Drumm-Hewitt, A. M., Dashow, E. M., Upadhyay, S. N., & Klin, C. M. (2016). Texting insincerely: The role of the period in text messaging. *Computers in Human Behavior, 55*(B), 1067–1075. doi:10.1016/j.chb.2015.11.003

Hancock, J. T. (2004). Verbal irony use in face-to-face and computer-mediated conversations. *Journal of Language and Social Psychology, 23*(4), 447–463. doi:10.1177/0261927X04269587

Hauser, M. (1996). *The Evolution of Communication*. Cambridge, MA: MIT Press.

Herring, S. C. (2018). Emergent forms of computer-mediated communication and their global implications. *LinguaPax Review, 2017*, 90–130.

Herring, S. C., & Dainas, A. (2017). "Nice picture comment!" Graphicons in Facebook comment threads. In *Proceedings of the Fiftieth Hawai'i International Conference on System Sciences* (pp. 2185–2194). Los Alamitos, CA: IEEE Press.

House, J. (2006). Constructing a context with intonation. *Journal of Pragmatics, 38*(10), 1542–1558. doi:10.1016/j.pragma.2005.07.005

Kalman, Y. M., & Gergle, D. (2014). Letter repetitions in computer-mediated communication: A unique link between spoken and online language. *Computers in Human Behavior, 34*, 187–193. doi:10.1016/j.chb.2014.01.047

Kiesler, S., Siegel, J., & McGuire, T. W. (1984). Social psychological aspects of computer-mediated communication. *American Psychologist, 39*(10), 1123–1134. doi:10.1037/0003-066X.39.10.1123

Konrad, A., Herring, S. C., & Choi, D. (2020). Sticker and emoji use in Facebook Messenger: Implications for graphicon change. *Journal of Computer-Mediated Communication, 25*(3), 217–235. doi:10.1093/jcmc/zmaa003

Kreuz, R. J., & Roberts, R. M. (1995). Two cues for verbal irony: Hyperbole and the ironic tone of voice. *Metaphor and Symbolic Activity, 10*(1), 21–31. doi:10.1207/s15327868ms1001_3

Langlotz, A., & Locher, M. A. (2012). Ways of communicating emotional stance in online disagreements. *Journal of Pragmatics, 44*(12), 1591–1606. doi:10.1016/j.pragma.2012.04.002

Lea, M., & Spears, R. (1992). Paralanguage and social perception in computer-mediated communication. *Journal of Organizational Computing, 2*(3), 321–341. doi:10.1080/10919399209540190

Locher, M. A., & Watts, R. J. (2005). Politeness theory and relational work. *Journal of Politeness Research, 1* (1), 9–33. doi:10.1515/jplr.2005.1.1.9

Madrigal, A. C. (2014). *The First Emoticon May Have Appeared in … 1648: The discovery would push back the pre-history of the emoticon by (at least) 200 years*. Retrieved March 26, 2021, from The Atlantic: https://www.theatlantic.com/technology/archive/2014/04/the-first-emoticon-may-have-appeared-in-1648/360622/

Miltner, K. M., & Highfield, T. (2017). Never gonna GIF you up: Analyzing the cultural significance of the animated GIF. *Social Media + Society*, 1–11. doi:10.1177/2056305117725223

Ong, K. K. (2011). Disagreement, confusion, disapproval, turn elicitation and floor holding: Actions as accomplished by ellipsis marks-only turns and blank turns in quasisynchronous chats. *Discourse Studies, 13*(2), 211–234. doi:10.1177/1461445610392138

Oxford Dictionaries. (2015). *Word of the Year 2015*. Retrieved March 27, 2021, from Oxford Languages: https://languages.oup.com/word-of-the-year/2015/

Pavalanathan, U., & Eisenstein, J. (2016). More emojis, less :) The competition for paralinguistic function in microblog writing. *First Monday, 21*(11). doi:10.5210/fm.v21i11.6879

Pohl, H., Domin, C., & Rohs, M. (2017). Beyond just text: Semantic emoji similarity modeling to support expressive communication 😀🐱💞😊🐱⌨️😊. *ACM Transactions on Computer-Human Interaction, 24*(1). doi:10.1145/3039685

Prada, M., Rodrigues, D. L., Garrido, M. V., Lopes, D., Cavalheiro, B., & Gaspar, R. (2018). Motives, frequency and attitudes toward emoji and emoticon use. *Telematics and Informatics, 35*(7), 1925–1934. doi:10.1016/j.tele.2018.06.005

Riordan, M. A. (2017a). Emojis as tools for emotion work: Communicating affect in text messages. *Journal of Language and Social Psychology, 36*(5), 549–567. doi:10.1177/0261927X17704238

Riordan, M. A. (2017b). The communicative role of non-face emojis: Affect and disambiguation. *Computers in Human Behavior, 76*, 75–86. doi:10.1016/j.chb.2017.07.009

Riordan, M. A., & Kreuz, R. J. (2010). Cues in computer-mediated communication: A corpus analysis. *Computers in Human Behavior, 26*, 1806–1817. doi:10.1016/j.chb.2010.07.008

Rudolf Von Rohr, M-T., & Locher, M. A. (2020). The interpersonal effects of complimenting others and self-praise in online health settings. In M. E. Placencia, & Z. R. Eslami (Eds), *Complimenting Behavior and (Self-) Praise across Social Media: New Contexts and New Insights* (pp. 189–212). Amsterdam: John Benjamins.

Sasamoto, R. (forthcoming). Perceptual resemblance and communication of emotion in the digital context: A case of emoji and reaction GIFs.

Scott, K. (2017). Prosody, procedures and pragmatics. In I. Depraetere, & R. Salkie (Eds.), *Semantics and Pragmatics: Drawing a Line* (pp. 323–341). Cham: Springer.

Scott, K. (2018). 'Hashtags Work Everywhere': The Pragmatic Functions of Spoken Hashtags. *Discourse, Context and Media, 22*, 57–64. doi:10.1016/j.dcm.2017.07.002

Scott, K., & Jackson, R. (2020). When EVERYTHING STANDS OUT, nothing does: Typography, expectations and procedures. In A. Piskorska (Ed.), *Relevance Theory and Figuration* (pp. 167–192). Amsterdam: John Benjamins.

Simpson, J. (2005). Meaning-making onine: Discourse and CMC in a language learning community. In A. Mendez Vilas, B. Gonzalez Pereira, J. Mesa Gonzalez, & J. A. Mesa Gonzales (Eds.), *Recent Research Development in Learning Technologies* (pp. 176–179). Badajoz: Formatex.

Skovholt, K., Grønning, A., & Kankaanranta, A. (2014). The communicative functions of emoticons in workplace e-mails :-). *Journal of Computer-Mediated Communication, 8*(4), 780–797. doi:10.1111/jcc4.12063

Thompson, D., & Filik, R. (2016). Sarcasm in written communication: Emoticons are efficient markers of intention. *Journal of Computer-Mediated Communication, 21*(2), 105–120. doi:10.1111/jcc4.12156

Tolins, J., & Samermit, P. (2016). GIFs ans embodied enactments in text-mediated conversation. *Research on Language and Social Interaction, 49*(2), 75–91. doi:10.1080/08351813.2016.1164391

Tschabitscher, H. (2021). *Writing in All Caps Is Like Shouting: You may think it's just for emphasis, but think again.* Retrieved April 9, 2021, from Lifewire: https://www.lifewire.com/why-not-to-write-in-all-caps-1173242

Vandergriff, I. (2013). Emotive communication online: A contextual analysis of computer-mediated communication (CMC) cues. *Journal of Pragmatics, 51*, 1–12. doi:10.1016/j.pragma.2013.02.008

Veszelszki, Á. (2015). Emoticons vs. reaction-Gifs: Non-verbal communication on the internet from the aspect of visuality, verbality and time. In A. Benedek, & K. Nyíri (Eds.), *Beyond Words: Pictures, Parables, Paradoxes* (pp. 131–145). Frankfurt am Main: Peter Lang.

Walther, J. B. (1992). Interpersonal Effects in Computer-Mediated Interaction: A Relational Perspective. *Communication Research, 19*(1), 52–90. doi:10.1177/009365092019001003

Wharton, T. (2009). *Pragmatics and Non-Verbal Communication.* Cambridge: Cambridge University Press.

Wilson, D. (2011). The conceptual-procedural distinction: past, present and future. In V. Escandell-Vidal, M. Leonetti, & A. Ahern (Eds.), *Procedural Meaning: Problems and Perspectives* (Vol. 25, pp. 3–31). Bingley: Emerald.

Wilson, D. (2017). Irony, hyperbole, jokes and banter. In J. Blochowiak, C. Grisot, S. Durriemann, & C. Laenzlinger (Eds.), *Formal Models in the Study of Language: Applications in Interdisciplinary Contexts* (pp. 201–220). Basel: Springer.

Wilson, D., & Sperber, D. (2012). Explaining irony. In D. Wilson, & D. Sperber, *Meaning and Relevance* (pp. 123–145). Cambridge: Cambridge University Press.

Wilson, D., & Wharton, T. (2006). Relevance and prosody. *Journal of Pragmatics, 38*(10), 1559–1579. doi:10.1016/j.pragma.2005.04.012

Yus, F. (2011). *Cyberpragmatics: Internet-Mediated Communciation in Context*. Amsterdam: John Benjamins.

Yus, F. (2014). Not all emoticons are created equal. *Linguagem em (Dis)curso, 14*(3), 511–529. doi:10.1590/1982-4017-140304-0414.

Zappavigna, M. (2012). *Discourse of Twitter and Social Media: How We Use Language to Create Affiliation on the Web*. London: Bloomsbury.

Zappavigna, M. (2015). Seachable talk: The linguistic functions of hashtags. *Social Semiotics, 25*(3), 274–291. doi:10.1080/10350330.2014.996948

Zappavigna, M. (2018). *Searchable Talk: Hashtags and Social Media Metadiscourse*. London: Bloomsbury.

6

THE PRAGMATICS OF MEMES

On March 21, 2021, a 400-metre-long container ship was blown off course while passing through the Suez Canal. It ran aground, blocking the canal for six days and causing significant disruption on one of the world's busiest trade routes. The story dominated news headlines around the world for several days, and various images were circulated online of the ship and of the attempts to free it. An example is shown in Figure 6.1. These images included several photographs showing excavation digger vehicles working alongside the container ship, dwarfed by the enormous vessel, and seemingly working away tirelessly to very little effect. One such image was posted on the Suez Canal Authority Facebook page (Suez Canal Authority 2021), and the sight of the little digger working hard at a seemingly impossible and never-ending task appeared to strike a chord with many users. This, and other similar images, were widely shared, and users soon began to edit them, adding text labels to the ship and to the digger. Users seemed to see themselves and their own situations reflected in the plight of the vehicles in the image. One user, for example, edited the image to label the container ship as 'my problems' and the digger as 'me'. Another was more specific and topical, labelling the container ship as 'my mental health during a global pandemic' and the digger as 'going for a lunch time walk'. The ship and the digger became visual metaphors for circumstances and situations in which one feels overwhelmed or helpless. The container ship represented the problem, and the digger represented efforts to overcome it and to keep going regardless. A meme had been born.

DOI: 10.4324/9781003254201-6

Figure 6.1. Example of Suez Canal Container Ship Image. Photograph by Engineer Studio / Shutterstock.com.

Memes such as the *Excavator Digging Out Suez Canal Ship* meme (KnowYourMeme.com) owe much of their success to the affordances of social media that we have discussed in previous chapters. They are multi-modal, combining text with an image, and they can be easily edited and adapted, and then quickly circulated to a wide audience. As Varis and Blommaert (2015, 38) note, social media users have shown themselves to be:

> extraordinarily creative in reorganizing, redirecting, and applying memic resources over a vast range of thematic domains, addressing a vast range of audiences while all the same retaining clear and recognizable intertextual links to the original memic sources.

In this chapter, we think about how memes fit into the wider landscape of digitally mediated communication. Memes can be thought about from a range of different social, cultural, and linguistic perspectives. This chapter starts with a brief overview of some of the previous work, and discusses some common types of meme. We will look at a range of examples and think about how they communicate meaning, both individually as meme tokens and collectively as part of a meme family. In the second half of the chapter, we work through the analysis of a case study example, to demonstrate how ideas from pragmatics can be applied to memes to help us understand how they convey meaning and how they are interpreted in context.

MEMES, MEANING, AND COMMUNICATION

What is a meme?

The term *meme* was first coined by evolutionary biologist Richard Dawkins in his book *The Selfish Gene* (Dawkins 1976). Just as biological features are passed from body to body via genes, so elements of culture can be passed from brain to brain. Dawkins explains that 'tunes, ideas, catch-phrases, clothes fashions, ways of making pots or of building arches' (192) can all be understood as cultural units that are transmitted from one person to another. Dawkins used the term *meme* to describe these culturally transmitted units. Some memes may be fairly short-lived, such as the fashion for flares and platform shoes, while others may endure for many generations. The tune and lyrics of the folk song Greensleeves were first recorded in 1580 and appear largely unchanged to this day (Kidson and Neal 1915). They have endured because they have been passed from brain to brain over the generations. The belief that King Henry the Eighth composed *Greensleeves* has, although untrue, also been passed from person to person. Both the tune and the idea are memes, in Dawkins' original sense.

The term *internet meme* has been adopted to describe digital cultural content that is shared, adapted, and passed between users online. Shifman (2014: 41–42) defines an internet meme as follows:

> (a) a group of digital items sharing common characteristics of content, form and/ or stance, which (b) were created with awareness of each other, and (c) were circulated, imitated, and/or transformed via the internet by many users.

On this definition, an internet meme is not a single post, video, or image, but a group of digital items. The members of this group share characteristics of some sort. In the discussion here, I will follow Shifman and refer to the group of items as a meme and individual items within that group as a meme token. For example, as Shifman explains, meme tokens which form part of the LOLcats meme 'share a topic (cats), form (photo + caption), and stance (humor)' (2014: 177). Each token consists of an image of a cat or kitten with an accompanying humorous caption describing the cat's behaviour in childish or broken English. Examples of tokens of this meme are given in (1) and (2).

(1)   Image of a cat sitting in a paper document folder.
       Top text: Im in ur folder
       Bottom text: Keruptin yr fylez

(2)   Image of a sleeping cat.
       Top text: I'm in ur bed
       Bottom text: zleeping

Meme tokens are not created in isolation. They exist as part of a meme family, and each token derives part of its meaning from being recognised as part of that family. LOLcat tokens could be circulated and appreciated individually as cute photographs. However, by adding a caption in idiosyncratic, stylised English, the creator is both signalling her awareness of the meme family and positioning her image as part of that family. Meme tokens within the same meme family share distinctive features, and these may be visual or verbal (Segev et al. 2015). Their status as part of a collection of texts is partly what sets meme tokens apart from viral posts. As Shifman (2014: 56) discusses, a viral post is a *'single cultural unit* (such as a video, photo, or joke) that propagates in many copies, [whereas] an Internet meme *is always a collection of texts'*. Users produce their own version of the meme, and adaptation and creativity are key to the spread and success of memes. As Marwick (2013: 13) explains, memes 'encourage a type of iteration, imitation, parody, and satire that can spawn literally thousands of variants'. They are the 'raw material for creativity' (Marwick 2013: 13) and form an important part of the participatory culture associated with new media discourses and literacies. As Yus (2021a) notes, posts may go viral without the original creator or author intending for that to happen. He gives the example of an online hotel review that unexpectedly goes viral. The author of the original review likely had in mind a fairly specific audience for the post. That audience probably included the owners of the hotel and prospective customers. The users who read the review as a result of the viral spread of the post are not the intended or imagined audience. A meme, on the other hand, is created with the hope and intention that it will be widely shared and seen by many.

Shifman's definition of a meme encompasses various types of digital items that are created, circulated, and adapted by users. She divides these into three groups (2014: 118). First there are memes which document a real-life moment. Memes in this category include video posts of participants taking part in a particular challenge or activity. In the summer of 2014, for example, the Ice Bucket Challenge spread across social media. Each participant made a video of themselves while a bucket of ice-cold water was poured over them. They then nominated a number of other people to complete the same challenge. Each video was linked by the theme, but was also unique to the individual creator. Shifman's second group is what she refers to as 'remix' memes. These 'are based on explicit manipulation of visual or audiovisual mass-mediated content' (118) and include lip-sync performances, recut trailers, and music parodies. The final category, on which we will focus our attention in this chapter, captures memes which, as Shifman describes, 'evolved around a new universe of digital and meme-oriented content'. These include the LOLcats memes, and we will explore more memes that fall into this category, including, image macros, object labelling memes, and phrasal template memes in the sections that follow.

Memes and communication

Imagine that you see a meme online. It strikes a chord with you, and you sit down at your computer and create your own new version. The new version that you have made shares features with the meme tokens you have seen online, and you created it with an awareness of those other tokens. So far, your creation meets two of Shifman's three defining characteristics for a meme. It is not, however, until you share your creation that it becomes part of the meme in any meaningful way. Memes are a collection of texts, and so to be part of the meme, your token must be added to the collection by posting and sharing it online. Sharing, as we discussed in Chapter 3, is an ostensive act of communication. Memes are therefore fundamentally communicative in nature. As it is the act of sharing that makes a meme token communicative, I make no distinction here between the original creator of a meme token and those people who go on to share that token subsequently. Whether you are sharing something you have created or rebroadcasting something created by someone else, you are communicating a message or messages. We can therefore use what we know about pragmatics to analyse how memes convey meaning and how other users interpret them.

Meme tokens are commonly used to express experiences and values. They may relate to topical events and involve cultural references, and they very often involve humour. These features make them tools for social bonding and community building. According to Zappavigna (2012: 101), 'Internet memes are deployed for social bonding rather than for sharing information'. Creating a new version of a meme is an 'act of semiotic belonging' and users share them to 'mark awareness of a particular aesthetic' (103), and to signal that they are privy to an inside joke. Recognising cultural references gives us what Zappavigna calls an 'intertextual pleasure' (117), and users bond around the value or opinion that is being expressed or the experience that is being described. As we saw with the reaction GIFs discussed in Chapter 5, this plays a role in creating an ambient sense of affiliation between users (Zappavigna 2012, 2015, 2018). We can see how common experiences and shared values might have motivated the creators of the Suez Canal meme tokens described at the start of this chapter. The Covid-19 pandemic understandably had a significant effect on many people's mental health. The user who labelled the excavating digger as 'going for a lunch time walk' is implying that the benefits of that small act of self-care are dwarfed by the wider circumstances in which people found themselves. Many viewers of the meme are likely to relate to these feelings, and this creates a sense of shared experience and of affiliation.

COMMON MEME TYPES

Twitter hashtag micro-memes

In Chapter 4, we saw an example of a meme that has emerged around the use of the hashtag #Failed90sRappers. For each meme token in this set, a user took the name of a rapper from the 1990s and altered it slightly to make it less serious, less impressive, and/or less dignified. Further examples of contributions to this meme include *The Notorious BFG, Tupacs of Biscuits*, and *Nice Cube*. The hashtag trended for 6 hours on January 2, 2014. It is an example of an emergent micro-meme, which is 'both adopted and abandoned in a short period of time' (Huang et al. 2010: 4). These Twitter micro-memes satisfy Shifman's definition. Each member of the meme family shares both a common theme and a common stance. The inclusion of the hashtag not only connects the different tokens together but functions as a signal that they are part of a family. That is, they are created with an awareness of each other. Finally, they are circulated on Twitter, with each participant contributing a new version to add to the collection. By creating a meme token for this meme family, users demonstrate both their knowledge of the 1990s rap scene and their ability to use wordplay and puns. In the case of *#Failed90sRappers*, the inclusion of the hashtag provides contextual information for use in the interpretation of the tweet, and the posts would be near impossible to understand without this. This is not necessarily the case with all micro-memes. The examples in (3) to (5) were all posted as part of the *#ICantDateYouIf* meme that circulated on Twitter in 2016.

(3)   #ICantDateYouIf You still stuck on your ex

(4)   #ICantDateYouIf you don't drive

(5)   #ICantDateYouIf you have more followers than me

If these messages were posted without a hashtag and with the subordinate clause in plain text instead, they would still make sense. However, they would simply be statements about who the speaker would and would not date. By including the hashtag, these tweets indicate an awareness of the other tokens of the same meme, and so the tweeter becomes a participant in a collaborative language game.

Phrasal templates

Phrasal template memes are text-based memes which follow a recognisable template with editable slots. Users customise the template by filling in the slots, and each example describes a different situation or scenario. Examples of the so-called *Hello, I'm a professor in a movie* phrasal template meme are given in (6) and (7) (KnowYourMeme.com).

(6)   Hello, I'm a professor in a movie, I only reach the main point of my lecture right as class is ending. Then I yell at students about the reading / homework as they leave.

(7)   Hello, I'm a writer in a movie. I write one piece a week and live in a two bedroom New York apartment with a walk-in wardrobe. Also I never actually pitch anywhere, the jobs just come to me.

Each meme token in this family is alike in that it ironically describes and mocks clichés associated with the portrayal of a character or character type in movies. To understand the intended meaning, a reader must both recognise the stereotype and understand that the clichés are inaccurate and ridiculous. The humour depends on recognising a discrepancy between the movie cliché described in the meme and the reality of working in that profession or having the described characteristic. This creates a sense of affiliation via awareness of shared assumptions and attitudes (Zappavigna 2012: 117). The meme also gently pokes fun at unrealistic characters, dialogue, and plotlines in movies. By creating a new version of the meme, users communicate that they recognise this and can provide further parallel examples. Phrasal template meme tokens share a common form and structure, and they often adopt a similar stance, in this case ironic. Each meme allows for creativity, innovation, and adaptation within the template, and they are circulated via social media networks.

Image macros

Image-based memes are multimodal. They generally combine images with text captions, and, as Yus (2018) discusses, both the image and text typically play an important role in the overall interpretation of the meme. Image macro memes consist of an image with some text overlaid. Often these memes have a line of text at the top of the image and a line at the bottom. In most meme tokens for a particular meme family, the image remains the same, and the text is varied from token to token.

A key concept in the communicative functionality of such memes is *resemblance*. Firstly, individual meme tokens resemble other meme tokens in the same meme family. Recognising a meme token as part of a meme family can play a key role in interpretation. Secondly, many types of memes use a resemblance between the meme content and a state of affairs in the world to convey meaning. Resemblance is not specific to memes, but rather is a key component in communication more generally. As Sperber and Wilson (1986/95: 226) explain, '[m]ost stimuli used in ostensive communication are representations'. We can use a representation of something to communicate ideas, because there is a resemblance between the representation and the thing itself. For example, we can draw a quick map on a napkin to indicate the best route to take to a particular destination. The sketch on the napkin is a representation, and it can be used to convey meaning because it visually resembles the actual route. As a further example, imagine sitting at a dinner table and discussing a recent sports match you watched. Perhaps someone moves cups, cutlery, and condiments around to represent players on the pitch. The relative positions of the various items on the table resemble the actual positions of the players and thus can be used to represent them. As Sperber and Wilson (1986/95: 227) explain, '[i]n appropriate conditions, any natural or artificial phenomenon in the world can be used as a representation of some other phenomenon which it resembles in some respects'. We will see that many image-based memes exploit resemblances to convey their meaning.

Meme tokens of the same image macro meme resemble one another visually, but also in terms of the emotion or attitude that they convey, and, in some cases, the narrative structure of the meme. To illustrate this, we will look at typical and widely circulated examples of an Advice Animal image macro meme: *Socially Awkward Penguin* (Dynel 2016; KnowYourMeme.com). In this meme, an image of a penguin walking awkwardly is shown against a blue background with editable text at the top and at the bottom. Examples are given in (8) and (9).

(8) Top text: Be polite, hold the door.
     Bottom text: They're slightly too far away.

(9) Top text: Phone vibrates.
     Bottom text   'Battery Low'.

Tokens of this meme tend to focus on a particular incident involving a feeling of awkwardness or embarrassment. The meme tells the story of the incident, and the narrative structure (Brewer and Lichtenstein, 1982) is consistent across the different uses. The text at the top describes the initiating event in the narrative. This is the action or event that initiates the story. In (8), it is the decision of the narrator to be polite and hold a door open for somebody else. In (9), it is the vibrating of a mobile phone. The text at the bottom then describes either a complicating event that occurs ('they are slightly too far away') or the outcome of the narrative ('battery low'). In either case, the bottom text describes a part of the story that makes the narrator feel awkward or embarrassed. The image of the penguin is a visual metaphor for how the narrator feels when this happens.

Another extremely popular image macro meme is the so-called *Success Kid* meme. This features a photograph of an 11-month-old baby boy looking smugly at the camera and doing what appears to be a fist pump with his right hand. As with the *Socially Awkward Penguin* meme, the *Success Kid* meme relates a short narrative and communicates the narrator's attitude to this. As examples (10) and (11) illustrate, the top line provides the initiating event for the narrative, and the bottom line provides the outcome.

(10) Top text: Late to work.
      Bottom text: Boss is even later.

(11) Top line: Thought today was Thursday.
      Bottom line: It's Friday.

In each case the outcome is better than expected in some way, and the image of the baby is a visual metaphor for how this made the narrator feel.

Notice that for each of these memes, the different meme tokens resemble each other in terms of the attitude that is expressed. While the incidents that they relate may be very different, they are connected via the attitude. Each creator has used the meme to communicate a time when they have felt that way.

Image macro memes are often, although by no means always, associated with humour and playfulness (Vásquez and Aslan 2021). They often poke fun at the participants in the narrative. In the *Socially Awkward Penguin* meme, for example, the humour is self-deprecating, and this also functions to communicate a feeling of solidarity derived from the idea that we have all felt socially awkward at one time or another. Yus (2021a, 2021b) found that image macro memes draw on a wide range of humorous strategies, and that the humour often arises from the process of incongruity resolution. A seemingly incongruous scenario is set up, and then the punchline resolves the incongruity (Dynel 2016; Yus 2021a). Many memes also involve word play and puns which are linked to pragmatic interpretation processes including reference resolution and disambiguation (Oswald and Maillat 2018; Zenner and Geeraerts 2018; Yus 2021a, 2021b).

MEMES AND METAPHOR: THE CASE OF THE DISTRACTED BOYFRIEND

Object labelling memes form a sub-category of image macros. Like standard image macros such as *Socially Awkward Penguin* and *Success Kid*, object labelling memes feature user-edited text laid over an image. However, rather than relating events in a narrative, in object labelling memes the added text serves as a label for the objects in the image. The Suez Canal memes discussed at the opening of this chapter are examples of object labelling memes, and another particularly successful meme of this sort is the so-called *Distracted Boyfriend* meme. In Scott (forthcoming), I discuss image-based memes as multimodal metaphors and I consider how the processes involved in interpreting verbal metaphors can help us to understand how memes convey meaning. In this section, we apply this analysis to the *Distracted Boyfriend* meme. The basic image for this meme is shown in Figure 6.2.

The *Distracted Boyfriend* meme features three characters: the eponymous distracted boyfriend, the girlfriend in blue and the passing woman in red. The distracted boyfriend is pictured turning to look admiringly at the passing woman in red, while his girlfriend in blue looks at him with anger and disbelief. The image depicts a fairly clichéd and stereotypical scenario of a man neglecting his partner to pay attention to someone else, with his partner noticing and reacting angrily. The reactions and emotions in the image are exaggerated and we can be in very little doubt about what is going on and how the characters are feeling. To produce a new token of this meme, a user labels each of these characters. By adding the labels, the user suggests that the

Figure 6.2. Distracted Boyfriend Meme Image. Photograph by Antonio Guillem / Shutterstock.com.

relationship between the people or items named in the labels resembles the relationship between the characters in the image in some way. Some examples of labelling from real tokens of this meme are given in (12) to (14).

(12)   Distracted Boyfriend: Me
       Woman in Red: New books at the bookstore
       Woman in Blue: The untouched, unread books on my book-
                               shelf at home.

(13)   Distracted Boyfriend: Me
       Woman in Red: Solar eclipse
       Woman in Blue: Scientific evidence supporting the dangers of
                               staring at the sun.

(14)   Distracted Boyfriend: Millennials
       Woman in Red: Avocado toast
       Woman in Blue: A stable career, property ownership, health
                               insurance, the financial stability to start a
                               family.

The Distracted Boyfriend is a multimodal object labelling meme, consisting of an image with overlaid labels. To process the information in the image, a viewer must first conceptualise what is represented in the picture. There are three characters in the image. We are likely to focus our attention on these three characters as they are in focus and highly salient. We must form some sort of mental representation of each so that we can think about them. Forceville and Clark (2014) describe this aspect of processing an image as a form of reference assignment. It certainly involves some sort of process of recognising or conceptualising the components in the image. The first time we see a token of this meme, and assuming we have not seen these characters before, we will construct a conceptual file for each of the characters in the image. We then use that file to store all of the information that we have about that character (Reboul 1998, 1999; Jackendoff et al. 2012; Recanati 2012, 2014; Scott 2020). When we first look at the image, the files are likely to contain only basic information about the visual appearance of the characters, along with some inferable assumptions about their relationships and perhaps about their behaviour in this particular moment. For example, the conceptual file representing the woman in blue will contain basic information about how she looks and what she is wearing, based on the information in the image. We may then add assumptions about her relationship with the man in the image based on the fact that they are holding hands, and we may add assumptions about how she is feeling in that moment based on an interpretation of her facial expression and the other things that we can see in the image. This process will be repeated for the other characters. We infer assumptions about their personalities, relationships, and feelings from the information in the image, and we add them to the corresponding conceptual file.

Interpreting the meme is not, however, just a matter of processing the information in the image. Object labelling memes are multimodal texts and the viewer must interpret the labels and image as a 'multimodal ensemble' (Jewitt 2013: 254–255). By labelling each character, the creator of the meme is actively directing our attention towards them. As such, the act of labelling is an ostensive act of communication. As viewers, we must infer what is being communicated by this act. Now let us consider the content of the labels that have been added. Taking the example in (12), the characters are labelled as 'me', 'New books at the bookstore' and 'The untouched, unread books on my bookshelf at home'. We process descriptions and referring expressions by mapping them onto conceptual files (Scott 2020). The most accessible interpretation of the pronoun 'me' is that it refers to the user who has shared the meme. Depending on where we encounter the meme and who has shared it, we may or may not already have a conceptual file representing this person. For the sake of discussion, let us assume that the meme has been shared by Jane. Jane is someone you know and you therefore already have a conceptual file representing her. That file contains all of the different assumptions that you hold about Jane. The other two labels in the image describe sets of objects. We may or may not have conceptualised these before. The use of the definite determiner in the label 'The untouched, unread books on my bookshelf at home' implies that these books are familiar or given in some way. However, we may have to construct a new conceptual file for them, even if we assume that they are familiar to Jane. The viewer now has two sets of conceptual files.

One set represents the characters in the image and the other represents the people and objects referred to in the labels. To interpret the meme, the viewer must work out how the image and labels work together as a multimodal text, and what the user of the meme intended to communicate by labelling the characters in this way.

Assuming a relevance-theoretic approach to utterance interpretation, the viewers will follow the relevance-theoretic comprehension procedure. They will test interpretations in order of accessibility and assume that the first interpretation that satisfies their expectations of optimal relevance is the intended interpretation. A highly accessible assumption to use in this process is that the meme user is referring to the characters in the image by the associated labels. She is saying that the characters in the image should be understood to be whatever is named in the labels. For example, Jane has labelled the male character in the image as 'Me'. The literal meaning of this act of labelling would be something along the lines of (15).

(15)   Jane is the distracted boyfriend.

Similarly, if taken literally, the other acts of labelling communicate something along the lines of (16) and (17).

(16)   New books at the bookstore are the woman in red.

(17)   The untouched, unread books on my bookshelf at home are the woman in blue.

Immediately, we can see that the act of labelling here is equivalent to using a metaphor. Jane is saying that the characters in the image are things that they clearly are not. Compare this non-literal act of labelling with the act of posting an old school photograph on Facebook and labelling it with an annotation indicating who is who in the image. The label on the school photograph indicates that the person named in the label and the person in the photograph are literally the same person. The two conceptual files will be merged together. However, when Jane labels the characters in the meme, she is creating a metaphorical relationship between the object in the image and the content of the label. The people or objects/ideas referred to in the labels (in this case, 'me', 'new books at the bookstore', 'unread books on my bookshelf at home') are the tenors (the subjects of the metaphors) and the characters/objects in the image (in this case 'distracted boyfriend', 'woman in red', 'woman in blue') are the vehicles (the figuratively used expressions or images).

When we interpret the acts of labelling in the meme, we are unlikely to even consider that they are intended literally. We know that Jane is not literally the man in the image, just as we know that she is not speaking literally when she meets with a friend in the park for lunch on a hot day and produces the hyperbolic utterance in (18) and the metaphorical utterance in (19).

(18)   I am starving.

(19)   I am so glad to be outside. My office is a greenhouse.

When she utters (18), Jane is using hyperbole to communicate that she is very hungry, and when she uses the metaphor in (19), she is communicating that her office is hot and stifling. In both cases she uses language non-literally to convey her message. There is no claim that she is literally starving, and neither is she claiming that her office is an actual and literal greenhouse. Rather these concepts are being used to convey something because they in some way resemble the proposition that Jane intends to communicate. In relevance-theoretic analyses of metaphor, this is known as interpretive resemblance. According to the relevance theory account, 'metaphor involves an interpretive relation between the propositional form of an utterance and the thought it represents' (Sperber and Wilson 1986/95: 231). As a multimodal metaphor, a meme involves an interpretive relation between the image and the thought that it represents. Thus to work out what Jane means when she creates and/or shares the meme in (12), we must infer in which ways the characters in the image resemble the people and objects named in the labels, and how the relationship between the characters resembles the relationship between the real-life people and objects.

In verbal utterances, whether spoken or written, the words that the speaker uses are clues to her meaning. They are not always used literally and neither do addressees expect them to be used literally. They simply expect them to be used in a way that is relevant. Relevance theory makes a distinction between the concept that is encoded by a word and the concept that is communicated by that word when it is used on a particular occasion by a speaker in context. This aspect of communicated meaning is explored in the field of lexical pragmatics, and it plays a key role in understanding metaphor. When she produces the utterance in (18), Jane uses the word *starving*. However, she does not use it to communicate the literal concept that it encodes. Rather she uses it to communicate that she is very hungry. This meaning is not encoded by the word *starving*. Rather the hearer must arrive at this interpretation by inferring what Jane meant when she used the word *starving* in that particular discourse context. The concept that *starving* conveys is inferentially derived and is specific to the context of use. This inferential process is known as ad hoc concept construction. When we represent concepts on the page, we write them in small capitals, and ad hoc concepts are indicated by adding an asterisk in the notation. Using this system, we can say that when Jane produces the utterance in (18) she is communicating the proposition in (20).

(20)   Jane is STARVING*

Here STARVING* communicates something like 'very hungry', and it is this concept that the hearer uses when constructing a hypothesis about Jane's overall meaning.

We can now apply this same interpretive process to the meme token from (12). The user who created and/or shared the meme is not communicating the literal proposition in (15), but rather the inferentially adjusted proposition in (21).

(21)   Jane is the DISTRACTED BOYFRIEND*

The ad hoc concept the DISTRACTED BOYFRIEND* in (21) is inferentially derived in the discourse context, and this process is guided by the principles of relevance. Again, we can see how this proceeds by thinking about how we understand verbal metaphors.

When a speaker uses a (content) word in a spoken, written, or signed utterance, assumptions are activated. For example, in the metaphorical utterance in (19), Jane's use of the words *office* and *greenhouse* will activate assumptions that the hearer holds about offices and greenhouses. The word *office* may, for example, activate assumptions about the typical ways in which offices are laid out and about the sort of things that people do in them. The speaker's use of the word *greenhouse* may activate assumptions about the typical activities that happen in a greenhouse, along with the typical conditions that we might find in this type of space. The assumption that greenhouses are hot and stuffy is likely to be amongst those assumptions. Furthermore, this easily combines with accessible assumptions from the discourse context about how indoor spaces might feel on a hot day. This leads us to conclude that Jane's office is like a greenhouse in terms of being hot and stuffy. Assumptions may be culturally specific, of course, and this is one way in which relevance-theoretic analyses allow for cultural variation in language use and interpretation. The underlying pragmatic processes are driven by human cognition and are the same cross-culturally. However, the assumptions that feed into the interpretive processes may vary, and when they do, this produces different interpretations, and can, on occasion, lead to misunderstandings.

Notice that interpreting the meaning of *office* in (19) is an inferential process and that we have to use contextual information to work out what Jane's likely meaning is. This involves inferring in which ways Jane's office resembles a greenhouse and constructing an ad hoc concept GREENHOUSE*. Notice that we do not take Jane to be implying that her office is full of plants or that it has walls made of glass. Even though these are typical characteristics of greenhouses and they feature in the assumptions that are activated by Jane's use of the word, they do not combine with any easily accessible assumptions from the discourse context to yield relevant implicatures. They are not part of the meaning of GREENHOUSE*. Contextual assumptions about what it is like to be stuck inside at work on a hot summer's day do, however, make assumptions about the temperature and air quality of a greenhouse highly accessible and these are likely to feature in the communicated concept GREENHOUSE*.

To interpret the verbal metaphor, the hearer looks for a resemblance between the vehicle and the tenor, and uses this to construct an ad hoc concept. Just as we looked for ways in which a greenhouse might resemble an office, so we look for ways in which the characters in the meme might resemble the objects and people in the labels that have been added to them. Use of a metaphor activates related notions, conceptions, and assumptions to do with the vehicle. Furthermore, the use of an image allows a very particular moment in time to be shown to the audience. We assume we are being shown this particular moment because it is relevant for the message that is being communicated. It is our job as the audience to find ways in which the depicted moment and the behaviour of the characters in that particular moment resemble the objects or people referred to in the labels and the relationship between them. We can then construct ad hoc concepts for the proposition in (21) and for the propositions in (22) and (23).

(22)   New books at the bookstore are the WOMAN IN RED*.

(23)   The untouched, unread books on my bookshelf at home are the WOMAN IN BLUE*.

These ad hoc concepts will be constructed as part of the overall interpretation process, and will be adjusted as part of the process of explicature formation. Remember that according to relevance theory, a speaker is looking for an overall interpretation that is optimally relevant and this will involve mutual parallel adjustment of explicature and implicature. For the meme token in (12), a viewer may construct ad hoc concepts, with the following features:

DISTRACTED BOYFRIEND*:	Easily distracted by WOMAN IN RED*;
	Finds the WOMAN IN RED* attractive and enticing;
	Does not appreciate the WOMAN IN BLUE*
WOMAN IN RED*:	New, interesting.
WOMAN IN BLUE*:	Familiar, available, not new.

Formulated in this way, the meme can be taken to communicate the propositions in (24) to (26).

(24)   I am easily distracted by new, interesting things. I find new, interesting things attractive and enticing. I do not appreciate familiar, available things that are not new.

(25)   New books at the bookstore are new and interesting.

(26)   The untouched, unread books on my bookshelf at home are familiar, available, and not new.

These combine to yield the implicature in (27).

(27)   I am easily distracted by new books at the bookstore. I find new books at the bookstore attractive and enticing. I do not appreciate the untouched, unread books on my bookshelf at home.

Of course, we might ask why Jane would decide to use a meme to communicate this message about herself and her relationship to books. Again, we can begin to answer this question by thinking about metaphors and metaphorical interpretations more generally. Jane might have chosen to make the same basic point by simply uttering something along the lines of (27). While this communicates the same basic message that we infer from the meme, there are several reasons why the meme might be preferred. It should be obvious that the paraphrase in (27) does not capture the full range of effects that we derive from the meme. Metaphors, and in particular creative and poetic metaphors, tend to generate a wide range of weak implicatures. The meme in (12) makes a range of further assumptions accessible that are not captured by the paraphrase in (27). For example, the two women in the photograph resemble one another physically. The ad hoc concepts might easily include this information, and this may well then lead the viewer to derive implicatures along the lines of those in (28) to (31).

(28)   The books in the bookstore are very similar to those books on my shelf at home.

(29)   It is the novelty of the new books that is distracting me, rather than a difference in quality.

(30)   I am always distracted by new, shiny things, and never appreciate what I already have.

(31)   I am likely to grow bored of the new books once I possess them and they are no longer new.

The precise content of the weak implicatures that are derived will vary from viewer to viewer. The meme functions as an extended metaphor, and as Wilson and Sperber (2012: 121–122) explain:

> [an] extended metaphor weakly implicates an ever-widening array of implications which combine to depict an atmosphere, a mood, achieving a powerful overall effect that varies from reader to reader and reading to reading.

The use of the meme is a highly efficient way to communicate this wide range of weak implicatures. To convey the same ideas, emotions, and attitudes verbally, would require either long explanations, or perhaps an extended verbal metaphor.

A further advantage of the meme format is that it allows the user to communicate a gentle, self-mocking attitude towards the scenario that she is representing via the metaphor. She is communicating that her behaviour towards her books is as superficial and perhaps ridiculous as the behaviour of the distracted boyfriend. We can see how shallow his reaction is in the moment depicted, and we are encouraged to see a resemblance between this and the user's tendency to be tempted by new books.

Finally, the meme token activates a further range of assumptions via its position as part of a meme family. While in the case of the example in (12), it is perfectly possible to interpret the image and metaphor in isolation, anyone familiar with the image as a meme is likely to access further implicatures. The fact that this same image can be modified and relabelled in so many different ways suggests that the situation depicted is a metaphor for a general scenario that many people can relate to. The experience of being distracted by something new and exciting when we should really be paying attention to what we already have is common. For the creator of this particular meme token, the experience plays out with books. However, the very fact that the token is part of a wider family, communicates an assumption that this is a common experience that many users will recognise and identify with.

Finally, notice that the interpretation of the meme depends on a combination of the information in the image and the information in the labels. They work together as a multimodal ensemble. If we change the labels, different features appear in the ad hoc concepts. The meme token in (13), for example, labels the characters as 'me', 'solar eclipse', and 'Scientific evidence supporting the dangers of staring at the sun'. The viewer may construct the following ad hoc concepts, resulting in implicatures along the lines of those given in (32) below.

DISTRACTED BOYFRIEND*:	Can't help looking at WOMAN IN RED*;
	Finds WOMAN IN RED* exciting and fascinating;
	Does not pay sufficient attention to WOMAN IN BLUE*
WOMAN IN RED*:	Exciting, fascinating
WOMAN IN BLUE*:	Sensible, boring, is good for DISTRACTED BOYFRIEND*

(32)   I can't help looking at solar eclipses. I find them exciting and fascinating. I find scientific evidence supporting the dangers of staring at the sun sensible and boring, even though it is good for me.

Different aspects of the depicted characters and their relationships are made accessible by the different labels, and the ad hoc concepts that are constructed differ accordingly. Both tokens of the meme use the characters in the image to communicate something about the people, objects, and ideas in the labels. However, the overall intended meaning communicated by the meme emerges from the image combined with the labels when they are interpreted in context and guided by the relevance-theoretic comprehension procedure and the principles of relevance.

CONCLUSIONS

Memes come in all shapes and sizes. They may be text-based or multimodal, and the meme tokens from the same family may be linked in various ways, including by a hashtag, by an image, or by a phrasal template. A defining characteristic of an internet meme is that it is shared and circulated online. As sharing is an ostensive act of communication, memes are fundamentally communicative devices. They may communicate a joke, a comment, or an opinion. However, they often also signal the creator's awareness of the values, experiences, and affiliations associated with the meme as a collection of texts. A meme token's status as part of a meme family often plays a role in its interpretation and may guide the viewer in the inferences they draw about the creator's intended meaning. Object labelling memes are multimodal metaphors which draw on the same pragmatic resources and processes that are used in the interpretation of verbal metaphors. They evoke interpretive resemblance relationships between the vehicles and the tenors, and this guides the viewer in the construction of ad hoc concepts. As with verbal metaphors, image-based memes encourage viewers to construct a wide range of weak implicatures related to the subject content. The images are often metaphors for common human experiences and emotions. The act of labelling them is a highly efficient and effective, while playful, way for a user to align themselves with the values and perspectives of the meme family while sharing their own, individual experiences.

REFERENCES

Brewer, W. F., & Lichtenstein, E. H. (1982). Stories are to entertain: A structure-affect theory of stories. *Journal of Pragmatics*, 6, 473–486. doi:10.1016/0378-2166(82)90021-2

Dawkins, R. (1976). *The Selfish Gene*. Oxford: Oxford University Press.

Dynel, M. (2016). 'Has Seen Image Macros!' advice animals memes as visual-verbal jokes. *International Journal of Communication*, 10, 660–688.

Forceville, C., & Clark, B. (2014). Can pictures have explicatures? *Linguagem em (Dis)curso*, 14(3), 451–472. doi:10.1590/1982-4017-140301-0114

Huang, J., Thornton, K. M., & Efthimiadis, E. N. (2010). Conversational Tagging In Twitter. In *Proceedings of the 21st ACM Conference on Hypertext and Hypermedia*. Toronto.

Jackendoff, R., Cohn, N., & Griffith, B. (2012). *A User's Guide to Thought and Meaning*. Oxford: Oxford University Press.

Jewitt, C. (2013). Multimodal methods for researching digital technologies. In S. Price, C. Jewitt, & B. Brown (Eds.), *SAGE Handbook of Digital Technology Research* (pp. 250–265). London: Sage.

Kidson, F., & Neal, M. (1915). *English Folk-Song and Dance*. Cambridge: Cambridge University Press.

KnowYourMeme.com. (n.d.). *Know Your Meme*. Retrieved July 31, 2019, from https://knowyourmeme.com/

Marwick, A. (2013). Memes. *Contexts*, 12(4), 13–14.

Oswald, S., & Maillat, D. (2018). Deceptive puns: The pragmatics of humour in puns. In C. Padilla (Ed.), *Perspectivas Sobre el Significado: Desde lo Biológico a lo Social* (pp. 145–171). La Serena: Universidad de la Serena.

Reboul, A. (1998). *A relevance theoretic approach to reference. Acts of the Relevance Theory Workshop* (pp. 45–50). Luton: University of Luton.

Reboul, A. (1999). Reference, agreement, evolving reference and the theory of mental representations. In M. Coene (Ed.), *Traiani Augusti vestigia pressa sequamur:studia 1 lingvistica in honorem L. Tasmowki*, (pp. 601–616). Padova: Unipress.

Recanati, F. (2012). *Mental Files*. Oxford: Oxford University Press.

Recanati, F. (2014). Mental files and identity. In A. Reboul (Ed.), *Mind, Values, Metaphysics: Philosophical Papers Dedicated to Kevin Mulligan*. Basel: University of Geneva.

Scott, K. (2020). *Referring Expressions, Pragmatics, and Style: Reference and Beyond*. Cambridge: Cambridge University Press.

Scott, K. (forthcoming). Memes as Multimodal Metaphors: A Relevance Theory Analysis.

Segev, E., Nissenbaum, A., Stolero, N., & Shifman, L. (2015). Families and networks of internet memes: The relationship between cohesiveness, uniqueness, and quiddity concreteness. *Journal of Computer-Mediated Communication*, 20(4), 417–433. doi:10.1111/jcc4.12120

Shifman, L. (2014). *Memes in Digital Culture*. Cambridge, MA: MIT Press.

Sperber, D., & Wilson, D. (1986). *Relevance: Communciation and Cognition* (2nd (with postface) ed.). Oxford: Blackwell.

Suez Canal Authority. (2021). *Suez Canal Authority Egypy - Official Page*. Retrieved April 12, 2021, from https://www.facebook.com/SuezCanalAuthorityEG/photos/415934016714302

Varis, P., & Blommaert, J. (2015). Conviviality and collectives on social media: Virality, memes, and new social structures. *Multilingual Margins*, 2(1), 31–45. doi: 10.14426/mm.v2i1.55

Vásquez, C., & Aslan, E. (2021). "Cats be outside, how about meow": Multimodal humor and creativity in an internet meme. *Journal of Pragmatics*, 171, 101–117. doi:10.1016/j.pragma.2020.10.006

Wilson, D., & Sperber, D. (2012). *Meaning and Relevance*. Cambridge: Cambridge University Press.

Yus, F. (2018). Multimodality in memes: A cyberpragmatic approach. In P. Bou-Franch, & P. Garcés-Conejos Blitvich (Eds.), *Analyzing Digital Discourse: New Insights and Future Directions* (pp. 105–131). Cham: Palgrave Macmillan.

Yus, F. (2021a). Incongruity-resolution humorous strategies in image macro memes. *Internet Pragmatics*, 4(1), 131–149. doi:10.1075/ip.00058.yus

Yus, F. (2021b). Pragmatics of humour in memes in Spanish. *Spanish in Context*, 18(1), 113–135.

Zappavigna, M. (2012). *Discourse of Twitter and Social Media: How We Use Language to Create Affiliation on the Web*. London: Bloomsbury Academic.

Zappavigna, M. (2015). Seachable talk: The linguistic functions of hashtags. *Social Semiotics*, 25(3), 274–291. doi:10.1080/10350330.2014.996948

Zappavigna, M. (2018). *Searchable Talk: Hashtags and Social Media Metadiscourse*. London: Bloomsbury.

Zenner, E., & Geeraerts, D. (2018). One does not simply process memes: Image macros as multimodal constructions. In E. Winter-Froemel, & V. Thaler (Eds.), *Cultures and Traditions of Wordplay and Wordplay Research* (pp. 167–194). Berlin: Mouton de Gruyter.

7

YOU WON'T BELIEVE WHAT'S IN CHAPTER 7!

If you have spent any amount of time on news or entertainment websites or on social media, then you have probably encountered clickbait. You will have seen those strangely compelling headlines and images which promise the latest celebrity gossip or which tease you with a taster of an extraordinary story that seems almost too amazing to believe. Perhaps you have been tempted to follow a link to find out which movie star you are most like or to discover whether you behave like a typical Cancerian or not. Clickbait has become a staple of the online world, and indeed, many websites depend on its success to drive the generation of advertisin revenue. Some typical examples of clickbait headlines are given in (1) to (4).[1]

(1)   17 Videos That Prove Kids Are Basically Just Drunk Adults

(2)   What Karaoke Song Should You Sing Based On Your Zodiac Sign?

(3)   I Let Twitter Run My Life For A Day, And Here's What Happened

(4)   Look At This Amazing Cat Who Goes On Adventures

We all know when we have fallen victim to clickbait. We will have followed a link to what looks like an intriguing article, but when we access the page, the

DOI: 10.4324/9781003254201-7

content is much less interesting than we expected. In some cases we may have to click through page after page to access the piece of information that was promised in the original link. As Biyani et al. (2016: 95) describe, clicking on clickbait links takes the readers to 'low quality content with misleading titles'. It is perhaps, then, not surprising that clickbait has been described as 'one of the pests of social media' (Potthast et al. 2018: 1506). It is hard to avoid clickbait, we dislike it, and yet it works. In a study into emotional arousal when reading clickbait, Pengnate (2016: 7) found that 'while online users express negative perceptions toward clickbait, they are still interested in clicking through the headlines'. Clickbait works. We know we are being clickbaited, we recognise the signs, and yet we continue to click.

How do the writers of clickbait headlines achieve this? How do they lure us into clicking, even when we have been disappointed before, and even when we recognise likely clickbait sources? Why do many readers not learn from experience, and what is it about clickbait headlines that makes them so tempting to so many readers? In this chapter, we consider what the language of clickbait might tell us about how it works, and we think about how clickbait strategies exploit our pragmatic processing systems to create a promise of information that many find irresistible.

DEFINING CLICKBAIT

Clickbait content tends to focus on certain topics. It tends to be light-hearted, popularist, and/or sensationalist. Writing coach and journalism teacher Roy Peter Clark (2014) discusses clickbait in his blog post for *The Poynter Institute for Journalism*. He notes that clickbait content is often focused on pop culture topics such as 'sex, celebrity, and miracle cures'. This sort of subject matter is also common in tabloid journalism, but not all tabloid journalism is necessarily clickbait. Popularist, sensational content alone is not enough to make something clickbait. When clickbait is not focused on celebrities, it is often focused on the readers themselves. The headlines frequently contain the promise of information that directly relates to the readers in some way. For example, we may be lured to click via the promise of a quiz or a test of some sort, which, we are led to believe, will reveal insights into our characters and personalities.

Clickbait links are designed to entice a user to click. However, the same can surely be said for all weblinks. Links are created to guide readers to relevant content. What makes clickbait different to other online links and other headlines? Clickbait links differ from other weblinks in that inducing a click is their sole purpose. Consider the motivations behind rebroadcasting that we discussed in Chapter 3. These were, on the whole, driven by the desire to share information. That is, the information was rebroadcast because the sharer wanted to communicate something, and because, we assume, she thought it would be interesting and relevant to the intended audience in some way. Writers of clickbait headlines are hoping to entice the readers to click, but they have very little interest in whether the readers then engage with the content of the main article or not. Once a user has followed the link, the clickbait has achieved its purpose. In this sense, any locutionary or illocutionary acts that clickbait headlines perform are secondary to the perlocutionary acts that they perform. Causing readers to click on the link is the primary purpose of a clickbait headline.

Peter Koechley is the co-founder of media site Upworthy (Upworthy.com, n.d.). He describes how headlines for the site are carefully constructed and tested to maximise reader engagement and clicks. As he explains:

> Upworthy curators come up with 25 headlines for every single nugget they want to post. Then the team narrows the list down to a few finalists, and finally we conduct a bunch of geeky experiments to determine the winner. We obsess over headlines because we want our content to go viral – and writing a brilliant headline is the easiest way to make that happen.
>
> (Koechley 2012)

While the headlines are carefully developed, tested, and refined in this way, the content in the articles themselves appears to be less important. Once a reader has clicked, the writer has achieved her aim. The sort of effort that is put into generating the headline is rarely replicated when producing the content itself. The quality of the associated articles themselves tends to be very low, and it is generally disappointing when compared with the promises that the headlines make.

Facebook has various policies and guidelines designed to reduce the amount of clickbait that appears on the platform. The site draws on the disconnect between the promise of the headline and the quality of the content to determine what is clickbait and what is not. Two key factors in making something clickbait are, according to Facebook, the length of time that people spend reading an article after they have clicked through, and the number of times that they share or discuss the content. If a user spends time reading an article and/or shares it with friends and contacts, 'it suggests they clicked through to something valuable' (El-Arini and Tang 2014). Users clicking through but then immediately returning to the previous page and choosing not to like, comment on, or share the article, is a key indicator of clickbait content.

This focus on inducing clicks, with little regard for how the users engage with the content post-click, helps to explain the low quality associated with clickbait content. Potthast et al. (2018: 1506) characterise clickbait as 'false or misleading', and Blom and Hansen (2015: 99) describe how clickbait strategies are 'used to provoke the reader into clicking by using presuppositions that seem improbable and cannot be substantiated in the full text'. Clickbait, therefore, is characterised by a discrepancy between what is promised and what is delivered. To bait someone is to lure them in by deception or trickery, and to clickbait someone is to do this via an online link.

ONLINE NEWS DISTRIBUTION AND CLICKBAIT

Social media and the internet have changed how we access and consume news. According to Statista.com (2020), 57% of 23- to 38-year-olds in the United States used social media daily to access news content. Meanwhile 44% of the same age group reported that they never read print newspapers. The move from print to online has meant a change both in the way we find and select what to read, and in the way that the producers of media content generate a profit. These changes have affected the language of the news media, and we can understand clickbait as content that is carefully crafted to attract the attention of readers and to entice them to click on a link.

The context in which we access and consume news necessarily affects the strategies that journalists and editors use to attract our attention and to encourage us to read their articles. Both online and print journalism providers need to attract readers if they are to generate a profit. However, the strategies that they adopt to achieve this are affected both by the means via which consumers access the content and by the profit generation models of the content providers. To generate a profit, producers of traditional print media such as newspapers and magazines must create a product that a consumer wants to buy. A newspaper is a bundle of stories and articles that readers choose to invest in. Magazine and newspaper editors prioritise attention-grabbing stories for their front pages to attract casual browsers in a shop, and they also work to build brand loyalty and encourage repeat custom by producing content that lives up to the promises of the front page and that speaks to their target audience. Thus headlines in traditional newspapers and magazines serve a specific purpose. They attract readers who are likely to go on and buy the publication. We see this purpose reflected in existing pragmatic analyses of traditional newspaper headlines.

Dor (2003) reports on the headline development process at the news-desk of an Israeli national newspaper. He identifies a series of strategies that the copyeditors use when writing headlines. This leads him to an analysis of headlines as 'negotiators between stories and readers' (720). They 'guide individual readers to those specific stories which would be worth their while to read in the full version'. Crucially, Dor concludes that a key role of a newspaper headline is to function as a 'selection mechanism' and summary of the story. Only readers who are particularly interested in the topic, or who enjoy reading news for its own sake, will go on to read the whole article. For Dor, headlines provide a label and/or summary so that readers can decide whether the rest of the content is likely to be relevant to them. Ifantidou (2009) also concludes that headlines function to give a quick and rough sense of what is going on in the news. Using a reader reaction study, she examines readers' interpretations of newspaper headlines. She explains that:

> Headlines are purposefully read for the sake of a quick and loose news update ... headlines are intended as autonomous meaningful constructions and are (or should be) designed to be interpreted as such.
>
> (702)

According to Ifantidou's analysis, while newspaper headlines are 'attention-getting devices' (717), they are also autonomous texts which can and should be interpreted in their own right. For both Ifantidou and Dor, newspaper headlines are self-contained texts. While they are associated with the content in the main article, they are not dependent on it for meaning. Consider the front-page headline in (5), taken from the *Guardian* newspaper from December 2020.

(5)   European states ban travel from UK as new Covid strain takes hold.

The headline in (5) provides the key points of the main story and can be fully understood in its own right without the need to read the accompanying article. While it lacks detail, it provides an overview of the story and the readers can be fairly confident about what they will find in the associated article.

   Unlike print journalism, most online news content is not paid for directly by the consumer at point of access. Rather online news providers generate a profit by selling advertising space on their news webpages. Online advertising is a profitable and growing industry. In 2016, in the US, internet advertising revenues surpassed television advertising for the first time (Interactive Advertising Bureau 2017), and the industry as a whole continues to grow year-on-year (Interactive Advertising Bureau 2019). Publishers of online content include advertisements on their pages and they earn fees from the advertisers based on the number of views the pages receive (Potthast et al. 2018). Therefore, it is in the interests of online content providers to encourage as many clicks on their pages as they can. We can see at least two strategies at play to achieve this. Many online versions of newspapers which were originally printed publications use the same type of headlines online that we find in the print version. We can see this in the examples in (6) and (7) which are both taken from the online versions of UK daily newspapers. The headline in (6) is from the *Guardian* newspaper, and (7) is from the *Daily Mail*.

(6)   France's ban on UK transport came as surprise, says Grant Shapps. (Walker et al. 2020)

(7)   JK Rowling WINS legal battle with 'utterly dishonest' former PA who used her credit card to splash out on coffee and toiletries – as Harry Potter author reveals she sued her to 'protect reputation of her staff'. (Keay and McManus 2019)

The two headlines represent very different sorts of articles. The headline in (6) covers a serious current affairs story, while (7) relates to celebrity gossip and scandal. In these cases, the headlines resemble those used in printed publications. Each provides an overview of the key points of the story and functions as a self-contained text. The commercial success of adopting this strategy online depends on maintaining the brand loyalty associated with the print publication. The online versions are designed to provide the same service that the customer would pay for with the print version, and to therefore encourage loyalty, subscriptions to the site's membership schemes, and return visits to the website. While established news brands can rely, at least in part, on loyalty from existing customers, other sites must drive users to their webpages by other means. A key strategy to do this is to create headlines that are so enticing that a large number of readers feel compelled to click on them when they might otherwise not visit the host site. It is this that has driven the use of clickbait and clickbait techniques.

We can begin to further understand why clickbait content has emerged in certain online news contexts and not in others, if we think about the means via which readers tend to come across news content online. Readers who are loyal to a news brand may visit a host site regularly to seek out news and articles that will be of interest to them. Other users find their way to the sites via keyword searches on search engines such as Google. Headline writers aiming to appeal to these readers construct their headlines to optimise search engine visibility. Consider the headline in (8), which Upworthy co-founder Peter Koechley (2012) provides as an example of this sort of headline.

(8)   Obama says gay marriage should be legal.

The headline in (8) contains strategic key words which are likely to match the search terms of users. A user who is interested in news about Barack Obama or who is interested in news about gay marriage, is, we can imagine, likely to include *Obama* or *gay marriage* in their Google search terms. By including these terms in the headline, the writer maximises the chances that her article will appear in search results. However, clickbait articles are not designed to be accessed via Google searches. Writers of clickbait articles and the headlines that go with them are not trying to satisfy an existing desire for a particular piece of information. Rather, they are trying to spark new interest. They want to connect with readers who did not even know they were interested in the topic until they saw the headline. According to boyd (2010: 53), 'in networked publics attention becomes a commodity'. Clickbait headline writers are vying for the attention of readers as a resource that can be monetised via advertising. Readers are likely to see a clickbait headline, not when they have searched for something on a search engine, but rather when they are scrolling through other online content. Clickbait headlines are posted as promoted posts on social media sites such as Twitter and Facebook, or they appear in sidebars or at the bottom of webpages. As users, we generally come across clickbait headlines when we are looking for something else. Perhaps you have opened a search engine to look for something, only to find yourself distracted by a promoted story that grabs your attention and entices you to click through to read more.

As we have seen, non-clickbait headlines provide a summary of the article, and based on that summary readers may decide to invest extra energy in reading the whole article. However, if they decide not to, they still have the key information. After reading (8) we know that Obama thinks that gay marriage should be legal. Compare the headline in (8) with the clickbait version in (9), again provided by Koechley (2012).

(9)   Now THIS is why I voted for Barack Obama.

Unlike (8), the headline in (9) does not give us an overview of the content of the article, and it also does not contain the same range of strategic keywords that we saw in the non-clickbait version. It was not written with search engine optimisation in mind. Instead, it was written to attract the attention and interest of as many social media users as possible as they scroll through a feed. This leads to a very different sort of headline.

Successful clickbait must do two key things. First, it must grab your attention, and it can do this by teasing information that seems more relevant than anything else that we might otherwise have been thinking about or planning to read. Second, it must entice us to click to find out more. A key strategy in achieving these two goals is to tell the readers part, but not all, of the story. The headline in (9) tells us that there is a reason why the writer voted for Obama, but it does not tell us what this reason is. This creates what is known as an information gap. Information gaps are, as we shall see, key in arousing curiosity and enticing a click.

INFORMATION GAPS AND CURIOSITY

Creating an information gap is key to the success of clickbait. Clickbait headlines need to grab the reader's attention and entice them to visit the associated site. As Koechley (2012) explains:

> a good social media headline seduces people to click through by telling them enough to whet their curiosity but not enough to fulfil it ... social headlines need to create a curiosity gap. Too vague, and nobody cares. Too specific, and nobody needs to click.

The headline needs to make readers aware of an apparent gap in their knowledge. This arouses curiosity, and the curiosity drives the readers to click. Loewenstein (1994: 75) proposes that curiosity is a 'cognitively induced deprivation that arises from the perception of a gap in knowledge or understanding'. The symptoms of curiosity are, according to Loewenstein (93), 'intensity of motivation, transience, association with impulsivity, and disappointment when information is successfully assimilated'. This characterisation of curiosity can help us to understand why clickbait works.

Headlines that create an information gap, rather than providing an overview of the whole story, increase the chances that the readers will feel an intense and impulsive, albeit transient, motivation to click on the link. Consider how this might work in the examples (10) to (13).

(10)   12 Mind-blowing Ways to Eat Polenta.

(11)   Stop Everything and Look at These Adorably Stylish Dogs.

(12)   Someone Calculated How Rich Harry Potter Was And The Answer is Surprising.

(13)   Are You More House Stark Or House Targaryen?

In each case, the headline tells us that apparently highly relevant information is to be found in the main article. However, unlike the non-clickbait examples, the clickbait headlines do not provide us with an overview or summary of this information. They simply promise us new and enticing information, which, if it lives up to the headline, would enrich our cognitive environments. The polenta information promised in (10) is described as 'mind-blowing', the dogs in (11) are so adorably stylish that it is worth stopping everything else to look at them, and the information about how rich Harry Potter is in (12) will, we are promised, be surprising. Finally, clicking on the link in (13) will tell you something about yourself by revealing which of the *Game of Thrones* families you most resemble. In each case, we are promised relevant information, although the details of that information are vague. According to Loewenstein (1994: 92–93), 'curiosity is driven by the pain of not having information' and 'is the feeling of deprivation that results from an awareness of the [information] gap'. Clickbait headlines arouse curiosity by telling us that highly relevant information exists while not actually providing us with the information itself. Instead, we are promised that it is just a click away. Clickbait headlines arouse our interest by hinting that the missing information will yield rich cognitive rewards, and they also promise us instant gratification of that interest if we read the associated article. In the rest of this chapter we look at the techniques and strategies that clickbait writers use to achieve this effect, and we think about why clickbait can be so hard to resist.

CLICKBAIT TECHNIQUES

To be successful, clickbait must attract the attention of the readers as they scroll through a social media feed or browse a website. Much of the existing work that has been done to identify clickbait strategies has been carried out with the aim of developing algorithms and software for detecting and avoiding content that is likely to be clickbait (Chen et al. 2015; Chakraborty et al. 2016; Potthast et al. 2016). To this end, Chen et al. (2015) examine both textual and non-textual features associated with clickbait. They identify a range of textual cues that can be used to recognise and flag potential clickbait content for readers. These cues include the use of forward-referring devices, unresolved pronouns, affective language and action words, suspenseful language, an overuse of numerals, and a use of reverse narrative.

Kuiken et al. (2017) consider clickbait from a journalistic perspective, with the aim of identifying which techniques have the most effect on the click through rate of a headline. They tested headlines in Dutch email newsletters for differences in the click through behaviour of readers. The click through rate was compared across headlines which either included or lacked certain features. They found that headlines performed significantly better when they included short words, signal words (translated as *hence, this, therefore, how, why, when, which, who,* and *like that*), pronouns, and sentimental words. Although often associated with clickbait, inclusion of questions was found to have a significantly negative effect on the performance of the headline, as was the inclusion of quotations. Despite the high frequency of numbered lists in clickbait headlines, inclusion of a number was found to have no significant effect on whether readers clicked through or not.

We explore a range of these cues further in the rest of the chapter and we think about what an understanding of pragmatic processes might be able to tell us about how and why they evoke curiosity.

Reverse narrative

Chen et al. (2015) found that the use of a reverse narrative structure was a reliable cue for detecting clickbait content. In a reverse narrative, the outcome of an event is presented before the initiating event. We can see this structure in the headline in (14).

(14)   A Little Girl Had A Total Meltdown After Her Dad Told Her She Doesn't Have A Boyfriend.

The headline describes two events. The father telling his daughter that she does not have a boyfriend, and the daughter having a 'meltdown'. The daughter having a meltdown is the outcome of the story and yet it is presented first, before the initiating event. This reverse structure has been shown to evoke curiosity in readers (Brewer and Lichtenstein 1982; Knobloch et al. 2004). From a pragmatic perspective, we can understand why this might be an effective strategy. When a writer uses a reverse narrative structure, she draws our attention to the outcome of the story. We assume that she has done so for good reason. The fact that our attention has been drawn to this carries with it the presumption that the story behind the meltdown will be worth hearing, and that reading it will lead to cognitive effects. However, without any further contextual information or details on the initiating events, we are unable to do much with this information. Children have what might be described as 'meltdowns' all the time, and without further details, we have no idea why this one is special, interesting, or relevant. Our attention has been drawn to it, we are expecting relevance, but we must read on to have our expectations satisfied. In the example in (14), the second half of the headline provides some information about the initiating event. However, the description we are given only raises more questions in the reader's mind. Why does a father have to tell his daughter that she does not have a boyfriend? Why does she think she does, and why is she wrong? For each of these points we infer that an answer can be found in the associated article, and so we are drawn to satisfy our curiosity by clicking.

Extremes and superlatives

Clickbait readers are presented with the promise that they will feel 'outraged', 'amazed', or 'inspired' by what they will see (Clark 2014). Affective language, action words, and suspenseful language are often used (Chen et al. 2015), and the content of the associated articles are presented in extreme and hyperbolic terms. I conducted a contrastive corpus analysis of clickbait and non-clickbait headlines to try to understand the distribution of terms associated with these hyperbolic qualities of clickbait (Scott 2021). The corpora were compared using the wmatrix corpus analysis and comparison tool (Rayson, 2008). The software tags each word in the corpora for part-of-speech and semantic field, and then calculates relative frequencies within the data. This provides an indication of whether a particular word, part-of-speech, or semantic field is overused or underused within one corpus relative to the other. The analysis revealed that when adjectives are used in clickbait headlines, superlatives are favoured to a statistically significant degree over general and comparative adjectives. That is, a clickbait writer will tend not to describe something as 'happy' or 'happier' if they can describe it as being 'the happiest'. They will tend not to describe something as 'good' or 'better' when they can present it as 'the best'. Examples to illustrate this are given in (15) and (16).

(15)   27 Of The Happiest Cats In The World.

(16)   13 Ways To Have The Best Valentine's Day.

Furthermore, when comparative terms were used, terms associated with being different and unusual (*weird, incredible, bizarre, mind-blowing, freaky, strange*) were found to be overused in the clickbait corpus in comparison to non-clickbait headlines. Clark (2014) included the advice that clickbait writers should put 'odd and interesting things next to each other' in his article outlining the 'Top 8 Secrets of How to Write an Upworthy Headline'. The corpus data suggest that this is indeed what clickbait writers do. Terms that are used to exaggerate or emphasise were also found to be overused in the clickbait corpus. These included maximisers and exclusivisers (*most, totally, perfectly*), and boosters (*extremely, enormously, as hell*). Examples from the corpus are given in (17) to (19).

(17)   How Chill Would You Be In Freaky Situations?

(18)   22 Faces That Perfectly Capture The Struggle Of Trying To Act Sober.

(19)   FYI, The New Power Rangers Are Hot As Hell.

We can demonstrate how these terms contribute to the creation of an information gap by looking more closely at a specific example. The headline in (10) promises its readers '12 Mind-blowing Ways to Eat Polenta'. When a user clicks on this link they are taken to a page which contains pictures of polenta dishes alongside links to external pages featuring polenta recipes. As is typical of clickbait headlines, we might feel that the headline has somewhat misled the readers in this case. Given the actual content, an alternative non-clickbait headline might be something along the lines of (20).

(20)   12 Recipes for Cooking with Polenta.

We can compare this alternative headline with the clickbait version to see how interpretation is likely to proceed in either case. First, notice that both (20) and its clickbait equivalent are grammatically parallel. They are both noun phrases, rather than full sentences, and so they function as labels for the webpages to which they link. When interpreting them, readers will form a hypothesis about what information is in the article and will use this to decide whether or not to click the link. The non-clickbait headline in (20) gives readers a clear idea of what they can expect to find in the article. They know that on the associated page there will be 12 recipes for cooking with polenta. On this basis readers can easily allocate themselves to one of two groups: people who are interested in reading about polenta recipes and people who are not. It seems likely that at any given point in time, the group of people who are specifically looking for polenta-based recipes will be reasonably small. Indeed, if they have gone online looking for a polenta recipe, use of a search engine seems a much more sensible strategy for finding one than scrolling through social media feeds. Remember, however, that the aim of the clickbait writer is not to satisfy curiosity, but to evoke it.

Now consider the clickbait version of the headline ('12 Mind-blowing Ways to Eat Polenta'). This headline does not promise recipes. Instead it promises 'mind-blowing ways to eat polenta'. The use of the phrase *mind-blowing* will activate in the readers a range of associations and impressions linked to the sort of things or events that generally warrant the description *mind-blowing*. Given the extreme and hyperbolic meaning of this phrase, it is reasonable to assume that readers will be envisioning amazing, incredible, and unexpected things. Having read the headline, readers must then make a decision about whether the contents of the article will be relevant for them, and therefore whether to invest further time and effort in clicking. However, now they are not asking themselves about polenta recipes. Now they are asking themselves whether they would like to find out 'mind-blowing' things about polenta and how it can be eaten. Suddenly, the pool of people who will answer *yes* to this question is much bigger than the pool of people who are interested in polenta recipes. Indeed, who wouldn't want to access such mind-blowing information, particularly as it is just a click away? The writer partly achieves this effect by putting unexpected things together. It is perhaps unlikely that many readers will have considered eating polenta to be amongst the set of things that can be described as mind-blowing. By doing so, the writer has encouraged the readers to ask themselves questions. What could these mind-blowing ways to eat polenta be? How might the process of eating polenta be appropriately described as mind-blowing? The answers to these questions are just a click away, we are told. Thus, the use of extremes, such as *mind-blowing*, and superlatives is one way in which a clickbait headline can attract the attention of the reader. By framing the content of the article in remarkable and unusual terms, the writer of the clickbait headline increases the number of people who will pay attention to it.

This use of language and this exploitation of our natural tendency to seek out relevance is part of the first step in creating an information gap and thus arousing curiosity. The clickbait writer baits the readers by telling them that highly relevant information exists. This creates the feeling of cognitive deprivation that Loewenstein describes. We have been told that this information exists, and so we feel unsatisfied until we have accessed it. It is this that entices the readers to click.

Forward reference

As we have seen, to fully interpret a clickbait headline readers tend to have to access the associated article. Clickbait headlines rarely provide a full overview of the story to which they link, and if readers do not click they are left with unanswered questions. A key strategy for creating this dependency on the information in the article is the use of forward-referring expressions and devices. Blom and Hansen (2015) conducted an analysis of headlines from Danish news websites and focused in particular on the role played by forward-referring techniques in 'creating anticipation and making readers click' (89). They identify eight manifestations of forward reference: demonstrative pronouns, personal pronouns, adverbs, definite articles, ellipsis, imperatives, interrogatives, and general nouns with implicit discourse deictic reference. We will focus more closely on the role played by definite referring expressions (demonstrative pronouns, personal pronouns, and definite articles) in the next section. First, however, we will briefly consider the other forward referring devices that Blom and Hansen associate with clickbait, and illustrate these with examples.

In clickbait headlines imperatives can be used to directly instruct readers to engage with the content in the main article, as in (21) and (22).

(21)   Look At This Amazing Cat Who Goes On Adventures.

(22)   Take This Quiz If You Want To Feel Better.

Other headlines use interrogatives, such as (23), implying that the answer to the question will be found in the article.

(23)   Which 'Jane The Virgin' Character Are You Based On Your Zodiac Sign?

Blom and Hansen describe the next strategy as 'general nouns with implicit discourse deictic reference'. This involves using a general noun phrase in the headline to refer to parts of the discourse in the article itself. That is, the headline refers to the article as a text, usually providing a label indicating what the readers can expect to find. Blom and Hansen (95) give the example in (24) (translated from the original Danish) to illustrate this.

(24)   VIDEO: Gigantic baby born in Texas.

In this example, the label is *VIDEO*, and the writer uses it to explicitly refer to the text in the linked article. This sort of forward reference often takes the form of numbered lists, as in (25) and (26). Again, a phrase from the headline refers forward, describing and labelling the text itself.

(25)   11 Awards All Nurses Deserve.

(26)   The 22 Most Important Celebrity Tweets Of All Time.

Blom and Hansen consider the ellipsis of obligatory syntactic phrases to be a forward-referring device, and they provide the example in (27) as an illustration from their corpus.

(27)   Vil bevæbne syriske oprørere (tv2.dk)
        Want(s) to arm Syrian rebels (95)

The missing subject, they claim, points forward to the argument in the article. We can imagine how the curiosity of readers might be aroused by the omission of an agent in an example like this, and how they might be motivated to click to find out who is responsible. No corresponding examples have yet been found in the English-language clickbait corpus, and so it may be this option is less grammatically acceptable in English. However, a similar technique is available in other contexts in English when a speaker or writer wants to be ostensively vague about who they are referring to (Scott 2013, 2020).

In example (28) the adverb *here* refers forward to the linked article, specifically pointing readers to the content.

(28)   Here's How To Actually Start Lifting Weights.

In this example, the forward-referring device is functioning in a similar way to demonstrative pronouns such as *this* and *that*, which point to where readers may find the information to fill a gap and satisfy their curiosity. Each of these forward-referring devices can be used to arouse the readers' curiosity by implying that information exists without actually providing the information itself. This creates the information gap which drives readers to click. Finally, Blom and Hansen discuss various categories of definite referring expressions. With the aid of comparative corpus analysis, we take a closer look at these in the next two sections.

Definite demonstratives

Definite referring expressions, as opposed to indefinite referring expressions, are used when it is assumed that the referent is given, rather than new (see Scott 2020 for further discussion). In headlines, they create a sense of familiarity and shared context. Compare the genuine clickbait headline in (29) with the alternative version in (30).

(29)   Anne Hathaway Comes To Jennifer Lawrence's Defense About That Phone Scolding Incident.

(30)   Anne Hathaway Comes To Jennifer Lawrence's Defense About A Phone Scolding Incident.

The use of *that* in (29) communicates an assumption that the readers are already familiar with the incident under discussion. It contributes to a sense of shared interests, knowledge, and perspective. The indefinite article in (30) communicates no such assumption, and indeed suggests that the incident is new information to the readers. Further examples of demonstrative determiners from the clickbait headline corpus are given in (31) to (33).

(31)   This Goat Has Been Bullying His Tiger Friend.

(32)   These Gadgets Will Make You Believe In The Future Of Food.

(33)   How Do You Get Rid Of Those Annoying Gray Hairs.

While previous work has identified demonstratives as a feature of clickbait generally, my close comparative corpus analysis compared clickbait headlines with non-clickbait headlines and allowed the individual use of the terms to be examined and compared. Proximal determiners, both singular (*this*) and plural (*these*), were overused to a statistically significant degree, when compared with headlines from non-clickbait sources. Indeed, the plural proximal determiner (*these*) was the most overused part-of-speech across the entire clickbait corpus. The singular distal determiner (*that*) was also overused, although not to the same degree as its proximal counterparts. There was no significant difference in the use of the plural distal demonstrative (*those*) across the two corpora.

The proximal demonstratives (*this* and *these*), as illustrated in (31) and (32), are forward-referring expressions in the way discussed by Blom and Hansen. They are used in the headlines to point us to the main article and indicate what we should expect to find there. If we follow the link in (31), we expect to find a story about a goat, and if we follow the link in (32), we expect to find a list of gadgets. The headlines create an information gap by telling us that the goat and the list of gadgets exist, and the demonstrative pronouns point us to a source of information which will, they imply, fill the information gaps, and satisfy our curiosity.

We saw the same technique used in example (9) above ('Now THIS is why I voted for Barack Obama'). The headline tells us that the writer of the article voted for Barack Obama and that she did so for a reason. The fact that the writer has drawn the reader's attention to this raises expectations that it will be relevant in some way. The information in the headline is not likely to lead to many cognitive effects in and of itself. After all, the readers were probably already aware that people voted for Obama and that these people did so for specific reasons, rather than randomly. The use of the demonstrative *THIS*, however, points readers to where their expectations of relevance will be satisfied. The reason for voting will be revealed in the article and this, it is implied, will provide relevance and hence the cognitive reward that the readers are expecting and hoping for. Recall that this headline was attached to an article about Obama's support for gay marriage, and yet the headline does not make mention of this. If it had, anyone not interested in Obama's stance on gay marriage, or indeed, anyone who was already aware of it, would be unlikely to follow the link. However, by keeping the content in the headline vague, and referring to the key topic simply as *THIS*, the writer creates an information gap for everyone who reads it. Nobody who reads it for the first time knows what *THIS* refers to, and yet everyone has their attention directed towards it and thus expects it to lead to relevance. In summary, proximal demonstratives *this* and *these* function in a similar way to the adverb *here* in examples such as (28). They point directly to the content in the linked-to article, and then as readers we are primed to find out why this content has been pointed out to us.

The distal demonstratives *that* and *those* that we find in (29) and (33) respectively have a different relationship to the information gap. Notice that both 'That Phone Scolding Incident' and 'Those Annoying Gray Hairs' refer to information outside of the text that readers are assumed to already have access to. That is, the distal demonstratives in these examples refer exophorically, communicating an assumption of shared, common knowledge. It is assumed that the readers have already heard about that phone scolding incident and have already thought about those annoying grey hairs. In part, this helps to construct the imagined audience for the article. The intended audience for (29) is anyone who is aware of an incident relating to phones and Jennifer Lawrence, and for (33) it is anyone who has ever thought about annoying grey hairs. However, the key to the creation of the information gap lies elsewhere in these examples. We click to find out how Anne Hathaway has come to Jennifer Lawrence's defence and to find out how to get rid of annoying grey hairs.

There is a difference in how the distal versus proximal demonstratives contribute to the information gap and thus to the success of clickbait in arousing curiosity. Proximal demonstratives play a more direct role in creating an information gap. Use of distal demonstratives depends on reference to shared context, and while this can draw the readers in, it may also exclude anyone who does not have access to those shared assumptions. This might suggest a reason for why we do not see the same degree of overuse in the distal demonstrative determiners in clickbait headlines as we do for proximals. Everyone is curious to find out how a goat could bully a tiger, but not everyone can relate to finding annoying grey hairs.

Personal pronouns

Personal pronouns are another type of definite referring expression. Like demonstratives, they are associated with given information and familiar referents. Use of personal pronouns in clickbait can be seen in examples (34) to (38).

(34)   Which TV Female Friend Group Do You Belong In?

(35)   How Intuitive Are You Really?

(36)   18 Animals Who Are Very Impressed With You And Your Life.

(37)   Leaving Home At 14 Was The Best Thing I Ever Did.

(38)   Running Helped Me Cope With Depression, But Then I Got Injured.

All personal pronouns were over-represented in the clickbait corpus to a statistically significant degree. This is perhaps understandable when we look more closely at the role that pronouns play in the headlines and in the information gap strategies that much clickbait adopts.

The headlines in (34) to (36) all use the second-person pronoun *you* to address the readers directly. This encourages the readers to position themselves as part of the intended audience. The headline is, it appears, addressed directly to us, and we are told that we will learn something about ourselves if we click on the link and engage with the content. The headlines in (34) and (35) ask the readers a question about themselves, and they imply that the answer can be found on the landing site. If you do not click on the links, you will never know how intuitive you are or which TV friend group you belong to. While these may seem trivial, and perhaps many readers will resist the urge to click, the headline writer has nonetheless created an information gap. She has made the readers aware that some information exists, but she has not provided them with the information itself. The headline in (36) takes a less direct approach, but nevertheless prompts us to ask questions about who these animals are and how they might be impressed with our lives. These animals, it is implied, think that something about our lives is impressive. Of course, we want to find out what that is. Use of the second-person pronoun contributes to the creation of an information gap, but not any old information gap. It contributes to an information gap about us, and that is something in which we are highly likely to see potential relevance.

In (37) and (38) we see examples of the first-person pronoun used in click-bait headlines. As with the second-person pronouns, use of first-person pronouns encourages a sense that the writer is speaking directly to the readers. In these examples it also frames the content as a personal narrative. To find something relevant, we need to accept it as true. The headlines promise not just any old story, but a first-hand account of something extraordinary. The writer is sharing something with us, and we are led to believe that highly relevant insights into the writer's experiences are just a click away.

CONCLUSIONS

The use of clickbait is perhaps an inevitable consequence of the changing models of news consumption that come along with an increasingly digitally mediated media landscape. To earn revenue, writers must drive users to a particular website, and to do so they must arouse curiosity in those readers. The strategies identified in the research provide insights into how clickbait continues to arouse our curiosity and entice us to click. By comparing corpora of clickbait headlines with more traditional headlines we can examine clickbait techniques in more detail and begin to understand how they exploit our pragmatic processes and our natural tendency to seek out information that is relevant to us. We have explored a few clickbait devices and techniques in this chapter. However, the corpus analysis revealed many more differences between the two sets of headlines. Furthermore, it should be clear from the examples in this chapter that one headline does not simply rely on one technique. Rather each headline is a carefully crafted piece of work, designed to create an information gap that many find impossible to resist.

NOTE

1 Unless otherwise stated, all examples of clickbait in this chapter are taken from the corpus compiled by Chakraborty et al. (2016).

REFERENCES

Biyani, P., Tsioutsiouliklis, K., & Blackmer, J. (2016). '8 amazing secrets for getting more clicks': Detecting clickbaits in news streams using article informality. In *Proceedings of the Thirtieth AAAI Conference on Artificial Intelligence (AAAI-16)* (pp. 94–100). Palo Alto, CA: AAAI Press.

Blom, J., & Hansen, K. R. (2015). Click bait: Forward-reference as lure in online news. *Journal of Pragmatics, 76*, 87–100. doi:10.1016/j.pragma.2014.11.010

boyd, d. (2010). Social network sites as networked public: affordances, dynamics and implications. In Z. Papacharissi (Ed.), *Networked Self: Identity, Community and Culture on Social Network Sites* (pp. 39–58). Abingdon: Routledge.

Brewer, W. F., & Lichtenstein, E. H. (1982). Stories are to entertain: A structural-affect theory of stories. *Journal of Pragmatics, 6,* 473–486. doi:10.1016/0378-2166(82)90021-2

Chakraborty, A., Paranjape, B., Kakarla, S., & Ganguly, N. (2016). Stop Clickbait: Detecting and Preventing Clickbaits in Online News Media. In *Proceedings of the 2016 IEEE/ACM International Conference on Advances in Social Networks Analysis and Mining (ASONAM)*. San Francisco.

Chen, Y., Conroy, N. J., & Rubin, V. J. (2015). Misleading online content: Recognizing clickbait as false news. In *Proceedings of the 2015 ACM Workshop on Multimodal Deception Detection,* (pp. 15–19).

Clark, P. R. (2014). *Top 8 Secrets of How to Write an Upworthy Headline.* Retrieved April 23, 2019, from Poynter.: https://www.poynter.org/reporting-editing/2014/top-8-secrets-of-how-to-write-an-upworthy-headline/

Dor, D. (2003). On newspaper headlines as relevance optimizers. *Journal of Pragmatics, 35,* 695–721. doi:10.1016/S0378-2166(02)00134-0

El-Arini, K., & Tang, J. (2014). *Click-baiting.* Retrieved March 30, 2021, from Facebook Newsroom: https://about.fb.com/news/2014/08/news-feed-fyi-click-baiting/

Ifantidou, E. (2009). Newspaper headlines and relevance: Ad hoc concepts in ad hoc contexts. *Journal of Pragmatics, 41*(4), 699–720. doi:10.1016/j.pragma.2008.10.016

Interactive Advertising Bureau. (2017). *IAB Internet Advertising Revenue Report: 2016 Full year Results.* PricewaterhouseCoopers Ltd. Retrieved October 7, 2019, from https://www.iab.com/wp-content/uploads/2016/04/IAB_Internet_Advertising_Revenue_Report_FY_2016.pdf

Interactive Advertising Bureau. (2019). *IAB Internet Advertising Revenue Report: 2018 Full Year Results.* PricewaterhouseCoopers. Retrieved April 20, 2021, from https://www.iab.com/wp-content/uploads/2019/05/Full-Year-2018-IAB-Internet-Advertising-Revenue-Report.pdf

Keay, L., & McManus, L. (2019). *JK Rowling WINS legal battle with 'utterly dishonest' former PA who used her credit card to splash out on coffee and toiletries - as Harry Potter author reveals she sued her to 'protect reputation of her staff.* Retrieved March 30, 2021, from Mail Online: https://www.dailymail.co.uk/news/article-6886399/JK-Rowlings-personal-assistant-PA-took-18-000-Harry-Potter-fraud-case.html

Knobloch, S., Patzig, G., Mende, A.-M., & Hastall, M. (2004). Affective news effects of discourst structure in narratives on suspence, curiosity, and enjoyment while reading news and novels. *Communication Research, 31*(3), 259–287. doi:10.1177/0093650203261517

Koechley, P. (2012). *Why The Title Matters More Than The Talk.* Retrieved April 20, 2021, from Upworthy Insider: https://blog.upworthy.com/why-the-title-matters-more-than-the-talk-867d08b75c3b

Kuiken, J., Schuth, A., Spitters, M., & Marx, M. (2017). Effective headlines of newspaper articles in a digital environment. *Digital Journalism, 5*(10), 1300–1314. doi:10.1080/21670811.2017.1279978

Loewenstein, G. (1994). The psychology of curiosity: A review and reinterpretation. *Psychological Bulletin, 116*(1), 75–98. doi:10.1037/0033-2909.116.1.75

Pengnate, S. (2016). Measuring emotional arousal in clickbait: Eye-tracking approach. In *Twenty-second Americas Conference on Information Systems,* (pp. 1–9). San Diego.

Potthast, M., Gollub, T., Komlossy, K., Schuster, S., Wiegmann, M., Garces Fernandez, E. P., Hagen, M., and Stein, B. (2018). Crowdsourcing a Large Corpus of Clickbait on Twitter. In *Proceedings of the 27th International Conference on Computational Linguistics,* 1498–1507.

Potthast, M., Köpsel, S., Stein, B., & Hagen, M. (2016). Clickbait detection. In N. Ferro et al. (eds.), *Advances in Information Retrieval. ECIR 2016. Lecture Notes in Computer Science,* vol. 9626. Cham: Springer. doi: 10.1007/978-3-319-30671-1_72

Rayson, P. (2008). From key words to key semantic domains. *International Journal of Corpus Linguistics, 13*(4), 519–549. doi:10.1075/ijcl.13.4.06ray

Scott, K. (2013). Pragmatically motivated null subjects in English: a relevance theory perspective. *Journal of Pragmatics*, 68–83. doi:10.1016/j.pragma.2013.04.001

Scott, K. (2020). *Referring Expressions, Pragmatics, and Style: Reference and Beyond.* Cambridge: Cambridge University Press.

Scott, K. (2021). You won't believe what's in this paper! Clickbait, relevance and the curiosity gap. *Journal of Pragmatics*, *175*, 53–66. doi:10.1016/j.pragma.2020.12.023

Statistic.com. (2020). *Statistic.com*. Retrieved December 21, 2020, from https://www.statista.com/statistics/1010456/united-states-millennials-news-consumption/

Upworthy.com. (n.d.). Retrieved April 05, 2021, from https://www.upworthy.com/

Walker, A., Henley, J., & Boffey, D. (2020). *France's ban on UK transport came as surprise, says Grant Shapps*. Retrieved December 21, 2020, from The Guardian: https://www.theguardian.com/world/2020/dec/21/france-ban-uk-transport-surprise-says-grant-shapps-covid

8

RESEARCHING ONLINE PRAGMATICS

New forms of media facilitate new means of interaction, and as they do so, new patterns of language use and even new communicative behaviours emerge. We have focused here on pragmatics as the study of language and communication in context, and, in particular, on the issues of (a) how online speakers and writers construct their messages and (b) how online hearers and readers interpret those messages. There are various questions we can ask about these issues and various ways in which we can attempt to find answers. Throughout this book, we have discussed the results of various studies into digitally mediated communication. In this chapter, we draw back the curtain a little more to consider the research methods that have been used to conduct these studies, and we think about how such studies help to progress our understanding of communication in digitally mediated contexts. The discussions here do not, of course, constitute an exhaustive survey of all of the methods available to those working in online pragmatics. However, hopefully, it will provide a taste of some of the ways in which these issues can be explored. What will also become apparent is that no research method is perfect. As we shall see, there are advantages and disadvantages to the various approaches, and results must always be considered in context and relative to the methodological limitations.

DOI: 10.4324/9781003254201-8

FINDING A RESEARCH TOPIC

Online research studies may start from a hunch. You may notice a particular trend as you browse your own social media feeds, or you may encounter words, expressions, or communicative devices that you have not come across before. You may even notice yourself using a particular device or strategy, and wonder what has motivated you to do so. These informal observations and reflections can be useful starting points for a research project. For example, my research studies on hashtags, discussed in Chapter 4, grew out of an initial observation that some hashtags appeared to have very little to do with the searchability of Twitter. This led me to ask questions about what contribution these non-search-related hashtags were making to the messages, and what was motivating the users to include them. Similarly, my research into the pragmatics of clickbait, discussed in Chapter 7, arose partly from my own frustration at being lured onto clickbait sites again and again. I wanted to understand why clickbait headlines were so effective, and my hunch was that pragmatics would have something to say about it. Both these pieces of research developed from informal observations of patterns in the way people use and interpret language and other communicative resources online.

Popular media discourse about language and social media can often provide the inspiration for research projects in online pragmatics. The influence of technology on language and communication has always caused passions to run high. Fears that technology is somehow damaging our ability to communicate or ruining language are as old as technology itself. Socrates (quoted by Plato) warned that the invention of the alphabet would 'create forgetfulness in the learner's souls ... they will be tiresome company, having the show of wisdom without the reality' (as cited in Baym 2010: 25–26). Similar worries about the 'linguistic and social status quo' (Tagg 2015: 3) have resurfaced with each new communicative technology. Linguistic and pragmatic innovation and the use of non-standard forms are often stigmatised and presented as cause for moral panic, or what Marwick (2008) calls 'technopanic'. Pragmatics and pragmatic theories can offer us a way to investigate these practices from an objective and dispassionate perspective, and to understand the communicative imperative that underlies them. Does the use of emoji, for example, signal a lack of linguistic ability or can we understand it in terms of linguistic creativity and innovation? To answer a pragmatics-focused research question or to investigate the pragmatics of an issue or practice we need two things. We need a theory of pragmatics and we need data. One without the other will only give us half of the picture.

USING PRAGMATIC THEORIES

Pragmatic theories provide a framework for understanding and analysing communicative behaviours. They are usually based on underlying assumptions about human communication, and they provide us with overarching guiding principles for understanding how language is used and interpreted. Working with a theory provides the researcher with certain assumptions as starting points for their investigations. It means that the researcher is not developing ideas or testing hypotheses in a vacuum. Rather the principles and assumptions of a theory give us starting points and parameters to use as we investigate the issue or question.

Several of the pieces of research discussed in this book have been driven by theory, and much of my own work in pragmatics has been based within the relevance-theoretic pragmatic framework (Sperber and Wilson 1986/95; Carston 2002; Wilson and Sperber 2012; Clark 2013). In Chapter 4, I outlined my relevance theory-driven work on the pragmatics of hashtags. My aim with this work was to understand why users sometimes include hashtags in their tweets when those hashtags appear to be of little or no use for searching for related content. Relevance theory provided me with several useful starting points for investigating this issue. First, relevance theory assumes that language is an ostensive stimulus. Hashtags involve language and can therefore be treated as part of an ostensive act of communication. Second, relevance theory assumes that when a communicator produces an ostensive stimulus, she is aiming at optimal relevance. Several key consequences follow from this, and these guided me in the questions that I asked about hashtag use, and in the predictions that I made about the range of uses that we should find in the data. First, a consequence of the definition of optimal relevance is that a communicator should not put her addressee to unrewarded effort. From this starting point, we can assume that when a hashtag is included in a tweet, it is contributing something to the relevance of the utterance. We can then look for what this contribution might be. Second, the relevance of an utterance is assessed on the basis of the speaker's overall intended meaning. This includes not just what the speaker states or asserts, but also what she intentionally implies. Previous work in relevance theory has demonstrated that (a) inference is involved in deriving all aspects of a speaker's meaning, implicit and explicit (Carston 2002), and (b) that speakers use devices and expressions to guide their addressee's inferential processes (Blakemore 2007; Wilson 2011). I was therefore able to form the hypothesis that non-search-related hashtags contribute to relevance by guiding inferential processes. This led to a prediction that I would find instances of hashtag use related to the full range of inferential processes that an addressee might need to perform to interpret an utterance. Once we have a prediction, we can test it against the data. The results of this process for my work on hashtags are summarised in Chapter 4.

My research into the pragmatics of sharing and rebroadcasting, as discussed in Chapter 3, was also driven by theoretical predictions based on the assumptions of relevance theory. If, as I have argued, rebroadcasting content is a case of attributive use, then we might expect to find the same range of attributive uses that we find offline also represented in online acts of rebroadcasting. To test this prediction, I looked for examples of rebroadcasting which achieved relevance via each of the three routes to relevance that have been identified in offline spoken and written discourse. Notice that, as with the hashtag research, my research on rebroadcasting makes no claims about how frequently each category is employed by users. Rather, the claim is simply that each variety of attributive use is attested in the data. Further work, using a corpus of data, is needed to establish how often each type of attributive use is found and whether there is cross-cultural or context-specific variation.

In Chapter 6, I outlined my analysis of object labelling memes as multimodal metaphors. Again, this analysis was driven by relevance-theoretic assumptions and principles. My research method, in this case, however, was different. To test the predictions that object labelling memes function as metaphors and are processed using the same inferential strategies, I focused on one particular instance of a widely circulated meme. I then used the machinery of relevance theory (the process of reference assignment, the relevance-theoretic comprehension procedure, and the notion of ad hoc concepts) to break down the interpretation process for various examples of the meme. In this way, I was able to demonstrate that the same theoretical concepts and interpretive processes which account for verbal metaphor interpretation in offline contexts can also explain how we interpret object labelling memes.

Good theory-driven research in online pragmatics not only reveals how users manage their interactions online and how they navigate context collapse, but also tests the theory on which it is based. Pragmatic analyses look at how communicators make use of the contextual resources at their disposal in order to convey their message. Online environments offer us a key opportunity to test existing theories by exploring human communicative behaviour in a specific environment. Theories are not static. They develop and change as our knowledge develops and changes. Finding data that cannot be explained using a particular theory or framework does not mean the data are necessarily wrong, and it also does not mean we should reject the entire theoretical approach. It should, however, send us back to (a) look at our data collection methods, and (b) reexamine the assumptions that the theory makes, to see if either can be improved.

Once we have applied a theory or framework, we can make predictions about what we expect to see in the data. At this point, we can collect data to test our predictions. Alternatively, we can draw on data that have been collected by other researchers, both within pragmatics and beyond. Work from a range of disciplines provides data which are relevant to pragmatic issues. Across this book and throughout my research, I have drawn on work from communication studies, media studies, cognitive science, and psychology, as well as more language- and discourse-focused research, to test theoretical predictions against data. In the next section, we discuss some of the ways in which digitally mediated data can be collected and used to test the theoretical predictions of pragmatic theories of communication.

TESTING THEORETICAL PREDICTIONS

Pragmatic theories and frameworks provide us with the structure and machinery to make predictions about how interlocutors will behave in different discourse contexts. As we have seen throughout this book, communicating in digitally mediated contexts brings with it both constraints and resources that differ from those that we typically find in face-to-face communication. Much of my work on online pragmatics has been rooted in the assumption that our basic interpretive processes and procedures remain the same whether we are communicating online or offline. A consequence of this assumption is the expectation that we should be able to understand differences in language use and interpretation in terms of the differences in the communicative context. There are various ways that we can test this prediction using data. In the examples discussed so far, the theoretical predictions were tested by looking for evidence of certain communicative behaviours in the data (examples of hashtags contributing to different inferential processes and examples of acts of rebroadcasting that achieve relevance in different ways) and by analysing typical examples of digital phenomena (for example, memes). In the rest of this section, I discuss some other means by which predictions can be tested, drawing on examples that have been discussed elsewhere in this book.

Free production tasks

One way to investigate the ways in which the discourse context affects language use, is to control the context, and ask users to produce utterances. We can then compare how users behave in different contextual conditions. As discussed in Chapter 5, Thompson and Filik (2016) found that emoticons were more likely to be used in sarcastic, rather than literal contexts. To establish this, they conducted two related free production task experiments. In the first experiment participants were shown a short exchange, and asked to imagine that it was a text message conversation between them and a friend. An example is given in (1) (Thompson and Filik 2016: 109).

(1) You: So how was the interview?
     Friend: I really can't tell …
     You: Well, you looked confident.

Some participants were then told that the final turn in the exchange (produced by 'You') had been intended literally, while others were told that it had been intended sarcastically. They were then all asked to make the final message clearer in terms of this intention, but they were asked to do so without adding or removing any of the words. The experimenters then analysed the use of emoticons in the responses to establish whether there were statistically significant patterns of use.

The second experiment followed a similar procedure using a new group of participants. On this occasion, the final 'You' turn was left blank, so that rather than editing the final message in the exchange, participants were asked to compose a reply. Some were instructed that they should write a reply which 'clearly shows you are being serious' while others were asked to compose a message which 'clearly shows you are being sarcastic' (Thompson and Filik 2016: 113).

Again, the researchers analysed the use of emoticons in the responses they received, looking for statistically significant patterns. Irony, sarcasm, and non-literal language use more generally, are key issues in pragmatics. Thompson and Filik's work suggests that users employ digital resources such as emoticons differently in sarcastic versus literal contexts. This in turn suggests that users are sensitive to the needs and perspectives of online audiences and that they adjust their utterances accordingly.

An advantage of this kind of production task is that the conditions can be carefully controlled. Thompson and Filik were able to see whether the difference in the instructions to the participants resulted in differences in language production. A drawback of such studies is that they are necessarily artificial in nature. Thompson and Filik describe how they set the task up to encourage participants to respond as they would to a friend. However, the participants were, of course, aware of taking part in an experiment, and they were producing responses in a non-natural scenario.

Judgement tasks

To understand how we make meaning in context, we need to understand the links between the form of an utterance and how that utterance is interpreted in context. One way to investigate this is to elicit judgements on different versions of utterances, and to use this to deduce the contribution that individual words, expressions, or non-verbal components make to the overall meaning. In Chapter 6, we discussed work by cognitive scientist Monica Riordan (2017a, 2017b). Riordan used this method to investigate the effect of non-face emoji on the interpretation of messages. In both her studies, Riordan showed her participants text messages. The texts were designed to be ambiguous, and they were created in several versions. In some, an extra word or phrase was added to remove the ambiguity and in others zero, one, two or three emoji were added. A final version containing both the extra word or phrase and the emoji was also created. Participants were then asked to rate a selection of the messages in terms of positivity and negativity. They were also given a list of eight emotions, and asked to indicate on a scale of one to seven how much each emotion was present in the message. Finally, participants were asked to rate how confident they were in their ratings for each message. Riordan's results supported her initial hypotheses that adding non-face emoji increases positive affect ratings. In her second study, Riordan (2017a) also asked her participants to rate how ambiguous they judged each text message to be. This provided insight into the role that emoji may play in disambiguation. She found that in some cases the addition of an emoji made a message less ambiguous than the addition of disambiguating extra linguistic material. While Riordan is not specifically working from the perspective of pragmatics, her findings have implications for our understanding of how users interpret online utterances. They specifically provide insight into the role that emoji can play in pragmatic processes such as disambiguation.

As with the free production tasks, these judgement and rating tasks use artificial stimuli, and are conducted under artificial circumstances. This allows the researcher to control the variables, but, as Riordan (2017a: 563) acknowledges, it is unlikely to fully capture the 'dynamic and flexible nature of emoji use'. Experimental studies of this nature necessarily exclude a range of contextual factors that might affect interpretation. As Riordan (2017b: 86) explains:

> Our interpretations of text messages are quite likely to vary depending upon from whom we receive the message and our understanding of the circumstances that may have led to the message, including past interactions with the message sender and the social roles we play with that person.

Here Riordan is acknowledging the central role that contextual factors play in interpretation, and that role is, of course, precisely what work in pragmatics is designed to explore.

User surveys

One way to investigate what people do when they communicate online and why they do so, is to ask them. This may seem an obvious and simple approach, but while the use of surveys can provide invaluable insight, careful planning must go into their use. Researchers must decide what sort of data they hope to elicit (quantitative or qualitative), how they plan to analyse it, and how it will answer a research question. Survey questions must be carefully worded for clarity and to avoid presupposing a particular answer or stance (Page et al. 2014: 151–152). We have seen work informed by surveys in the course of the discussions in this book, and these examples helpfully illustrate both the potential of surveys and their limitations. Communications and social media scholars Marwick and boyd (2011) investigated how Twitter users envision their audience, and how they decide which topics to tweet (and crucially to not tweet) about. They posted questions to their own Twitter followers and to a sample of other active accounts. The key to this approach was that Marwick and boyd were very clear about their goals, and they were realistic in terms of the type of data they were collecting. In their discussion of their methodology, Marwick and boyd (2011: 117–118) explain that they were aiming to 'elicit potentially diverse perspectives' rather than getting 'a representative sample of Twitter users', and they acknowledge that their data would not 'account for all potential perspectives'. However, the responses they received provided insight into 'core differences in conceptualizing audience', and could be built on in future empirical work.

A research team also including danah boyd used a similar approach as part of their research into the practice of retweeting, as discussed in Chapter 3 (boyd et al. 2010). They asked boyd's Twitter followers why they think people retweet content and what sort of content they were most likely to retweet.

Again, the key to interpreting data collected via this sort of approach is an awareness and acknowledgement of the limitations. The sample in this case is a convenience sample, and the responses 'are not representative of all Twitter users nor do they reflect all possible answers' (4). Furthermore, the respondents are self-selecting and, as boyd et al. (2010) discuss, are likely to be disproportionally 'reflective tech-savvy adults interested in social media, education, and technology' (4). While danah boyd and her colleagues are not linguists and do not work specifically in pragmatics, their survey work can provide a useful perspective when investigating pragmatic questions. In my work on rebroadcasting, discussed in Chapter 3, their survey results provided a useful starting point for understanding the range of motivations that users have for retweeting. When formulating my analysis of rebroadcasting as attributive use, I had to consider whether the motivations from the user survey could be accounted for within the categories of attributive use that we find evidenced elsewhere. Had I not been able to reanalyse the motivations in pragmatic terms, I would have had to revisit my proposal that rebroadcasting is an act of attributive use.

Finally, it is important to be aware that a limitation of using surveys of this sort is that they collect data about what users report that they do. There are all sorts of reasons why this might not represent actual behaviours and practices. Survey data tells us what users think they do and what they are willing to tell us that they do. Other methods must be used to confirm whether this is, in fact, what they actually do.

Corpus analysis

A corpus is a collection of texts which is usually large and structured in such a way that it can be easily searched. Corpus analysis research is generally focused on investigating language as it is used by speakers in naturalistic and authentic settings (Bernardini et al. 2006). We might be tempted to think of the World Wide Web itself as the ultimate corpus. However, as Page et al. (2014), following Sinclair (2005), caution, we know very little about the dimensions and parameters of the internet, and, furthermore, it is constantly changing. For this reason, researchers tend to build their own corpora. Researchers can apply for academic access to the Twitter API (Application Programming Interface) to access and study data, and there are plans to make curated datasets available for research purposes (Developer.twitter.com, n.d.). Corpora might be random samples of posts from a certain time period, or they might follow particular users or particular themes. Michele Zappavigna (n.d.) provides descriptions on her website of the various corpora she has built. These range from a 100-million-word corpus of tweets from 2009, to the entire Twitter stream of a particular user.

Online discussion boards and forums are also a source of corpora, and have been used to explore topics including trolling (Jenks 2019), (im)politeness, and relational work (Landone 2012; Wang and Taylor 2019; Rudolf Von

Rohr and Locher 2020). When studying a particular phenomenon, it might be appropriate to collect together a number of examples for analysis and comparison, creating a mini corpus. Dynel (2016), Yus (2021), and Vásquez and Aslan (2021) each used this method to explore humour in memes. When investigating politeness in WhatsApp group chats, Flores-Salgado and Castineira-Benitez (2018) compiled a relatively small but focused corpus of messages. They asked informants from two WhatsApp groups to send them chats, from which they then extracted all instances of requests. These requests formed their corpus. Petitjean and Morel (2017) used a similar method to compile a WhatsApp corpus to investigate the use of transcribed laughter ('*hahaha*') to manage interactions.

From a pragmatic perspective, corpus analysis can be used to establish whether language is used differently in different contextual conditions, and is particularly useful when those contextual conditions can be defined and controlled. For example, we might want to know if language is used differently on different platforms or by different groups of users. In my work on clickbait, I wanted to establish whether the language in headlines on news websites associated with clickbait was significantly different to the language used on more traditional news websites. I adopted a corpus analysis approach because this allowed general patterns of use to be examined and comparisons to be made. As discussed in Chapter 7, clickbait is not defined by one or two specific features. Rather, writers of clickbait carefully construct their headlines and draw on many techniques. Similarly, it is not the case that expressions and parts of language associated with clickbait are never used in non-clickbait content. Analysing one or two, or even scores of clickbait headlines would not necessarily reveal reliable patterns in the language that is used. However, corpus analysis allows us to look at a large dataset and compare the frequencies with which particular words and expressions are used.

The corpora that I used in my analysis were compiled by Chakraborty et al. (2016). The clickbait corpus contained headlines from Buzzfeed, Upworthy, ViralNova, Thatscoop, Scoopwhoop, and ViralStories. While not everything on these sites is necessarily what we would stereotypically think of as clickbait, the corpus consists of headlines from sites which rely heavily on advertising revenue. The non-clickbait corpus, on the other hand, contained headlines from online versions of traditional news publications (*The New York Times*, *The Guardian*, and *The Hindu*) and from Wikinews, which is written by volunteers and has a strict style and content guide (Wikinews, n.d.). While there is no guarantee that these publications will never employ any clickbait tactics, the basis on which the corpora had been compiled meant that headlines could be compared based on the business models of the host publications. A comparison between these two large corpora of headlines allowed statistically significant patterns of overuse and underuse to be established in one corpus, relative to the other. Having established these patterns of use, I was then able to conduct close analyses on individual headlines from the clickbait corpus. This allowed me to apply the relevance-theoretic pragmatic framework to try to understand the underlying reasons for the differences that we see in the data.

In Chapter 5, we discussed the findings from Riordan and Kreuz's (2010) corpus study of non-verbal cues. Various existing corpora of computer-mediated communication were combined for this study, and the researchers then used text analysis software to categorise each word according to various dimensions. From this, they were able to compare the use of various non-verbal cues across the different corpora, and to identify the function of the words with which the cues occurred. They concluded that capitalisation was the most commonly used non-verbal cue. This might seem surprising to readers now given the widespread use of emoji in digitally mediated discourse. However, we need to interpret Riordan and Kreuz's work relative to the time in which their data were produced. The corpora in their study covered the period between 2001 and 2010 and included only English-language texts. As we saw in Chapter 5, emoji and emoji keyboards did not become widely available outside of Japan until after the end of this period. Their work provides a snapshot of how users co-opted the textual resources available to them during a very specific time period. Given the speed of development of digital technology and software, and the pace at which users adapt to these developments, it is crucial to always consider the context in which data were produced when interpreting results. This brings us to some more general points about corpora and their use in pragmatics research.

Corpora are datasets, and any research needs to allow for the fact that 'the composition of the dataset influences the analysis and interpretation of results' (Page 2014: 33). This needs to be considered when choosing or compiling a corpus or other dataset for research. For example, Page (2012) compiled a corpus to carry out comparative work looking at the discourse styles used by different groups of users on Twitter. The corpus sampled data from accounts which represented those groups of interest. Page (2014) then drew on this same corpus for her work on corporate apologies on Twitter. As Page discusses, this provided useful data and allowed general comparisons to be made, but there are inevitable limitations to using a dataset that was not compiled with the specifics of the research in mind. Limitations need to be considered in any corpus work, and should be acknowledged and allowed for in any analysis and discussion.

ETHICS IN ONLINE RESEARCH

Social media sites make an enormous amount of data very easily available. On average, 6000 tweets (Internet Live Stats n.d.) and 995 Instagram photographs (Omnicore 2021) are posted every second, and some sort of access to these data is usually no more than a few clicks away. Just because we can access data, does not, however, mean that we should, and it does not give us free reign to use those data however we please. In this section, we think about some of the ethical issues related to research into the pragmatics of digitally mediated communication. This brief discussion does not pretend to provide a comprehensive overview of all of the ethical issues and considerations that arise when we study language use and communication online. The topic is complex, nuanced, and constantly developing and evolving. However, ethical considerations must be at the heart of any research methodology, and those conducting research into online pragmatics must consider the possible implications of the methods they use and the analyses that they conduct.

As Page et al. (2014: 59–61) note, the principles that underlie ethical research were developed in relation to offline research activities, and there is no single set of agreed guidelines governing research into the use of social media. The British Association for Applied Linguistics (BAAL) provides recommendations on good practice with specific points relating to internet research (BAAL 2017). As these guidelines note, however, opinions differ on what may be considered to be publicly available data online, and this impacts on the decisions that researchers make around informed consent, privacy, and confidentiality. As we shall see, these issues are not unrelated to the contexts in which online data tend to be produced and thus to the ideas that we have explored more generally in this book, including context collapse, and imagined audiences.

For some of the data collection methods discussed in this chapter, the requirements around informed consent and confidentiality are likely to be similar to those that apply when conducting offline research using the same methods. Participants in experiments, surveys, and interviews must understand what they are taking part in, and they must give informed consent to their participation. That is not to say that there are not complexities involved in obtaining consent that is genuinely and fully informed. Cases must be considered carefully, individually, and relative to the context. However, issues around informed consent become even more complicated when research methods involve the collection of naturally occurring online data. A researcher may have access to a wide range of online data, much of which may be publicly available. As Page et al. (2014: 64) explain:

> the researcher must consider where the materials or interactions they want to analyse are situated because the context in which the social media materials are produced or published influences the ethical aspects of accessing that material in the first place.

As they go on to discuss, however, the lines between what is public and what is private can often become blurred when we move online. Different sites afford their users different degrees of control over who can see what, and it is not always a simple case of data being either public or private. While Twitter and Instagram accounts are either open to the public or protected, Facebook allows users to control who sees what to a more fine-grained degree. Just because the researcher has access to a post, does not mean that it is publicly available or that the user who produced it intended it to be so.

It is also far from a case of 'one-size-fits-all' when it comes to the ethics of research into digitally mediated communication. Consider, for example, my work on clickbait headlines discussed in Chapter 7. The data for this research were drawn from a range of news websites and were intended for public consumption. Given that clickbait headlines are designed to attract and entice readers, reproduction of them elsewhere is fairly low risk. Furthermore, the headlines were analysed as a set and the focus was on significant differences in word frequencies across the two corpora. Illustrative examples were discussed. However, most of the analysis abstracted away from individual utterances. Both the nature of the data and the analytical method used made this study fairly straightforward from an ethical perspective. Contrast this, however, with the ethical issues that are likely to arise when, for example, researching communication between private individuals, or when using public data that deals with a sensitive topic. When the subject content of a study is more sensitive and/or the users involved are more easily identified, the issues become more complicated and nuanced.

Even when material is publicly available, the perspectives of the users who produced the content still need to be carefully considered. As we have seen, the imagined audience for a post might be very different to the actual audience for that post. While the users might not have taken technical precautions to restrict a post, that does not mean that they intended the content to be available for general consumption and analysis. Zimmer (2010: 323) calls for a 'better understanding of the contextual nature of privacy in these spheres'. As he explains, 'just because personal information is made available in some fashion on a social network, does not mean it is fair game for capture and release to all'.

Much of my own work has been focused on Twitter, and, in most cases, the examples that I have used to illustrate my arguments have been used without the explicit consent of the users who posted the original content. While all of these tweets are publicly available, I have taken various precautions to mitigate the risks that might be posed to the users from my discussion of their posts. I have anonymised tweets that were posted by private individuals. I have not, however, anonymised tweets when the posting account belongs to either an institution or organisation (such as the BBC or Sport Relief) or to public figures, such as politicians, journalists, and celebrities. I have then made a case-by-case decision about whether to reproduce the content of the tweet verbatim or to paraphrase it. Twitter is searchable, and removing the usernames from a manuscript means very little in terms of anonymity if the original tweets can easily be retrieved via a keyword search. In cases where the content is uncontroversial and appears to have been intended for as wide an audience as possible, I have retained the original wording. However, when tweets were part of a conflict, disagreement, or included discussion of a sensitive topic, I felt that the nature of the discourse context in which they were posted gave me a responsibility to protect the identity of the user. In these cases I have paraphrased the content of the tweet so that the original post cannot easily be found.

Page (2017) discusses cases from her own research where the original source of the data has been deleted or where the user who created the original content has now died. Extracts of the content, in this case blogs, remain available in Page's printed publications, and she expresses unease at the risks that this could pose to the users or to their friends and relatives. She explains that she would make different decisions were she to conduct the same research now. Page discusses a range of examples of researchers changing their approaches to digital ethics over the course of a project or career, and she stresses the importance of taking a reflective approach to ethical decision-making and the 'need to respond to unforeseen developments as the research process unfolds' (317).

When using online data there is often a tension between protecting the identity of users and giving proper credit for content. Should we be treating content producers as authors and citing their work, or should we be treating them as informants and protecting their anonymity? As with the issues around informed consent and privacy, there is not necessarily a single answer to this dilemma. Opinions differ and cases must be considered individually and in context. Consider, for example, the memes discussed in Chapter 6. In the case of image macros, each token consists of an image with captions overlaid. As such, each is a creative collaboration between at least two people: the photographer and the writer of the captions. However, the images are often used and disseminated without the explicit permission of the copyright owner, raising ethical and legal issues around intellectual property rights. Should each token of a meme be considered a work in its own right, and should the creators be anonymised to minimise risk or should they be credited as artists? Of course, the sharing, remixing, and rebroadcasting may detach a piece of content from its creator(s). However, just because we cannot trace the creator of a piece of content, does not mean we can use, reproduce, and analyse it freely.

Such dilemmas are at the heart of ethical decision-making, and indeed, if the answers were easy, straightforward, and universally appropriate, they would not be matters of ethics. As Ess and the Association of Internet Researchers (2002: 4) point out in their recommendations on ethical decision-making and internet research, ethical problems are ethical problems, 'precisely because they evoke more than one ethically defensible response to a specific dilemma or problem. Ambiguity, uncertainty, and disagreement are inevitable.'

DIVERSITY IN ONLINE RESEARCH

Research into the pragmatics of digitally mediated communication attempts to answer questions about how we communicate online. However, the conclusions that we draw from research are only as representative as the diversity of the participants in the studies. Sampling is, of course, a necessary part of research design. We cannot include the whole internet in a corpus, and we cannot survey or interview everyone who uses a particular platform or service.

Just as we must understand communication relative to the context in which it occurs, so too must we interpret research relative to the context in which it was conducted.

For practical and ethical reasons, much of the research into digitally mediated communication has focused on data that are publicly available. This has consequences for work in pragmatics, of course. We cannot assume that the way users behave in private discourse contexts will be the same as the way they behave in public discourse contexts. When drawing conclusions about how users interact and communicate in online spaces, we must be mindful that we may only be seeing a fraction of their online lives. Private communication remains under-explored (Georgakopoulou 2011), and looks likely to be a rich area for further investigation in the future.

The World Wide Web gives us access to a wide and diverse range of voices, opinions, and practices. However, this diversity is rarely reflected in the research that we find published in academic journals and books. For ethical reasons, participants in experiments tend to be volunteers, and, for practical reasons, they often end up being undergraduate students from Universities in 'Western, educated, industrialized, rich and democratic (WEIRD) societies' (Azar 2010). Furthermore, while in theory anyone can make their voice heard via social media, certain voices tend to dominate. Christian Fuchs (2014: 121) argues that despite the apparent democratic and participatory nature of social media and Web 2.0, the reality is quite different. He argues that:

> [c]ontemporary social media are not participatory: large companies that centralize attention and visibility and marginalize politics, especially alternative politics, dominate them.

Lists of the most followed accounts on Twitter, Facebook, and YouTube reveal that it is mostly high-profile entertainers, politicians and corporations that are actually being listened to (Fuchs 2014). This is likely to affect the data to which we have most access and which are therefore most likely to be included in our studies. Gosling et al. (2010) take a slightly more optimistic stance. They suggest that the internet is a promising tool for reaching wider audiences. As access to technology and infrastructure increases, they suggest, the internet can help in increasing the diversity in research samples.

Much of the work discussed in this book has focused on English data. Cognitive pragmatic approaches such as relevance theory aim to uncover general patterns in human behaviour and communication. As such, the conclusions in this field of pragmatics generally abstract away from factors relating to the language of use and the specifics of the cultural context. Our overall understanding of how language is used online can, however, only be enriched by including analyses of language and discourse from a more diverse range of languages and cultural contexts. There is a growing body of work in online pragmatics which analyses online discourse in languages other than English. For example, Zhang et al. (2020) analyse emoji on the Chinese social media site WeChat from an intercultural pragmatics perspective (Kecskes 2014), while Oberwinkler (2019) analyses emoticon use by Japanese Facebook users, and Sampietro (2019) looks at them in WhatsApp in Spanish. Issues of politeness and impoliteness have also been considered in a range of languages and cultural contexts. Wang and Taylor (2019) look at mock politeness in Chinese and British online forums, and both Flores-Salgado and Castineira-Benitez (2018) and Landone (2012) consider online politeness strategies in Spanish. Depraetere et al. (2021) compare Belgian French and French French Twitter complaints, focusing on directness and indirectness as impoliteness and politeness strategies. Online speech acts have been considered in Chinese contexts (Wenjie et al. 2021), while Ren and Fukushima (2020) compare requests online in Chinese with requests online in Japanese. Speech acts are considered from a multilingual perspective by Tsoumou (2020), who examines Facebook status updates and comments in Congo-Brazzaville. Other recent work from an interaction and intercultural pragmatics perspective includes research on Dutch (Piepers et al. 2021), Italian (Labinaz and Sbisà, 2021), Spanish (Bou-Franch 2020), and Hebrew (Hirsch 2020). This is just a small sample of some recent work in intercultural and interpersonal pragmatics, and provides a taster of some of the non-English work that has been conducted. Further research into pragmatics (cognitive, interpersonal, and intercultural) from a cross-linguistic and cross-cultural perspective is needed, and it has huge potential to enrich our understanding of digitally mediated communication and online behaviours.

Finally, we must always be aware of our own biases when conducting research. Researchers of digitally mediated language are likely themselves to be users of online platforms and social media sites. When you are researching something as an insider, it can be tempting to assume that you are a typical user. It is easy to assume that the way that you use social media is the way that everyone uses it, and that the sort of content and language that you come across, is representative of digitally mediated communication as a whole. Obviously, the content that we see on our own social media feeds depends on the digital connections that we have in our networks, and on the topics and people that we have chosen to follow. Promoted content may appear on our timelines based on demographic information and internet search history. Our experiences of the digital world are tightly curated by filters and algorithms, and in reality any one user is only seeing a tiny slice of the digitally mediated world (Pariser 2011; Bozdag and van den Hoven 2015). While we may not be able to easily change this, an awareness of the limitations of what we see online is a first step to ensuring that we interpret data and analyse results in an appropriate context.

CONCLUSIONS

Developing our understanding of digitally mediated communication and online pragmatics requires rigorous use of appropriate research methods, underpinned by a theoretically robust framework. This chapter provides a brief insight into some of the methods that underlie the research discussed in the rest of this book. As should be clear, each method has its advantages, disadvantages, and limitations. Findings and analyses must be considered relative to those limitations, and the context in which data are collected must always be kept in mind. No one study or project is going to tell us everything we might want to know about how we communicate in digitally mediated contexts. However, a carefully constructed research question, underpinned by theoretical assumptions, and systematically explored via the data can expand our knowledge and understanding of how pragmatic processes play out in online contexts. Finally, rigorous research methods and diversity of participants are crucial if we are to draw conclusions that hold outside of our online echo chambers and our content filter bubbles. I hope the discussions in this chapter, and in this book more generally, will inspire further research into digitally mediated communication and the pragmatics of language use online.

REFERENCES

Azar, B. (2010). Are your findings 'WEIRD'? *Monitor on Psychology*, *41*(5).

BAAL. (2017). *Recommendations on Good Practice in Applied Linguistics*. Retrieved April 16, 2021, from https://baal.org.uk/wp-content/uploads/2017/08/goodpractice_full.pdf

Baym, N. K. (2010). *Personal Connections in the Digital Age*. Cambridge: Polity Press.

Bernardini, S., Baroni, M., & Evert, S. (2006). A WaCky introduction. In *Wacky! Working Papers on the Web as Corpus*. Bologna: GEDIT.

Blakemore, D. (2007). Constraints, concepts and procedural encoding. In N. Burton-Roberts (Ed.), *Pragmatics* (pp. 45–66). Basingstoke: Palgrave Macmillan.

Bou-Franch, P. (2020). Pragmatics and digital discourse in Spanish research. In D. A. Koike, & J. C. Félix-Brasdefer (Eds.) *Routledge Handbook of Spanish Pragmatics: Foundations and Interfaces*. London: Routledge.

boyd, d., Golder, S., & Lotan, G. (2010). Tweet, tweet, retweet: Conversational aspects of retweeting on Twitter. In *Proceedings of the 43rd Hawaii International Conference on System Sciences* (pp. 1–10). Honolulu, HI: IEEE.

Bozdag, E., & van den Hoven, J. (2015). Breaking the filter bubble: Democracy and design. *Ethics and Information Technology*, *17*, 249–265. doi:10.1007/s10676-015-9380-y

Carston, R. (2002). *Thoughts and Utterances: The Pragmatics of Explicit Communication*. Oxford: Blackwell.

Chakraborty, A., Paranjape, B., Kakarla, S., & Ganguly, N. (2016). Stop Clickbait: Detecting and Preventing Clickbaits in Online News Media. In *Proceedings of the 2016 IEEE/ACM International Conference on Advances in Social Networks Analysis and Mining (ASONAM)*. San Francisco.

Clark, B. (2013). *Relevance Theory*. Cambridge: Cambridge University Press.

Depraetere, I., Decock, S., & Ruytenbeek, N. (2021). Linguistic (in)directness in twitter complaints: A contrastive analysis of railway complaint interactions. *Journal of Pragmatics*, *171*, 215–233. doi:10.1016/j.pragma.2020.09.026.

Developer.twitter.com. (n.d.). *Products for Researchers*. Retrieved April 9, 2021, from https://developer.twitter.com/en/solutions/academic-research/products-for-researchers

Dynel, M. (2016). 'Has Seen Image Macros!' Advice Animals Memes as Visual-Verbal Jokes. *International Journal of Communication*, *10*, 660–688.

Ess, C., & the Association of Internet Researchers. (2002). *Ethical Decision-making and Internet Research: Recommendations from the Aoir Ethics Working Committee*. Retrieved April 16, 2021, from www.aoir.org/reports/ethics.pdf

Flores-Salgado, E., & Castineira-Benitez, T. A. (2018). The use of politeness in WhatsApp discourse and move 'requests'. *Journal of Pragmatics, 133,* 79–92. doi:10.1016/j.pragma.2018.06.009.

Fuchs, C. (2014). *Social Media: A Critical Introduction.* London: Sage.

Georgakopoulou, A. (2011). "On for drinkies?": Email cues of participant alignments. *Language@Internet, 8,* 4. Retrieved June 15, 2021, from https://www.languageatinternet.org/articles/2011/Georgakopoulou

Gosling, S. D., Sandy, C. J., John, O. P., & Potter, J. (2010). Wired but not WEIRD: The promise of the Internet in reaching more diverse samples. *Behavioral and Brain Sciences, 33*(2–3), 94–95. doi:10.1017/S0140525X10000300

Hirsch, G. (2020). Humorous and ironic readers' comments to a politician's post on Facebook: The case of Miri Regev. *Journal of Pragmatics, 164,* 40–53. doi:10.1016/j.pragma.2020.04.012.

Internet Live Stats. (n.d.). *Twitter Usage Statistics.* Retrieved April 2, 2021, from Live Internet Stats: https://www.internetlivestats.com/twitter-statistics/

Jenks, C. J. (2019). Talking trolls into existence: On the floor management of trolling in online forums. *Journal of Pragmatics, 143,* 54–64. doi:10.1016/j.pragma.2019.02.006.

Kecskes, I. (2014). *Intercultural Pragmatics.* Oxford: Oxford University Press.

Labinaz, P., & Sbisà, M. (2021). The problem of knowledge dissemination in social network discussions. *Journal of Pragmatics, 175,* 67–80. doi:10.1016/j.pragma.2021.01.009.

Landone, E. (2012). Discourse markers and politeness in a digital forum in Spanish. *Journal of Pragmatics, 44* (13), 1799–1820. doi:10.1016/j.pragma.2012.09.001.

Marwick, A. (2008). To catch a predator? The MySpace moral panic. *First Monday, 13*(6). doi:10.5210/fm.v13i6.2152

Marwick, A. E., & boyd, d. (2011). I tweet honestly, I tweet passionately: Twitter users, context collapse, and the imagined audience. *New Media and Society, 13*(1), 96–113. doi:10.1177/1461444810365313

Oberwinkler, M. (2019). Emoticons in social media: The case of Japanese Facebook users. In E. Giannoulis and L. R. A. Wilde (Eds.), *Emoticons, Kaomoji, and Emoji: The Transformation of Communication in the Digital Age* (pp. 104–123). Abingdon: Routledge.

Omnicore. (2021). *Instagram by the Numbers: Stats, Demographics & Fun Facts.* Retrieved April 16, 2021, from https://www.omnicoreagency.com/instagram-statistics/

Page, R. (2012). The linguistics of self-branding and micro-celebrity in Twitter: the role of hashtags. *Discourse and Communication, 6*(2), 181–201. doi:10.1177/1750481312437441

Page, R. (2014). Saying 'sorry': corporate apologies posted on Twitter. *Journal of Pragmatics, 62,* 30–45. doi:10.1016/j.pragma.2013.12.003

Page, R. (2017). Ethics revisited: Rights, responsibilities, and relationships in online research. *Applied Linguistics Review, 8* (2–3), 315–320. doi:10.1515/applirev-2016-1043

Page, R., Barton, D., Unger, J. W., & Zappavigna, M. (2014). *Researching Language and Social Media: A Student Guide.* Abingdon: Routledge.

Pariser, E. (2011). *The Filter Bubble: What The Internet Is Hiding From You.* London: Viking.

Petitjean, C. & Morel, E. (2017). "Hahaha": Laughter as a resource to manage WhatsApp conversations. *Journal of Pragmatics, 110,* 1–19. doi: 10.1016/j.pragma.2017.01.001

Piepers, J., van de Groep, M., van Halteren, H., & de Hoop, H. (2021). "Amsterdam, you're raining!" First-hand experience in tweets with spatio-temporal addressees. *Journal of Pragmatics, 176,* 97–109. doi:10.1016/j.pragma.2021.01.032.

Ren, W., & Fukushima, S. (2020). Comparison Japanese and Chinese: Comparison between Chinese and Japanese social media requests. *Contrastive Pragmatics 2* (2), 200–226. doi:10.1163/26660393-BJA10017

Riordan, M. A. (2017a). Emojis as tools for emotion work: Communicating affect in text messages. *Journal of Language and Social Psychology, 36*(5), 549–567. doi:10.1177/0261927X17704238

Riordan, M. A. (2017b). The communicative role of non-face emojis: Affect and disambiguation. *Computers in Human Behavior, 76,* 75–86. doi:10.1016/j.chb.2017.07.009

Riordan, M. A., & Kreuz, R. J. (2010). Cues in computer-mediated communication: A corpus analysis. *Computers in Human Behavior, 26,* 1806–1817. doi:10.1016/j.chb.2010.07.008

Rudolf Von Rohr, M-T., & Locher, M. A. (2020). The interpersonal effects of complimenting others and self-praise in online health settings. In M. E. Placencia, & Z. R. Eslami (Eds), *Complimenting Behavior and (Self-) Praise across Social Media: New Contexts and New Insights* (pp. 189–212). Amsterdam: John Benjamins.

Sampietro, A. (2019). Emoji and rapport management in Spanish WhatsApp chats. *Journal of Pragmatics*, 143, 109–120. doi:10.1016/j.pragma.2019.02.009.

Sinclair, J. (2005). Corpus and text - basic principles. In *Developing Linguistic Corpora: A Guide to Good Practice* (pp. 1–16). Oxford: Oxbow Books.

Sperber, D., & Wilson, D. (1986). *Relevance: Communciation and Cognition* (2nd (with postface) ed.). Oxford: Blackwell.

Tagg, C. (2015). *Exploring Digital Communication: Language in Action*. Abindgon: Routledge.

Thompson, D., & Filik, R. (2016). Sarcasm in written communication: Emoticons are efficient markers of intention. *Journal of Computer-Mediated Communication*, 21(2), 105–120. doi:10.1111/jcc4.12156

Tsoumou, J. M. (2020). Analysing speech acts in politically related Facebook communication. *Journal of Pragmatics*, 167, 80–97. doi: 10.1016/j.pragma.2020.06.004

Vásquez, C., & Aslan, E. (2021). "Cats be outside, how about meow": Multimodal humor and creativity in an internet meme. *Journal of Pragmatics*, 171, 101–117. doi:10.1016/j.pragma.2020.10.006

Wang, J., & Taylor, C. (2019). The conventionalisation of mock politeness in Chinese and British online forums. *Journal of Pragmatics* 142, 270–280. doi:10.1016/j.pragma.2018.10.019.

Wenjie L., Lin L., & Wei R. (2021). Variational pragmatics in Chinese social media requests: The influence of age and social status. *Journal of Pragmatics*, 178, 349–362. doi: 10.1016/j.pragma.2021.04.002

Wikinews. (n.d.). *Wikinews: Style guide*. Retrieved April 7, 2021, from https://en.wikinews.org/wiki/Wikinews:Style_guide

Wilson, D. (2011). The conceptual-procedural distinction: Past, present and future. In V. Escandell-Vidal, M. Leonetti, & A. Ahern (Eds.), *Procedural Meaning: Problems and Perspectives* (Vol. 25, pp. 3–31). Bingley: Emerald.

Wilson, D., & Sperber, D. (2012). *Meaning and Relevance*. Cambridge: Cambridge University Press.

Yus, F. (2021). Incongruity-resolution humorous strategies in image macro memes. *Internet Pragmatics*, 4(1), 131–149. doi:10.1075/ip.00058.yus

Zappavigna, M. (n.d.). *Corpora*. Retrieved April 9, 2021, from http://www.michelezappavigna.com/p/corpora.html

Zhang, Y., Wang, M., & Li, Y. (2020). More than playfulness: Emojis in the comments of a WeChat official account. *Internet Pragmatics*. doi:10.1075/ip.00048.zha

Zimmer, M. (2010). 'But the data is already public': On the ethics of research in Facebook. *Ethics and Information Technology*, 12, 313–325. doi:10.1007/s10676-010-9227-5

INDEX

Note: Page numbers followed by 'n' refers to notes numbers.